Exigent Psychoa

MW00779992

Exigent Psychoanalysis: The Interventions of Jean Laplanche offers a bold exploration of the contemporary psychoanalytic field by focusing on key issues through the lens of one of this century's most exacting and invigorating psychoanalytic theorists.

Deliberately taking an integrative approach that spans a vast range of psychoanalytic ideas – with particular focus on the enduring tension between Freudian and Relational paradigms – Ashtor shows how a rigorous close reading of Laplanche's work can disrupt stale binaries and forge new possibilities for revolutionizing the foundations of psychoanalysis. Organized as pointed interventions on such topics as metapsychology, motivation, the unconscious and psychic structure, Ashtor integrates cutting-edge research on Affect theory and sexuality to demonstrate the potential for fieldwide innovation.

Of interest to established and emerging clinicians alike and aimed at addressing a broad spectrum of theoretical positions, *Exigent Psychoanalysis* offers the first extensive clinical and theoretical study of Laplanche's work, thus facilitating a timely and cutting-edge intervention in contemporary psychoanalytic debates.

Gila Ashtor, PhD, LP is a critical theorist, psychoanalyst, and writer. She teaches at Columbia University and is in private practice in New York City. She is the author of *Homo Psyche: On Queer Theory and Erotophobia* (Fordham UP, 2021) and *Aural History* (Punctum, 2020). She trained at the Institute for Psychoanalytic Training and Research (IPTAR) in New York City and is an editor at Studies in Gender and Sexuality.

"*Exigent Psychoanalysis* offers a brilliant and erudite argument for a profound transformation of psychoanalytic theory in light of Laplanche's revolutionary project. Ashtor's compelling case for Laplanche's theory underscores the importance of his radical insistence on the Copernican revolution within Freud's thought – the fact that we develop a mind by revolving around others whose unconscious communications live as an other within. Readers will be engrossed and enlightened by Ashtor's wide-ranging, acute exposition of the links between our new theorizing of affect and the Laplanchian task of revising the foundations of metapsychology."

Jessica Benjamin, author of *Beyond Doer and Done To: Recognition Theory, Intersubjectivity and the Third*

"Laplanche 'puts Freud to work'. Ashtor puts Laplanche to work. Laplanche's object is Freud. His close reading and critique of Freud's writing reveals what is implicit and potential developments. Ashtor's object is US psychoanalysis, its development, conflicts and splits. Her object is well chosen. For 50 years after Freud's death, Anglophone psychoanalysis was dominant. Freud's writing was known through the Standard Edition; US and UK analysts filled the journals, the thinking of European and Latin American colleagues was largely known in English translation. With rigor and pleasing clarity, Ashtor explains past and current controversies – including their origin in Freud – wisely focusing on sexuality, metapsychology, motivation and the structure of the mind."

Jonathan House

"Ashtor's book will be widely anticipated, once it's announced that it's coming, and widely read when it arrives. It is incredibly timely, and I feel confident in its depth and astuteness."

Donnel Stern

Exigent Psychoanalysis

The Interventions of Jean Laplanche

Gila Ashtor

Routledge
Taylor & Francis Group

LONDON AND NEW YORK

First published 2022
by Routledge
2 Park Square, Milton Park, Abingdon, Oxon OX14 4RN

and by Routledge
605 Third Avenue, New York, NY 10158

Routledge is an imprint of the Taylor & Francis Group, an informa business

British Library Cataloguing-in-Publication Data
A catalogue record for this book is available from the British Library

Library of Congress Cataloging-in-Publication Data

Names: Ashtor, Gila, author.
Title: Exigent psychoanalysis : the interventions of Jean Laplanche / Gila Ashtor.
Description: Milton Park, Abingdon Oxon ; New York, NY : Routledge, 2021. | Includes bibliographical references and index.
Identifiers: LCCN 2021006096 (print) | LCCN 2021006097 (ebook) | ISBN 9781032039763 (hardback) | ISBN 9781032039770 (paperback) | ISBN 9781003190042 (ebook)
Subjects: LCSH: Psychoanalysis. | Laplanche, Jean.
Classification: LCC BF173 .A698 2021 (print) | LCC BF173 (ebook) | DDC 150.19/5--dc23
LC record available at https://lccn.loc.gov/2021006096
LC ebook record available at https://lccn.loc.gov/2021006097

ISBN: 978-1-032-03976-3 (hbk)
ISBN: 978-1-032-03977-0 (pbk)
ISBN: 978-1-003-19004-2 (ebk)

Typeset in Times New Roman
by MPS Limited, Dehradun

Contents

Acknowledgments   *vi*
Abbreviations   *ix*

Introduction: Innovation and deviation in
psychoanalysis   1

1   *Metapsychology* – Mytho-symbolic versus
    metapsychology   50

2   *Sexuality* – Laplanche's theory of the unconscious   77

3   *Seduction* – Laplanche's theory of psychic structure   115

4   *Translation* – Laplanche's theory of motivation   149

    Index   *185*

Acknowledgments

Although perhaps all books can be said to be products of their time and place, I feel the historical conditions of this project with particular acuteness. In one sense, this is because as a critique of psychoanalytic theory – as it exists today – it takes for granted the major and trenchant critiques wagered in generations before me. While taking these critiques for granted may seem hasty or even immodest to some, it has not been the aim of this book to focus on the achievements of the brilliant clinicians who have enriched and transformed the field. On the contrary, the critical angle of *Exigent Psychoanalysis* requires me to focus on the limitations that remain after so many changes have taken place. That said, I want to take this opportunity to express gratitude for the courageous thinkers and clinicians who have taken on the challenge of asking, and often answering, the deep psychological questions at the heart of our field. I am inspired by more thinkers than I could name, and hope this work testifies to my sustained engagement.

This book feels specific to this moment in another sense as well, which has to do with my experience undertaking formal analytic training in New York City in the second decade of the twenty-first century. While training at an institute that identified itself as "contemporary Freudian," I was at the same time deeply immersed in the conversations and events of NYU's postdoctoral program, where so many self-identified Relational and Interpersonal analysts taught and supervised. The easy and casual crossover between these communities has for a while now been greeted with considerable optimism and relief but what struck me in particular was the palpable sense, shared by many in *both* circles, that neither faction had all the answers. Moreover, it often seemed to me that there was a growing appetite for new angles and interventions that would transcend some of the more familiar binaries, and a clear feeling, however implicit, that a new generation of analysts like me – brought up on Freud and on the spirited and vigorous critiques of Freud that arose in the past 40 years – were specially poised to initiate the next stage of theoretical development. I hope this book provides an invitation to that process.

I read Laplanche for the first time in college, in a collection of essays that was published as *Essays on Otherness* (Ed. John Fletcher). I sat at Peet's Coffee in Cambridge, Massachusetts highlighting every other paragraph, trying to grasp, intellectually, what was resonating powerfully in the words. I was intrigued and overwhelmed by what I was reading, and I understood that it would take a few years (and a few more degrees) before I could make productive use of what I read. I was extraordinarily fortunate that by the time I returned to Laplanche nearly a decade later, there was a vast collection of new translations and still more translations on the way. I am so grateful to Jonathan House for making Laplanche widely accessible, and for being such a passionate, rigorous, and generous interlocuter over the years. His willingness to engage with me on questions at the heart of this project has been a tremendous source of support, and I am incredibly grateful for his wisdom and kindness.

I also want to thank Jessica Benjamin for years and years of enthusiastic debate and encouragement. Her willingness to be a source of unflagging support has made up for early deficits of that sort, and I can't even begin to imagine engaging the psychoanalytic field without her. Even though we may not always agree, I am grateful for her playfulness with ideas, her curiosity, and her tenacity.

I am grateful to *Studies in Gender and Sexuality* for providing an early platform for my experimentation with writing about Laplanche, to Lisa Baraitser for important conversations about Laplanche and the intersection of clinical and critical theory, and for the friendship and camaraderie of Katie Gentile, whose steadfast commitment to interdisciplinary dialogue creates new possibilities for innovation in our field. I am grateful to the faculty and supervisors at the Institute for Psychoanalytic Training and Research (IPTAR), where I undertook my psychoanalytic training. The warmth of my colleagues and fellow candidates made the labor of analytic training a positive experience. I am especially grateful to Alan Bass for the Respecialization program, which made it possible for academics and scholars to undertake clinical training. His close readings of Freud were a highlight of my training, and his passion for psychoanalysis is always palpable and moving.

I want to thank Donnel Stern, whose enthusiasm for this project shepherded it through to publication, and whose formidable work on topics at the heart of metapsychology have long been an inspiration to me. I am grateful to many clinicians, across a range of orientations, for nourishing conversations over the years.

And in my personal life, which is of course inextricable from the work that happens here, I am as always and ever grateful to Jonathan, who makes everything possible.

Abbreviations

Frequently cited works have been identified by the following abbreviations:

Laplanche, Jean

UCR	The Unfinished Copernican Revolution
STA	A Short Treatise on the Unconscious
II	Implantation, Intromission
IDH	Interpretation between Determinism and Hermeneutics: a Restatement of the Problem
TPA	Transference: Its Provocation by the Analyst
FS	Freud and the Sexual
TOB	The Temptation of Biology
NFP	New Foundations for Psychoanalysis

Introduction: Innovation and deviation in psychoanalysis

"Putting Freud to work, or, in other words, 'interpreting Freud with Freud' (Laplanche, IDH, 1968), does not meant trying to find a lesson in him – still less an orthodoxy. Nor is it a matter of choosing one Freud against another, or of 'fishing' here and there for a formulation which suits me. Putting Freud to work means demonstrating in him what I call an exigency, the *exigency* of a discovery which impels him without always showing him the way, and which may therefore lead him into dead ends or goings-astray. It means following in his footsteps, accompanying him but also criticizing him, seeking other ways – but impelled by an *exigency* similar to his" (Laplanche, IDH, 147).

The "self-reflective" turn

Psychoanalysis has a vexed and confounding relationship to change. While as a treatment methodology, healing is equated with self-transformation, as an intellectual discourse psychoanalysis reveals itself to be a discipline that consistently resists its own development. At the heart of Jean Laplanche's interventions is the relentless determination to confront these defensive tendencies within psychoanalysis. Refusing either to excuse the field or abandon it entirely, Lapalnche treats psychoanalysis *psychoanalytically*; which is to say, he identifies areas of limitation and sets out to discover what anxieties are involved.

The field's antagonistic relationship to innovation manifests most explicitly in an extensive history of violent schisms and splits that began with Freud and continue, in somewhat more tempered form, into the present. Within psychoanalysis and the broader history of science, this pattern of behavior has been the subject of considerable scholarly attention, leading some critics to designate psychoanalysis a religion rather than a science, and others to insist on the necessity of abandoning psychoanalysis' humanistic origins in favor of empirical methods instead. But while it has become commonplace to bemoan the field's long history of intolerance, and either impugn the discipline wholesale or call for radical revisions, so far little progress has been made in understanding *why* innovation – which is a natural and necessary step in the progression of new knowledge – remains so problematic for the field. Why, in other words, does the field remain more or less informally divided between those who are reluctant to challenge Freudian concepts directly and those who are comfortable criticizing Freud but reluctant to develop an alternative theory of mind? And while these two kinds of intellectual reluctance manifest differently, what makes the *reluctance to innovate* such an enduring feature of psychoanalytic discourse?

To be clear, it is not as though major changes in the field have *not* occurred since Freud. In fact, as Arnold Cooper observed in a classic paper entitled, "Psychoanalysis today: new wine in old bottles or the hidden revolution in psychoanalysis" (1986), "there has been a quiet, largely unadvertised, revolution in the way psychoanalysis is conceived" (52) that is all the more remarkable for having occurred *without* engendering substantive changes to Freud's original terms. And while in one sense, trenchant critiques of drive (Fairbairn, 1952; Sullivan, 1953; Tomkins, 1962; Greenberg and Mitchell, 1983; Bowlby, 1969, 1973, 1980), gender (Benjamin, 1988, 1995, 2005; Harris, 2005; Corbett, 2009), and analytic neutrality and technique (Aron, 1996; Bollas, 1987; Jacobs, 1990; Bromberg, 1998) can hardly be said to be "hiding," what Cooper aptly describes is the peculiar phenomena by which even vigorous challenges to Freudian ideas *do not* effectuate changes to psychoanalytic terminology or theory of mind. In fact, as a measure of just how much the psychoanalytic field has changed since its inception, Cooper conducted a survey of eminent analysts from a variety of persuasions to find out what ideas and techniques informed their practice and discovered that, "a two-person psychology and some version of a comprehensive intersubjective or relational point of view have superseded traditional resistance analysis as the core theoretical and technical viewpoint for most of our profession in the United States. The representational world, conceived as internalized object relations, has superceded drive-defense configurations as primary determinants of mental life. The intrapsychic focus on the patient has to a great degree given way to or at least been supplemented by scrutiny of the interpersonal-intersubjective-relational transactions between patient and analyst.... The change from the concept of neutrality toward the emphasis on mutual enactment, viewing transference and countertransference as a total situation describes a new form of psychoanalysis" (2008, 249). Observing that the sum total of all these changes become a "newer overall view of psychoanalysis" (248), Cooper notes that "basic ideas have changed radically in response to our vastly expanded clinical experience as well as to researches in ethology, infant observation, and psychoanalytic process, but little of this is reflected in the ordinary discourse of psychoanalysis. The changes in psychoanalysis are of a magnitude that most fields would consider a major paradigm shift" (52). And yet, instead of advertising our innovations as practitioners in other disciplines might, "psychoanalysts cling to Freud's language as one part of our clinging to our identification with Freud. It takes a courageous and perhaps foolish psychoanalyst to willingly break away from such a magnificent identification" (54). Using "transference," the "Oedipal complex" and the "analytic situation" as examples, Cooper notes that, "the unchanging words, each of them clinical at root, have been screens hiding their constantly changing meanings and applications" (52). This is why even the most sustained critiques of Freud can be said to stop short of systematic conceptualizations; because even when thinkers are comfortable denouncing certain theoretical formulations, they refrain from rebuilding a new framework *tout court*. Perhaps nowhere is this tendency more acutely felt than in the peculiar pattern Cooper identifies whereby innovations, when they *do* occur, are nevertheless made to conform to Freud's original terminology as if we "cannot bring ourselves to talk a language other than the one Freud taught us" (1986). How else can we explain that words like "transference," "Oedipus complex," and "neutrality" persist long past persuasive challenges to their scientific and clinical utility? What can explain this hesitation to devise a new set of terms that differ from Freud's original ones? And moreover, how do we understand the confounding disconnect between considerable changes in our practice, on the one hand, and on the other, the persistence of Freud's metapsychological "bedrock" (Cooper, 2008).

While congratulating ourselves on our progress is commonplace in the field, Cooper rejects such a short-sighted approach; in an assessment, which I share, Cooper writes that, "the continuing use of traditional language" effectively "disguise[s] the changing ideas of psychoanalysis" and has deleterious consequences for the field's intellectual development. The refusal to change our theoretical models and maps is even more problematic in the context of science since "it is a psychoanalytic task to provide the biologists with a comprehensive and accurate model of the mind and its functions – conscious and unconscious – and we must assure that this map is available in its up-to-date version" (1986, 61). He writes, "our failure to announce clearly our changing ideas has hindered our educational activities, has slowed the acceptance of psychoanalysis among the sciences, and has interfered with the most fruitful collaboration with the disciplines at our boundaries" (62). What is more, the refusal to modify Freud's original language – even when the meanings of these terms have undergone dramatic transformations – belies the field's genuine and substantive dynamism. Indeed, so effective are the field's camouflages that no efforts are made to develop a "newer overall view of psychoanalysis" that would systematically formalize and represent the discipline's major shifts. Lest it seem as though only our scientific credentials are imperiled by this disconnect, it is worth pointing out that the ultimate scope and scale of our progress is jeopardized as well. After all, how truly different and enlightened can contemporary psychoanalysis be said to be, if all the words for describing mental life remain unchallenged and unchanged?

In recent years, existential questions about the future of the field have emerged from other angles as well. In what may be thought of as a "self-reflective" turn, many voices in contemporary psychoanalysis describe a wish for deeper engagement with neighboring disciplines and greater sensitivity to the changing norms of academic and political discourse. Exasperated with the "holy wars" that have divided the field into rival "schools," and skeptical about the capacity of pluralism to facilitate difficult conversations, the contemporary landscape is marked by a new willingness to "implement our own model of inquiry by turning an eye on ourselves" (Aron et al., 2018). Observing the paradox of our field as one wherein "we ask our patients to revisit their life narratives" and hail "self-examination and self-critique" as the "conduit for growth" but as a clinical/intellectual field "haven't used our own methodology," Aron, Grand, and Slochower's recent intervention, *De-Idealizing Relational Theory* (2018), calls on present-day practitioners to obtain some distance from the field's behavioral patterns and rhetorical tropes. Their plea for a new mode of argumentation that abstains from the familiar charges of "rebellion, antagonism, and hostility" (2) joins a growing chorus of clinicians who express disenchantment with the current state of psychoanalytic theory (Cooper, 2008; Westen, 2002; Boesky, 2005). No longer satisfied with pluralism as the preeminent antidote to rejectionism, and less sanguine about the prospects of genuine progress, there is palpable momentum for new approaches to self-critique.

In particular, recent attention has focused on the limits of postmodernist approaches to psychoanalytic knowledge-building. While initially celebrated as offering a corrective to the field's outdated positivist roots, in recent years, critics from multiple angles have pointed out that postmodernism is not the remedy we thought it could be. As Aner Govrin writes, there is actually "a heavy price psychoanalysis might pay if the majority of analysts adopt postmodernism as their preferred epistemology. The contention is that only analysts who thought they "knew the truth" created the classical, interpersonal, self-psychological, ego psychological, Kleinian, Bionian, Fairbairnian, Winnicottian, and other schools of thought. These positivist perspectives gave rise to compelling and complex theories of the mind. Their creators believed that their formulations corresponded to reality" (2006, 508). Govrin distinguishes between "two eras in psychoanalysis – the positivist era of the schools and the postmodern era" (509) in order to show that in postmodern psychoanalysis "truth is no longer perceived as an ideal toward which to strive" and the analyst "acknowledges uncertainty and embraces the impossibility of recognizing one truth, or the inability to generate objective truths independent of historical context and culture" (510). While on the surface, this approach seems exciting and unproblematic, one significant effect of treating all knowledge as subjective and contextual is that there is little opportunity for clinicians to generate new ideas that attempt to describe something "true" about the mind. In her recent book on the importance of introducing affect into psychoanalytic theory, Virginia Demos (2019) has adumbrated a set of related concerns that center on how a generalized pluralist approach actually functions to *prevent* psychoanalysis from rigorously challenging its own problematic ideas.

This new focus on the limits of theoretical pluralism, in tandem with a series of broader shifts in intellectual discourse, has dramatically altered the landscape of contemporary psychoanalysis. Calling for a new openness to "self-critique" that privileges innovation, authenticity and rigor over loyalty to established "guilds," a growing number of clinicians express an appetite for theoretical introspection that explores the limitations of psychoanalytic theory from *within*. Alongside this increasing interest in self-examination, the psychoanalytic field is undergoing major shifts in its clinical and conceptual priorities. As one significant example of this development, issues pertaining to sexuality, gender, and identity are no longer seen as peripheral to psychoanalysis but as fundamental to the field as whole (Gherovici, 2017; Giffney and Watson, 2017; Atlas, 2018) and topics such as race and class which were once considered "political" (and therefore not directly pertinent to depth psychology) are now acknowledged to be inseparable from clinical work (Layton, 2020; *Division Review*, Summer 2020). Taken together, these shifts conduce to a crucial change in the climate of psychoanalytic discourse; whereas efforts to challenge psychoanalytic doxa were once greeted with "knee-jerk" suspicion and hostility and treated as an "assault" on Freud's precious legacy (Cooper, 2008), today preeminent journals routinely feature calls to radicalize psychoanalysis by reinventing its metapsychological "bedrock." But while this new openness signals a welcome break with the field's intellectual conventions, there is as yet no clear path toward the kind of "self-reflective" inquiry today's clinicians describe. Moreover, while it is relatively straightforward to assail the "bad old days" of psychoanalysis in which arguments took place "under a virtual intellectual reign of terror" (Cooper, 2008, 237), it remains unclear whether the field's relationship to innovation has been fundamentally altered. In fact, efforts to localize the problem to a particular era (1950s) or a specific style of thought (positivism) seem instead to perpetuate habits of looking externally, rather than internally, for sources of the field's flaws.

Introducing Jean Laplanche

Enacting a radical and decisive break with these defensive tendencies in psychoanalytic thought, the French clinician and philosopher Jean Laplanche (1924–2012) is uniquely suited to meet the needs of the present moment. At once insistent on preserving the psychoanalytic discoveries which are truly revolutionary *and* affirming the urgent necessity of "putting psychoanalysis to work," Laplanche coins the phrase "faithful infidelity" to describe his distinctive style of relating to the discipline's core formulations. The particular meaning of this phrase will be appreciable through a firmer grasp of the field's enduring conflicts around innovation/deviation; for now, it suffices to point out that by putting two opposing words together Laplanche favors tension over easy conciliation, and substantive confrontation over rejection. Indeed, whereas generations of psychoanalytic thinkers have grappled (often unsuccessfully) with how best to navigate the father–son dynamic endemic to nearly all attempts at relating to Freud, Laplanche sidesteps this familiar drama almost entirely by separating "Freud," the founder of a scientific discipline, from the "object" of psychoanalysis, which is sexuality and the unconscious. This deft and relentless insistence on a necessary *gap* distinguishing Freud (the individual) from psychoanalysis (the science) creates the philosophical conditions for Laplanche to undertake a systematic critique of everything in psychoanalysis that impedes its development as a radical theory of internal life. In an essay aptly titled, "In Debate with Freud," Laplanche explains that "'doing justice' to a great text, means not masking but restoring its contradictions, its weaknesses, its moments of hesitation and imprecision, and even its incoherences... Speaking personally, it is these decisive junctions, these points of 'going astray' in the Freudian oeuvre which fascinate me, and I have set myself the task of opening up a discussion of just what is at play in such moments: what then becomes of the *exigency* which magnetizes the entire movement of this strange body of thought? For me it is a matter of putting Freud back to work, of making his work 'work' (of making it creak perhaps) by working with it" (FS, 277).

As this book will show, Laplanche's determination to "put Freud to work"[1] is unparalleled in its rigor and unprecedented in the opportunity it represents for the field. While there have certainly been many inventive clinicians in the decades since Freud, the reluctance on the part of these thinkers to challenge Freud directly or criticize him on his terms has contributed to the sense, expressed so well by Cooper, that no matter how much psychoanalysis purportedly changes, it nevertheless always seems to stay the same. By refusing to proclaim himself either a faithful adherent or a heretic, Laplanche accomplishes a rare feat in psychoanalytic theory: a systematic critique of psychoanalytic foundations that fortifies, rather than abandons, Freud's speculations on sexuality and the unconscious. As such, Laplanche can be said to be *both* Freud's critic and psychoanalysis' defender, a position he achieves by reading Freud exactingly while simultaneously criticizing moments of crucial incoherence. In addition to his scrupulous close reading of Freud, Laplanche introduces a series of metapsychological concepts that are explicitly intended to reorient psychoanalysis from its *auto*-centric model of the mind toward one in which the *other* person is at the center. By invalidating those concepts which impede the field's potential as a radical theory of mental life and introducing several major new ideas – specifically, *enlarged* sexuality, seduction, and translation – Laplanche rebuilds psychoanalytic theory on thoroughly *other*-centered grounds. And lest these innovations seem like just another minor corrective to Freud's original vision, Laplanche assures us that attempts to conform our findings to psychoanalytic doxa are misguided since it is more often than not *Freud himself* – not subsequent followers – who strays from the radical potential of psychoanalytic discoveries.

The road *half*-taken: two paths for psychoanalysis

In order to demonstrate the two possible directions for psychoanalytic theory, Laplanche establishes "sexuality" as the essence of Freud's radical discovery and then meticulously reads Freud's entire oeuvre in order to identify the specific moments when Freud either moves *toward* or *away* from this essential discovery. Dubbing these competing tendencies "Copernican" (*toward* sexuality) and "Ptolemaic" (*away* from sexuality), Laplanche uses a metaphor of "centering" and "decentering" to track the movement of Freud's thought. Whereas a common trope portrays Freud as the victim of later misreadings (for example, Lacan's castigation of ego psychology as betraying Freud's radical vision), Laplanche instead contends that "if Freud is his own Copernicus, he is also his own Ptolemy" (UCR, 60). Determined to sustain the radicalism of sexuality's "decentering" as against Freudian theory's constant "self-centering and self-begetting," Laplanche insists on an attitude of "*faithful infidelity*. A fidelity with respect to reading and translation, restoring to Freud what he means – including his contradictions and his turning points; an infidelity with respect to the interpretation of Freud's *goings-astray*, in order to try to find what I call 'New Foundations for Psychoanalysis'" (FS, 285). As such, a "*rigorous metapsychology …* would be a metapsychology that certainly has its origins in Freud, but which, as the outcome of a working through, does not hesitate to make choices and propose important reconfigurations" (FS, 36). Addressing the role of his critical method in developing the foundations for a rigorous metapsychology, Laplanche explains that, "putting Freud to work means demonstrating in him what I call an *exigency*, the exigency of a discovery which impels him without always showing him the way, and which may therefore lead him into dead ends or goings-astray. It means following in his footsteps, accompanying him but also criticizing him, seeking other ways – but impelled by an exigency similar to his" (IDH, 147). What *is* this exigency which impels both Freud and Laplanche? According to Laplanche, the "exigency" which "impels" Freud is the "discovery" of *enlarged* sexuality, which he defines in the following way: "1. A sexuality that absolutely goes beyond genitality, and even beyond sexual difference; 2. A sexuality that is related to fantasy; 3. A sexuality that is extremely mobile as to its aim and object; and 4. (a point on which I myself lay great emphasis) a sexuality that has its own 'economic' regime in the Freudian sense of the term, its own principle of functioning, which is not a systematic tendency towards discharge, but a specific tendency towards the increase of tension and the pursuit of excitation. In short, it is a sexuality that exists before or beyond sex or the sexed, and which may perhaps encompass genitality but only under the very specific modality of the phallic" (FS, 142).

The remarkable clarity with which Laplanche identifies *enlarged* sexuality as the privileged object of psychoanalysis belies the difficulty of consistently maintaining this object in view. Whereas in chemistry, for example, it is technical limitations alone which may hinder scientific progress, in the case of unconscious sexuality the complexity of the topic and resistances it provokes are what make it difficult for the clinician to look too *closely* for fear of what he'll find. Therefore, while Freud repeatedly located resistance to his findings out "there" – in the general public of naïve and religious-minded readers or in rival clinicians who were timid and suggestible – Laplanche instead contends that the most enduring resistances originate "within" Freud's own ideas. It is Freud who struggles and fails to sustain the meaning of *enlarged* sexuality, and Freud alone who builds a theory which systematically undermines its own powerful discovery. It is Freud who introduces the concept of an *enlarged* sexuality and then proceeds to more or less drain sexuality of any genuinely radical meaning, and Freud who utilizes an array of rhetorical and conceptual tools to dilute, distort, and undo the force of his most original contributions. These facts prompt Laplanche to suggest that although Freud compared himself to Copernicus, he was often his own Ptolemy instead. In a magisterial essay, "The Unfinished Copernican Revolution," Laplanche explains that contrary to common sense assumptions, "the opposition between Ptolemy and Copernicus, geocentrism and heliocentrism is a simple, pedagogical one; but let us remember that a revolution is never as revolutionary as it thinks – it has its forerunners in the past, and what it offers as a new opening also carries with it possibilities for potential relapses" (UCR, 53).

Laplanche reminds us that "it is well known that on several occasions Freud compared the discovery of psychoanalysis to the Copernican revolution" (60) and was rarely modest in his self-assessment of the scientific contributions he perceived himself to be making. While for decades following Freud's death, psychoanalytic writers reproduced these statements uncritically – fiercely protective of Freud's scientific credibility and the legitimacy of psychoanalysis as a discipline[2] – Laplanche avers that "my vision of Freud's 'Copernican' revolution coincides only partly with what he says about it himself at the time" (60). Establishing a more critical approach to Freud's success, Laplanche observes that there is not a single, courageous, "Copernican" revolution but a "double history of innovation and going-astray" such that, as in astronomy, there are "some intuitions of truth almost from the start, but also an initial going-astray" (60). By using the phrase "going-astray" Laplanche refers to those moments when instead of moving *toward* an elaboration of *enlarged* sexuality, Freud moves *away* from it. Accordingly, the "wrong path [is] taken each time there was a return to a theory of self-centering, or even self-begetting" (60).[3] Indeed, this oscillation is so constant and so powerful that "in Freud, one should speak, at almost every period, of an alternation between relapses into Ptolemaism and resurgences of the Copernican, other-centered vision" (60).

What *is* this "other-centered vision" of psychoanalysis that Freud recurringly approaches and avoids? According to Laplanche, the radical innovation of psychoanalysis – the *true* equivalent to the Copernican breakthrough – is the discovery that *we revolve around other people* and *not* the other way around. In this view, Ptolemaism is actually a natural and commonsense idea because it confirms our subjective experience of ourselves as at the center of our own lives. Not only is it extremely difficult to *experience* the *non*-centrality of oneself, but the machinery of perception is more or less designed to hide this fact from view. Self-centeredness is therefore not merely a preference but a functional necessity of language and communication; our inability to genuinely inhabit other minds means that we are prone to see ourselves as the origin and cause of our experience. But while putting ourselves at the center of the solar system confirms how we feel and wish to see ourselves, it is, in actuality, as psychologically inaccurate as Ptolemaism was astronomically false. Just as heliocentrism represented a radical break from the geocentrism of early astronomy, *enlarged* sexuality demands a totalizing reversal in how we understand the basic organization of internal life. It is not we who are stationary and at the center of our lives, but other people whom we revolve around. As such, what makes *enlarged* sexuality such a powerful concept has less to do with the superficial sensationalism of genital activity than with how it violates our every effort at "self-begetting." Sexuality is neither inherently revolutionary nor automatically scandalous and if all psychoanalysis could be said to reveal was that sexuality is a repressed wish or forbidden act then its explanatory potential would be demonstrably narrow. If, however, sexuality can be *enlarged* beyond genitality, and situated in the context of psychic development and relationality, then it dissolves familiar illusions of our autonomy and attunes us to the presence of the *other-in-us*.

As Laplanche will show, the primacy of *otherness* is the radical innovation of psychoanalysis, even if Freud himself did not consistently understand this. Not merely is man no longer the center of his own universe, but he is not even the primary source of his own sexuality. Through the elaboration of several key concepts, Laplanche demonstrates that each individual is *preceded* by an adult and this precedence, while seemingly banal, actually has staggering developmental consequences, one of which is that biopsychical development is now a process that fundamentally depends on the unconscious communications of an*other* human being. It is this immutable fact that sets each person on a psychological course that may *feel* private but is fundamentally oriented to the *other* person on whom one's development depends. While each part of this logic will be extensively elaborated in great detail later, it is important for now to show that the central point Laplanche seeks to make is that there are two totally different versions of the story you could tell about sexuality: the first – and Ptolemaic version – is that the individual's psychic life is dominated by repressed sexual wishes. The second – Copernican version – is that the individual's psychic life develops in *relation* to the unconscious sexuality of his earliest objects. The Ptolemaic story locates the genesis of sexuality within each individual, and as such runs into considerable incoherence in its attempt to account for the *cause* of sexuality's origins. In sharp contrast, the Copernican reformulation says that in spite of how personal my sexuality *feels* to me, it actually comes *at* me, first, from another person. With this categorical distinction firmly in place, Laplanche becomes able to identify what constitutes the specifically Copernican discovery – the primacy of *otherness*-in-*me* – versus what merely seems revolutionary but is in reality yet another iteration of Ptolemaic ideology.

Reproblematization of the whole

In sharp contrast to the typical conventions of psychoanalytic discourse, Laplanche is not shy about the uncompromising nature of this critical heuristic. Whereas Cooper observed the field to have undergone a "hidden revolution," Laplanche is not preoccupied with minimizing or "hiding" the scale of his critique. While many creative theorists have added major new ideas while promising to leave the core tenets of Freud's metapsychology unchanged, and others disclaimed the scope of their contributions by categorizing them as mere additions, expansions or improvements, Laplanche relentlessly demonstrates that what needs to change about psychoanalysis is nothing short of its *foundations*. Toward the end of Laplanche's essay on the "Unfinished Copernican Revolution," he writes: "To show that one can go further than Freud, that one can sustain more effectively than him the 'Copernican' aspect of his discovery, is the most important dimension of what we have named the 'new foundations' for psychoanalysis. This would be an inadequate claim if it simply referred Freud back to his mistakes, his blindness or even the inadequacy of the conceptual tools at his disposal. The correction of a going-astray, as I understand it, goes beyond the mere refutation of error, or even the explication of its contingent causes" (81). What's needed, Laplanche suggests, is (1) the elaboration of "new foundations for psychoanalysis" and (2) recognition that the Ptolemaic re-centering we see in Freud's own theory is "a parallel to the ineluctable narcissistic closure of the apparatus of the soul" (82). This latter point is particularly crucial because in it Laplanche suggests that one reason for the field's conflicted relationship to change has to do with the Copernican discovery itself; namely, it is not only Freud who struggled to sustain his own focus on sexuality but the very problem of *decentering ourselves* which makes the required theorizations so difficult to establish and maintain. In fact, it is precisely because the discovery of *enlarged* sexuality is neither neutral nor straightforward that resistances are not merely occasional but actually bound to arise. This is why Laplanche insists that it is the "duty of the analyst" to safeguard the Copernican potential of psychoanalysis by drastically rewriting our concepts so that they accurately convey "the permanence of the unconscious, the primacy of the address of the other" (83). Laplanche believes in the power of more accurate and courageous theoretical formulations to sustain the Copernican discovery and this belief prompts him to introduce major new concepts – among them, *enlarged* sexuality, seduction, and translation – in the hope these will fortify the radical potential of psychoanalysis.

Lest these interventions seem like yet another localized revision of Freudian ideas, Laplanche is adamant that we should not be satisfied with merely *tweaking* our existing model. In fact, Laplanche is so determined to differentiate his own approach from the usual critiques that he spends considerable time explaining why our tendency to revise local ideas rather than problematize the foundations functions to curtail far-reaching progress. Returning to the example of Ptolemy and Copernicus, Laplanche explains that although the Ptolemaic system suffered from a total inability to explain the movements of stars, for "fourteen centuries" astronomers resorted to convoluted mathematical formulas to preserve Ptolemaic hypotheses rather than conceding that a new underlying framework was required. In a system "where the earth remains the center of reference" it was impossible to explain the movements of planets without complicated and elaborate recourse to a "whole series of accidental movements" (55). Although "highly mathematical hypotheses" were concocted to justify keeping the earth at the center – hypotheses which "mobilize the ingenuity, even the genius, of astronomers" (55) – these hypotheses were all derived "from a basic hypothesis which is false" (55) and thus the strenuous mathematical ingenuity of astronomers was really an attempt to forestall a more comprehensive change in how the solar system needed to be understood. Unsurprisingly, "the immediate result of heliocentrism, the perspective adopted by Copernicus, is an immense simplification" (55) because once the earth is decentered, no "ingenious" hypotheses are required to explain the stars.

Brining these insights to bear on the conditions of psychoanalytic theory, Laplanche suggests that the situation *since* Freud resembles astronomy *before* Copernicus; in order to maintain the basic premises of Freud's theorizations, a vast amount "of supplementary excess baggage" (55) is required. "Is it possible," Laplanche asks, "to load the Freudian vessel with all this supplementary excess baggage – Kleinian positions, foreclosure, false self or omnipotent self, transitional space, etc., etc., – without the whole thing capsizing? Is there no place for moving from local questions to a re-problematization of the whole?" (55). Like Ptolemaic astronomy, psychoanalysis continues to be "a system in which each unexplained detail, far from bringing the whole in question, was made the object of a supplementary *ad hoc* hypothesis. Overload, blockage – one thinks of what became of Freudian metapsychology at a certain level of complication, when it began to fill out certain inadequacies with new concepts, without bothering to determine whether they were congruent with the whole or whether it was not rather the whole which should have been reconstructed" (55). For Laplanche, psychoanalysts resemble the "ingenious" astronomers who for "fourteen centuries" chose to update the Ptolemaic "Bible of astronomy" instead of asking whether "it was not rather the whole which should have been reconstructed." Such a view of the field echoes similar observations made by Cooper when in his study of psychoanalytic theory, he notices a "hidden revolution" whereby terms *do* undergo tremendous shifts *with the proviso* that the true extent of these shifts is minimized and "hidden" from view. In one of the most confounding illustrations of this situation, Cooper reflects on the field's bizarre usage of "classical" to designate a superior method of practice, writing that, "when the Renaissance rediscovered classical Greece, its great artists used the classic models as a source of inspiration for new experiments in art and for the construction of new aesthetic ideals; they did not do classical sculpture" (1984, 41).

This preoccupation with preserving psychoanalysis (in spite of time, progress, and the natural development of knowledge) is not an isolated problem but the field's preeminent mode. Cooper traces the origins of this attitude back to Freud himself whose "interest was in some ways more proprietary than scientific" (2008, 237), as evidenced by the constant requirement that "shibboleths" be used to separate analysts from nonanalysts. Whether the "secret password" was the Oedipus complex (Freud, 1905), the theory of dreams (Freud, 1937), or the unconscious (Freud, 1937) (236), Cooper sees such an extensive reliance on "shibboleths" as indicative of Freud's mistaken priorities and draws the link between Freud's preoccupation with distinguishing "analysis" from "non-analysis" and the field's subsequent wars over "true" belief. Indeed, among the most explicit consequences of this legacy is the field's custom of organizing different schools according to degrees of "orthodox" adherence. Cooper writes, "that generations of psychoanalysts were willing to label themselves as "orthodox," meaning that they would not overturn any of Freud's basic ideas but would at most provide addenda to his thoughts, seems an extraordinary admission of mistrust concerning the scientific power of his theories and the identity of our profession" (2008, 241). Evaluating what this behavior reveals about our field, Cooper decides that such faithful "clinging" to archaic language with "abandoned" meanings is neither benign nor accidental but in-dicative of a profound failure – perhaps even a deliberate refusal – to "distinguish oneself by going beyond and overthrowing the father" (241). Cooper concludes that "it is as if we cannot bring ourselves to talk a language other than the one that Freud taught us" (1986, 53) and speculates on the possible reasons for this continued "clinging to Freud": "(1) the power of Freud's language; (2) the difference be-tween the language of human behavior with its inherent ambiguity and the language of a more positive science, whether operational or action language; (3) the desire to preserve Freud from potential de-stroyers; (4) the desire to remain identified with Freud; and (5) the need to prove that one has remained within the orbit of psycho-analysis" (53). Cooper's list of possible "causes" is provocative and courageous not least because it subtly but emphatically makes the following declaration: the field of psychoanalysis suffers from un-resolved conflicts in its attachment to Freud, and cannot advance scientifically or clinically until it works through these powerful anxieties.

Cooper is not the first to notice that the field struggles in its re-lationship to Freud, but he is unique for bringing an "analytic," even diagnostic, sensibility to bear on this problem. Whereas critics of psychoanalysis routinely disparage the field on the basis of its re-semblance to a religion (Crews, 2018; Roustang, 1982; Sulloway, 1979) and defenders decry the comparison as unsubstantial "Freud-bashing," Cooper, a psychoanalyst himself, urges members to take these comparisons seriously and become more self-reflective, "ana-lytic" even. Like an experienced analyst who is unpersuaded by the kinds of minor improvements that keep a patient's underlying de-fensive apparatus completely unchanged, Cooper does not see a "hidden revolution" as better than no revolution at all because it is precisely the felt need to keep the revolution "hidden" that *is* such a major problem in the first place. "If we are making claims as healers, charging for our services and claiming that we can enable people to alter their lives in more positive directions, then we must, sooner or later, demonstrate that our ideas are in accord with findings from neighboring disciplines" (2008, 246), and we cannot keep "hiding" our changes from others and ourselves for fear acknowledging our progress is tantamount to *deviating* from Freud. Besides, why *shouldn't* our theories deviate from Freud? Isn't development the aspiration of a dynamic science? And whether we deviate or not, do we understand why *deviation* is how *innovation* feels? Unsatisfied with the "hidden" aspect of our revolution, and determined to help psychoanalysts look inward, Cooper paves the way for an in-depth exploration of the field's abiding conflict around innovation. In what follows, we will see how these conflicts are constitutive of the field, and in what ways Laplanche's attitude of "faithful infidelity" achieves a breakthrough in existing patterns of our relationship to Freud.

Psychoanalysis and the "Sinai complex"

In an effort to gain traction on this enduring problematic, it is crucial to develop a coherent explanation of *why* psychoanalysis finds itself in this peculiar position with respect to change and innovation. In an interview with Stephen Mitchell, the historian Peter Rudnytsky addresses this situation and asks, "whether Freud didn't bequeath a curse on the history of psychoanalysis that needs to be taken into account" (2000, 112). After Mitchell says no, "that seems too harsh to me" – Freud was a "towering genius" and we must be sympathetic to his limitations – Rudnytsky contrasts Freud's behavior with Darwin's intellectual generosity and says it, "leads me to wonder whether Freud's personality didn't lead psychoanalysis in an unfortunate direction by abandoning a scientific ethos by which people revise their hypotheses if they find that they are contradicted by evidence ... didn't Freud paradoxically steer psychoanalysis in a direction that was antiscientific despite his desire to ground psychoanalysis in natural science?" (116). Although Mitchell repeatedly resists these "harsh" characterizations, Rudnytsky doubts Mitchell's optimistic assessment, even wondering whether Mitchell's contention that Freud has been successfully transformed from a "ghost" into an "ancestor" (borrowing Loewald's formulation) (1993) is accurate, or merely wishful thinking. Although they ultimately agree to disagree, the exchange is exemplary of how Freud's extraordinary influence on the field is routinely described in supernatural terms. That is, while Rudnytsky occupies the position of historian in this debate – neutral, unsentimental, an outsider to the field – his attempts to rationally draw attention to the problem are suffused with references to occult forces (curses, spells, etc.) as if Freud's personality was so powerful, forbidding, and transcendental that psychoanalysis, as a professional field, is fated to remain eternally a horde of followers, traumatically tethered to their ancient king. According to this view, contemporary psychoanalysis continues to be traumatized by Freud's violent treatment of rivals as "defectors" Rudnytsky, 2000) such that to date, *still* no one dares to challenge basic psychoanalytic tenets for fear they will be "cast out" of the community as a whole. One perhaps cannot help but wonder if the author of *Moses and Monotheism* wouldn't be privately amused by this comparison, and precisely be- cause it confirms the primitivity of the field's behavior, it can be extremely narratively persuasive. Indeed, even as the account por- trays the field in baldly mystical terms – its rhetoric of Freud's "curse" evoking the logic of Greek tragedies or Biblical stories where a rootless, superstitious cult is "marked" by their immutable bond to a punitive father/king – it nonetheless carries the advantage of treating the relationship between the field and its founder in *emotional* terms.

By contrast, and as evidenced when asked about the topic directly, Mitchell avoids this line of thinking entirely by downplaying the problem, choosing instead to see the fact of changes in the field as proof enough that we are cured of whatever early fixations we once suffered from (2000). As if determined to sidestep this oedipal drama completely, Mitchell instead advocates for a pluralism of ideas that loosens the grip of theoretical orthodoxy. But while such a position effectively facilitates greater *flexibility* with respect to how Freud's ideas are followed, there is a meaningful difference between following *less* stringently and rigorously dismantling a flawed theory of mind. Remarkably, it is the latter activity that remains as off-limits today as it did 100 years ago because even though the field has undergone manifold changes, Freud's original language remains nearly completely unchanged. Writing after the interventions of Mitchell's Relational school, Cooper notes that the field's changes are of a magnitude that would constitute a paradigm-shift for any other science and yet this has not translated into a "newer overall view of psychoanalysis": "in the United States a two-person psychology and some version of a comprehensive intersubjective or relational point of view, have superseded traditional resistance analysis as the core theoretical and technical viewpoint for most of our profession in the United States. The representational world, conceived as internalized object relations, has superseded drive-defense configurations as primary determinants of mental life. The intrapsychic focus on the patient has to a great degree given way to or at least been supplemented by scrutiny of the interpersonal-intersubjective-relational transactions between patient and analyst" (2008, 249). As such, although it *feels* radical to follow Freud more loosely that originally permitted, pluralism might *not* actually be the assault on psychoanalytic orthodoxy that either side claims it to be. A closer engagement with the history of metapsychology in the next chapter will reveal that underneath the proclaimed scandal of multiplicity is in fact an enduring theoretical homogeneity. Differences among Klein, Winnicott or Kohut – vast as they often may seem to be – are confined to the *narrative* plane that ultimately preserves the fundamental ontology of Freudian *metapsychology* intact.

Perhaps this is why Mitchell always seems to strenuously qualify his deviations from traditional psychoanalysis as "different" rather than "better," as when he says, "I think the relational model is better; I don't think it's "right" ... I think the drive theory is anachronistic; I don't think it's Wrong, with a capital "W" (2000, 118). Such a qualification not only avoids direct confrontation with psychoanalytic foundations, but makes plain that the only possible way of relating to Freudian orthodoxy isn't to call it "wrong" but to merely alter the *degree* of one's wholesale fidelity to it. Mitchell's intervention in American psychoanalysis is indeed exemplary here. By emphatically drawing a sharp distinction between "drive" versus "relational" theory, Mitchell successfully reorganized the discourse into competing claims about human motivation that left practitioners free to decide which account of psychic life they preferred (1983). But while Mitchell positions "relational" psychoanalysis as a better, more useful and updated version of psychoanalysis, he nevertheless shies away from any categorical rejection of Freud's original model or terminology. For example, when asked in an interview whether relational theory should supercede older views, he replies that the Freudian model "was a great explanatory framework at a particular point in intellectual and clinical history. Now it doesn't work very well. The success of the relational turn in psychoanalysis is mostly due to the fact that it's more useful" (2000, 118). Although Mitchell draws on the philosopher Richard Rorty to justify his vision of a comparative psychoanalysis, the reluctance to say that the "drive" model is "Wrong" but simply less "useful" is not quite as rhetorically innocent as his appeal to pluralism suggests because what it ultimately prevents is a meaningful effort to *link* the major problems in psychoanalytic theory with major flaws in Freud's theoretical model. Instead of making these requisite connections, Mitchell repeatedly demurs, preferring to treat "drive" theory as a reasonable "choice" (among many) for individual clinicians to make. When asked about Freud's influence, or how he thinks Freud's intolerance of "disloyalty" handicapped the development of theory, Mitchell says, "It's hard for me to villainize Freud" because "he didn't have basic elements that are available to us now" and that although "there's no question that it was antiscientific in that ultimately his authority was law," it's more helpful to "see Freud in terms of his advantages and disadvantages" (2000, 112–7).

This repeated recourse to what's "useful" about a given interpretation belies Mitchell's discomfort with the fundamental objective of criticism, which is to discover the logical contradictions of a given theory so as to develop new ideas on firmer ground. His repeated contention that *now* "drive theory doesn't work very well" but it *was* correct "at a particular point in intellectual and clinical history" is a benevolent gesture that completely distorts the goal of scientific development which is to *supersede* "anachronistic" ideas because they are wrong, then as now. In this vein, it is worth noting that for many contemporary clinicians, it is no longer sufficient to merely say (as many psychoanalysts once did) that the patients Freud treated no longer exist (but if they did, his theory/technique would be applicable) because that even in Freud's day, the patients he treated did not actually exist as he perceived them. This is to say that there is substantial clinical value to adjudicating between "right" and "wrong" theoretical ideas and that the merits of a particular idea should be replaced when they are "wrong" and *because* they are wrong, whether or not Freud had limitations or not. To return to the relational example, Mitchell's magnanimity toward even those theories he considers "anachronistic" is consistent with a more general inclination to avoid substantive criticism, as if all criticism automatically leads to the violent "holy wars" of early psychoanalytic history. It is understandable that in the 1970s and 1980s, having only recently emerged out from under the oppressive hegemony of 1950s ego psychology, practitioners might be reluctant to erect yet another system of adjudicating "right" from "wrong" psychoanalytic theory. It is also understandable for clinicians to associate judgment with orthodoxy and to have feared the emergence of yet another monistic system. However, linking critical judgment or the capacity to adjudicate which ideas are right and wrong with rigid orthodoxy fundamentally misses what makes orthodoxy so pernicious, which isn't that it upholds a reasonable framework for deciding the difference between right and wrong, but that it judges *all* development strictly on the basis of its adherence to existing dogma.

Moreover, it is neither scientifically generous nor ethically benign to preserve and perpetuate old ideas simply because we cannot bear to challenge them. This need to preserve wrong ideas for the sake of avoiding conflict reflects a field-wide aversion to critical judgment. In this vein, we could view Mitchell's earlier modesty about the ultimate "truth" of his school's accomplishments as related to the problem of meaningful critique, and how the refusal to critically judge which ideas are right or wrong significantly hinders the capacity for innovation. While in the context of psychoanalytic history it is understandable that even a gesture of minor disobedience has come to feel dangerous and even risky, such a perception reflects the extreme prohibition against change, in *any* form, that governed the field's first generations rather than an objective appraisal of the substantive distance taken from orthodox views. Therefore, and despite the scale of its ambition and range of its interaction with other fields, the structural innovations of "relational" theory are limited precisely *because* they are circumscribed to merely telling different stories of human motivation rather than developing comprehensive new

models of unconscious psychic life. While major technical and theoretical changes certainly follow from different ideas of human motivation, such that whether you believe the human infant is primarily
seeking attachment or discharge begets substantively contrasting
technical procedures, it nevertheless remains the case that none of
these rival narratives challenge the original Freudian organization of
the mind. More importantly, none of the paradigms as they have
been elaborated since Freud amount to a new biopsychical ontology
that can meaningfully accord with contemporary science. While brain
researchers of the past thirty years have made astonishing contributions to our understanding of mental life, these findings have not led
psychoanalysis, as a discipline, to substantially revise its core conceptualizations of how unconscious life is *mechanically* structured.

Mitchell's particular way of negotiating theoretical innovation (by
emphasizing pluralism and sparing the original foundations) brings
us back to the problem of deviation in psychoanalysis. How are we to
understand the enduring prohibition against substantive critique? If
pluralism is not the solution one hoped it would be (Aron et al., 2018)
and calling the field "cursed" lacks explanatory depth (Rudnytsky,
2000), then we need a cogent articulation of why the field remains
caught in a dynamic of loyalty versus heresy with respect to psychoanalytic innovation. While Freud's singular role in the construction of psychoanalytic identity cannot be underestimated, and while
it is certainly the case that entire generations of analysts were shaped
by their identifications with him, it is time to go beyond the familiar
tropes of Freud's villainy and the field's victimization because such
accounts still completely fail to explain the psychological *reason* for
this particular identificatory sequence in the first place. That is, the
field's repetition of a certain pattern with respect to Freud still does
not explain why the field relates to Freud this way to begin with.
Cooper touches on this aspect of the situation when he speculates
that the field's continued "clinging" to Freud stems from the "power
of his language" but while suggestive, the phrase remains vague –
what makes his language so powerful? Powerful *how*? In the interest
of deepening our grasp of this emotional dynamic, what if we
brought a richer perspective on attachment to bear on this exercise in
"self-reflection" by presuming that the intensity of our "clinging"
exposes something vital about Freud's insecurities and our own.

To wit, perhaps Freud has such a prominent place in our imaginations because he brought order to a vital dimension of our experience that was, until then, uncodified, unstructured and unavailable to scientific observation. Although Freud did not, properly speaking, "invent" the unconscious, therapy or the fascination with dreams, his unique capacity to synthesize information and organize different ideas into a coherent picture of mental life created psychoanalysis as a *field* with a specifiable *object* of study. In this role as the field's progenitor, Freud functions less as the oft-cited Jewish God who announces *he* is Truth and demands obedience, than God's emissary Moses. In the biblical story with which Freud was exceptionally familiar, Moses is the reluctant redeemer of the Jewish people, a man of mysterious lineage who is chosen by God to liberate his people from bondage. In one of Exodus' most harrowing scenes, Moses, who has just spent forty days and nights with the burning bush receiving God's laws, finally emerges with the finished tablets and is eager to share the tablets with his people, who he imagines have been waiting patiently. When instead, he is met with the spectacle of the Jewish people worshipping a golden calf, he is furious and devastated and instead of coming down the mountain with God's tablets in tow, he smashes them, rebuking the Israelites (who had just been saved from Egypt) for their impatience and ingratitude. As a punishment for their crime, the Israelites are cursed to wander the desert until the generation of idol-worshippers dies out.

Freud's fascination with Moses is well known; in fact, within Freud studies, a minor sub-field is devoted to investigating the biographical dimension of Freud's interest in Moses, his relationship to Judaism and the potential impact of these ideas on psychoanalytic theory.[4] But to date, few efforts have been made to link Freud's identification with Moses to his self-image as founder of the psychoanalytic field. Moreover, although psychoanalysis specializes in the interpretation of phantasmatic life, little consideration has been made of how Freud's fantasied self-identification with Moses consigns psychoanalysts to being his "people." Accordingly, the transmission of an idea say innovation = deviation, for example, is less mysterious than it initially seems since we know from decades of clinical writing and research that unconscious parental fantasies have the power to organize a child's internal psychic life, whether these fantasies are ever made explicit or not. In fact, one of Laplanche's singular insights will be to emphasize the "realism of the unconscious," by which he means that the child's unconscious derives from "messages" transmitted by the unconscious of the parent. In this view, the mechanism which enables present-day psychoanalysts to perpetuate behavioral patterns initiated a century ago is not particularly mystical (the result of a "curse" or "spell") but rather the direct result of how psychoanalysts are positioned as the "people" rescued from ignorance/bondage by their fearless leader Freud. In this telling, Freud represents a kind of Moses who liberated us from superstition and devised laws that emancipated us from centuries of ignorance about psychic experience. What remains less immediately clear is why the Moses-Israelite matrix should necessarily conduce to such a powerful fear of deviation.

This is where the drama of the golden calf may be instructive because although most historians of the field assume that our anxiety about change is a learned reaction to Freud's violent treatment of "heretics" as idol-worshippers, such an explanation completely misses our own endogenous disinclination to deviate from Freud's original laws lest in doing so we compromise our only access to the template that promised comprehension. After all, Freud's journey into the subject of psychic life produced a body of knowledge that made a certain kind of inquiry newly possible. Rather than trying to psychoanalyze Freud's fantasies about this endeavor, what interests me is the effect on psychoanalysts of experiencing psychoanalytic knowledge as a vocabulary they stand at risk to lose. From this perspective, the endurance of Freud's influence has less to do with some mythical paternal force than with the fact that he represents our only access to the critical exploration of unconscious life. It is tempting to associate this word-giving role with the maternal function but I think juxtaposing "maternal" and "paternal" in this way ultimately obscures the extent to which our attachment to Freud is really about our experience of him as the "one who brought us out of ignorance," and concomitantly, our anxiety about deviance expresses the fear that by being doubtful, impatient and childish, we risk inadvertently jeopardizing our newfound liberation. In other words, perhaps popular characterizations of the field as suffering from an "Oedipal complex" completely misconstrue the nature of our anxiety toward deviation, mistakenly attributing to Freud a constellation of feelings that originate in us. If we accept that studying unconscious psychic life inevitably generates considerable anxiety, and that this anxiety, while common to all intellectual endeavors is acute when the object of study is not easily accessible to standard scientific procedures, then we might begin to imagine how the enduring fidelity to Freud is more usefully seen as a *symptom* rather than a *cause* of the field's vexed relationship to change. Viewing the problem this way permits a level of analytic complexity that is otherwise absent from accounts which focus exclusively on simplistic narratives of Freud's tyranny and the field's submission.

Furthermore, accurately appreciating our role in the trajectory of psychoanalysis clears a path for critically reflecting on the dynamics at play in the development of our field. Specifically, we might observe that one major effect of the refusal to invalidate any of Freud's original terms, and corresponding determination to preserve all his terminology even when words have undergone significant transformations, has been the inability to develop new models of the mind that more accurately represent what we know about psychic life today. As Cooper observed, "analytic theory and technique have undergone vast change from the simple task of making the unconscious conscious or undoing infantile repressions or resolving infantile conflict. Currently we consider an *enlarged* panorama of early and later faults, failures, deficits, deprivations, and their consequences, as well as conflict resolutions, and the enormous changes wrought during the course of development upon earlier conflicts that may no longer be germane. In this new light it is hard to give a meaning to 'infantile neurosis' or to 'transference neurosis'" (1986, 59). The rigid "clinging" to archaic terms not only forces all scientific innovation to be funneled through outdated language, but in so doing, systematically prevents the construction of any comprehensive new working models. While this situation has been predominantly attributed to "Oedipal" anxiety about overthrowing Freud-the-Father, a more nuanced interpretation of why the field "changes without changing" is enabled by understanding that Freud functions as a Moses-like figure whose law-giving actions transformed the ignorant Israelites into an organized, coherent and exclusive nation. What if psychoanalysts are frightened that they don't know – in advance – which Freudian ideas are immutable versus which are up for grabs? Within this dynamic, psychoanalysts may often feel like Israelites who think they are behaving reasonably only to find that their innovations are equivalent to idol worship. This "Sinai complex" whereby we do not know which ideas will jeopardize our status as adherents of psychoanalysis helps explain why innovation resembles "new wine in old bottles," and why clinicians invested in psychoanalytic ideas are anxious about how changing *some*thing could inadvertently compromise everything.

Extensive scholarly studies have demonstrated that Freud's behavior in the construction of psychoanalysis – rarely citing sources, attributing all discoveries to his own autonomous intellectual journey, exiling anyone who disagreed with him – consolidated the myth that he was Moses the law-giver, a reluctant but unambiguous "deliverer" who speaks to ordinary people from the Truth of what he alone has directly seen, and that his aggressive self-mythologization effectively shaped the field into a "movement" rather than an academic discipline. For the most part, these observations have led critics to conclude that psychoanalysis operates like a religion rather than a science and to disregard it accordingly. But these well-rehearsed criticisms make little progress in penetrating the dynamic relationship between Freud and subsequent generations of psycho-analysts, meaning that calling it a religion leaves totally unanswered the psychological *reason* why generations of analysts abide by Freudian/Mosaic decrees. In other words, what if our fidelity is not *caused* by our religion but by our conviction that deviating could cost us our relationship to what *is* true about our science. The hardline dichotomy between "religion" and "science" is an effective tool for derogating psychoanalysis but it fails to capture how the transmission of a difficult truth (such as the unconscious) *is* indeed an idiosyncratic feature of psychoanalytic theorizing. What if psychoanalysis is our name for the study of unconscious, erotic life, and our conflicted experience of innovation expresses our fear that straying will lead to the loss of our object of study?

Indeed, it is worth observing that asking this question about the transmission of psychoanalysis reenacts Freud's enduring question about Judaism: "what gave Judaism its extraordinary hold over the Jews, with all its "fateful consequences?" (Yerushalmi 1991, 29).

As Yosef Haim Yerushalmi has so skillfully demonstrated, "the force and longevity of religious tradition cannot be apprehended if tradition is presented essentially in terms of the history of ideas, or the history of education, or even as a system of symbols whose mythical, material and social referents can be decoded, while its psychological dimensions are ignored" (87). As such, it is these "psychological dimensions" which the "Sinai complex" aims to elucidate. Specifically, explaining the motivation of contemporary clinicians in maintaining fidelity to Freud is a radical departure from those popular explanations which suggest that some kind of collective unconscious process accounts for our current behavior. Yerushalmi notes that contrary to Freud's notion of how Judaism has been transmitted, "one cannot explain the transmission of a tradition at any time as a totally unconscious process. Though much of the process of transmission may be nonverbal, that is not tantamount to its being unconscious. The basic modalities in the continuity of a religious tradition are precept and example, narrative, gesture, ritual, and certainly all of these act upon, and are interpreted by, not only consciousness but the unconscious. The true challenge for psychoanalysis is not to plunge the entire history of tradition into a hypothetical group unconscious, but to help clarify, in a nonreductive way, what unconscious needs are being satisfied at any given time by living within a given religious tradition, by believing its myths and performing its rites" (89). As against prevailing notions that subsequent generations have passively submitted to Freud out of some mysteriously transmitted trauma of having once been idolatrous, we might consider instead that our attachment to psychoanalysis involves our acceptance of the emotional bargain Freud proffered.

When in his essay on the field's agonizing relationship to innovation, Cooper mentions Freud's abiding fascination with the biblical figure of Moses, he does so in order to ask whether "it stretches the imagination, but perhaps not too far, to think that Freud, brilliant scientist and amazing scholar, might transfer some of his deep personal belief in the basic immutability of Jewish character, an underappreciated and enormously important part of his own identity, into a wish for and an effort to do all that he could to assure the constancy and immutability of his personal creation – psychoanalysis. A speculation such as this one does not, of course, shed any

light on the need for conformity among so many of Freud's followers" (2008, 238). In this passage, Cooper cites Freud's well-
documented conviction that the Jews possessed certain immutable
traits throughout history in order to speculate about Freud's ambi-
tions for psychoanalysis but somehow stops short of making the link
between Freud's self-mythologization as Moses and the "the need for
conformity among so many of Freud's followers." In other words,
Cooper's evocation of Moses, although apt, nevertheless misses the
drama at the heart of the biblical tale which is that after Sinai, the
Israelites *become* Moses' followers by foreswearing idol worship and
promising to trust him as their leader from now on. If then, as Freud
believed, the Jews retained certain attributes throughout history it
wasn't by some mystical or accidental transmission of the laws but
because they accepted the terms of Moses' leadership (i.e. "follow
everything I say, or I abandon you in the desert"). The "Sinai complex" aims to describe precisely the effect on Freud's followers of his
self-perception as Moses; in particular, it intends to explain why the
"conformity" among psychoanalysts that frustrates and confuses
Cooper can be most clearly understood as the natural consequence of
our field's discursive origins.

In the final paragraphs on his imaginary monologue with Freud,
Yerushalmi confesses: "I carry within me a pent-up feeling, an intuition, that you yourself implied something more, something that
you felt deeply but would never dare say. So I will take the risk of
saying it...In short, I think you believed that just as you are a godless
Jew, psychoanalysis is a godless Judaism. But I don't think you intended us to know this" (99).[5] What if a better relationship to psychoanalysis wasn't the usual choice between orthodoxy vs. heresy but
the "faithful infidelity" Laplanche describes, whereby we don't have
to change our field into a totally unrecognizable empirical discipline
on the one hand, or abandon our scientific ambition and consider our
work a hermeneutic exercise on the other, but are able to rigorously
ascertain *which* ideas preserve the development of our field and
generate principles that are faithful to those ideas? Could our
"faithful infidelity" finally transform psychoanalysis into the kind of
"godless Judaism" Freud experienced in his own relationship to
tradition? Would our transformation into "godless Jews" finally

liberate us to bring to our science all the creativity and ruthlessness that genuine engagement requires?

"Slipping the knife" into psychoanalysis: Laplanche's approach to critique

When situated in the context of this constitutive emotional matrix, the discipline's longstanding anxiety about innovation and deviation requires us to put pressure on the trope, popular among clinicians today, that the so-called "bad old days" of psychoanalysis are over, and that our current pluralistic discourse signals an enlightened emancipation from the religious-type battles of the field's early generations. Aron, Grand and Slochower allude to this idea as well when in their essay calling for a "self-reflective" turn, they acknowledge that in spite of the "relational" school's privileging of mutuality over hierarchy and multiple perspectives over univocity, they too have succumbed to bitter divisions and a lack of self-critique. Therefore, rather than advocating for yet another variation of pluralism or historicization, this project draws on Laplanche to "put psychoanalysis to work" by getting rid of ideas which contradict what we've learned clinically and theoretically and inventing "new foundations for psychoanalysis" which sustain the "realism of the unconscious." While getting rid of flawed ideas may, for some, have violent connotations, neither our discipline, nor our patients, are well-served by our anxieties about aggression. Cooper provides a helpful distinction between scientific strategies, "lumping" and "splitting." "The lumper finds underlying unity in superficially diverse phenomena. The splitter explores hidden differences among seemingly similar phenomena. Lumping was important early in our history. For example, it was important to demonstrate that the Oedipus complex was universal. I believe that at the present time, however, splitters have a greater contribution to make" (1984, 44). For reasons that are, perhaps, not unrelated to its evocations of a primitive defense, "splitting" has negative connotations in psychoanalysis. And yet, as Cooper points out, splitting has a vital function in the development of new knowledge. While it is not a goal in and of itself, splitting plays a crucial role in establishing the coordinates of scientific inquiry by configuring what actually belongs within a given conceptual paradigm. Splitting, insofar as it aims to get rid of flawed assumptions and terms, can be a productive tool in the service of theory-building. As such, what's needed is a two-step process that, first, conducts a thorough critique that proficiently identifies problematic areas in our current model of the mind and second, provides a rigorous appraisal and integration of contemporary research. Such an undertaking promises a genuinely new set of formulations to work with that draw out what is currently latent in so much clinical writing and thinking but remains stifled by the pressures of a long-standing resistance to change.

Even though there is tremendous resistance to retiring old terminology, or even to calling it "wrong," there is a natural limit to how much the discipline can evolve if it sees its task as merely upgrading Freud's original language. Cooper reminds us that, "we do have some old-fashioned guidelines to help our evaluation of theory. The classical rules indicate that a theory should be elegant (i.e. parsimonious, using the least number of propositions and constructs required for its subject); it should be consonant with knowledge and theory in other sciences (i.e. there would have to be compelling reasons to contradict established knowledge, and the theory is strengthened if it can draw on other sciences); and it should be useful (i.e. it should lead to further ideas and activities that will yield new knowledge)" (1983, 33). Using these guidelines, we have a scientific and ethical obligation to "alter conceptions that no longer stand up to such examination" and to re-shape our inquiries based on what we've learned. In sharp contrast to the field's behavioral conventions – of preserving Freud's original map of the mind by updating the meaning of specific terminology – there is new urgency to taking a sharper, more ruthless approach that is willing to get rid of those foundational tenets which we can demonstrate to be logically, scientifically, and clinically unsound.

In the search for "splitters" to perform a crucial analytic function, Laplanche is unique for making his "faithful infidelity" to Freud the centerpiece of his critical approach. Whereas his teacher and former analyst Jacques Lacan claimed his own readings to be a "return to Freud," Laplanche proclaims to be neither rehabilitating nor condemning Freud so much as "putting him to work," by which he means that he is interested in testing which ideas can be said to promote the Copernican discovery of *enlarged* sexuality and which ideas get in the way. Laplanche repeatedly calls for "new foundations for psychoanalysis" but it is not as though this means that *all* of psychoanalysis since Freud has "gone astray" or that all of contemporary psychoanalysis is irredeemably wrong. Instead, what Laplanche has observed is that as a result of Freud's original and systematic "going-astray," the field is built on foundations which are deeply and substantially flawed. What is more, and as Cooper has observed regarding the field's relationship to change, there is a constant pressure on any new ideas to conform to Freud's original structure of the mind such that increasingly complicated phrases and conceptualizations are sooner added than a comprehensive re-formulation of the basic model is undertaken. In other words, while there is a powerful tendency to merely amend Freud's original maps (and while this tendency operates like adherence to some tacit prohibition against creative evolution), Laplanche observes that in point of fact the field *has* already generated a plethora of new insights only without a coherent foundation to unify and explain them. Even a cursory overview of contemporary psychoanalytic theory attests to Laplanche's accuracy on this point:[6] the increasing popularity of terms like "enactment" or "unconscious communication" – even among so-called traditional Freudians[7] – reveals the extent to which the major focus among clinicians has shifted toward theorizing processes that have always been at the fringe of mainstream doxa because they were seen to challenge, rather than simply compliment, Freud's basic formulations. This widespread intellectual phenomenon – of normalizing ideas which were once seen as hearsay – reflects how far the field has needed to move beyond its original conceptions (presumably in order to maintain intellectual and clinical viability), even if there remains a deep-seated reluctance to actually extrapolate from these variegating local ideas into a more far-reaching "re-problematization of the whole." The problem with maintaining "an old official stance" is not only then, as Cooper warns, that it "hampers our taking a fresh look at behavior in the light of newer knowledge"(1986, 59) but that in failing to build a new "vessel" that could legitimately contain the knowledge we have developed, psychoanalysis remains stubbornly tethered to fundamental misunderstandings of the psyche as a whole.

For this reason, Laplanche aims to establish a firm basis for future development by substantially reconfiguring the discipline's underlying foundations. To do so, Laplanche undertakes a multi-leveled critique that a) demonstrates what makes a given idea *Ptolemaic*, b) identifies the Ptolemaic *pull* of a particular theoretical concept, and c) articulates a distinctly *Copernican* alternative. Upon completing this exercise for an array of central psychoanalytic ideas, Laplanche then gathers together the Copernican version of each idea – the proverbial roads-not-taken – in order to erect an entirely new path that now has, at its foundations, Copernican (rather than Ptolemaic) formulations. The end result of Laplanche's critical reformulation far exceeds any of the particular individual theoretical revisions he makes. Therefore, whereas Laplanche is often used today to improve a particular psychoanalytic concept (Fletcher, 1999; Stein, 2008; Silverman, 2015; Saketopoulou, 2014),[8] I read Laplanche's critique as more urgent and comprehensive: to fundamentally reorient the basic foundations of the discipline. In this way, Laplanche's innovations are not merely limited to his rigorous reinterpretations of familiar concepts but to the overall *new* scene that emerges as a result of his systematic rejection of flawed thinking and reimagination of central concepts along rigorously radical lines.

It is of special importance to recognize the emergence of a new psychological *scene* as such, because one of Laplanche's singular achievements is to have elaborated a thoroughly Copernican theory of human development that is capable of standing alone as the new center of all subsequent theoretical formulations. Whereas the adult-infant relationship is at the center of many prominent thinkers since Freud, and while many have already advocated for its promotion within metapsychology, Laplanche is unique for working out a version of this scene that is, at once, entirely focused on the development of *enlarged* sexuality and at the same time, provides a radically new understanding of the unconscious as it relates to *affective* life. Furthermore, Laplanche's meticulous elaboration of the sexual-affective dimension to adult-infant relationality is all the more remarkable for being – although strictly psychoanalytic – totally compatible with the findings of contemporary neurobiology. While the question of how psychoanalysis ought to relate to brain research has long been the subject of intense controversy, and while Laplanche repeatedly insists that psychoanalysis is a self-sufficient discipline with the tools to independently develop and evaluate its own ideas, there seems to be little justification for perpetuating a theory which either contradicts or cannot maintain a genuine dialogue with current scientific research. As such, it is one of Laplanche's greatest strengths that, even though he draws from external disciplines when necessary, his theoretical paradigm compliments and extends so much of what we have learned in evolutionary biology, neuroscience, attachment theory, affect studies, and neurobiology.

A third way: Laplanche's interventions in contemporary theory

In their illuminating genealogy of French psychoanalysis, Dana Birksted-Breen and Sara Flanders observe, "while psychoanalysts all over the world recognize their Freudian origins, it is undeniable that psychoanalysis has developed along different lines of interest in different geographical areas due to cultural phenomena and to the influence of important or charismatic figures" (2010, 1). As a consequence of its discursive regionalism, the field has long had difficulty putting geographically or culturally heterogeneous psychoanalytic thinkers in conversation with each other. More often than not, major debates in the field are localized to a discrete geographical or linguistic area with few bridges between questions that arise in one place with answers arrived at in another. When efforts *are* made to introduce or integrate foreign thinkers, there is a tendency to fetishize and idealize these new ideas as though they are totally detached from ongoing debates, so that instead of retracing a thinker's unfamiliar steps, new terminology is simply imported wholesale and without deeper exploration. The results are of limited long-term use since without a firm grasp on how new ideas fit in with and respond to existing concerns, they function merely as shiny terminology that has no lasting bearing on the substance of our arguments. Such a tendency is all the more tempting in the case of Laplanche since until fairly recently most of his essays have been untranslated into English and, as a thinker, Laplanche often takes the shared context of his arguments for granted, rarely walking the reader through how his ideas correspond to contemporary issues concerns. That said, Laplanche is also a thinker who seems unique among psychoanalysts for relishing vigorous debate and who seldom softens the edges of his arguments for the sake of easy harmony.

Indeed, although Laplanche is not always explicit about the specific targets of his critiques, the philosophical rigor of his arguments manifests most clearly in a pattern of orienting his contributions as "interventions" in ongoing debates. As such, even if he doesn't frame his theories in direct contrast to Klein or attachment theory, for example, it is nevertheless possible to reconstruct how his argumentative moves perform a purposeful intervention in relevant work.

When reading Laplanche, I often have the sensation of being shown "answers" without a clear delineation of the corresponding "questions." While I mostly enjoy the reconstructive task this style entails, the absence of a clear "here's the problem, now here's the solution" structure can make it difficult to appreciate the scale and boldness of Laplanche's interventions. In order to draw out this element of Laplanche's style, and to maximize the impact of his original ideas, this book is structured as an encounter between Laplanche and the field of contemporary Anglo-American psychoanalysis as it exists today. As such, I organize this book as a set of questions – about *psychoanalytic theory*, the *unconscious*, *psychic structure*, and *motivation* – and then explore how Laplanche's concepts – of *metapsychology*, *sexuality*, *seduction*, and *translation* – provide possible answers.

The first chapter concerns the status of psychoanalytic theory, asking what this term means, and how it operates to enable or prevent theoretical innovation. Since one's approach to psychoanalytic theory is implicitly, if not always explicitly, structured in relation to one's ideas about theory-building generally, the first chapter deals with why **metapsychology** continues to be such a problematic term and why a revised approach to psychoanalysis as a scientific field is the first precondition to rigorous theoretical development. After establishing the general terms of psychoanalytic theory, the second chapter sets out to consider the meaning and operation of the **unconscious**. Since the term remains at the center of psychoanalysis even while having undergone significant transformation over the past several decades, this chapter explores what specific kind of psychic entity and process the "unconscious" is meant to explain. Such an inquiry will involve a comprehensive exploration of sexuality, its relationship to unconscious life and why *enlarged* sexuality must remain the privileged object of psychoanalytic treatment and study. In chapter three, this book investigates how **psychic structure** is conceptualized, especially as different positions on this topic correspond to different views about the origin and cause of mental suffering. Tracking how existing ideas about what causes conflicts and psychopathology revolve around vigorous arguments that nevertheless neglect the role of actual "otherness," this chapter establishes the necessary link between the subject's "individual" psychic structure and the ineluctable fact of alterity in the intersubjective sphere. The fourth and final chapter looks at continual debates about **motivation** and links the field's difficulty formulating a coherent and scientifically viable motivational theory with its enduring neglect of affect. This chapter delves into the findings of contemporary affect theories in order to devise a basic set of assumptions about mental functioning that turn out to contradict existing psychoanalytic formulations. By putting affect at the center of all biopsychical processes, and introducing Laplanche's idea of the "translation" process, it then becomes possible to grasp Laplanche's "general theory of seduction" as the basis of all psychic development.

As even this cursory description indicates, these topics are some of the broadest and most fundamental concerns of psychoanalysis since its inception. Not only have these questions preoccupied the field for generations, but every attempt to answer them involves going right to the heart of psychoanalysis' deepest concerns. In its simplified form, these topics can be said to correspond to the field's most rudimentary questions, such as 1) *what* is the nature of psychoanalytic theory (chapter 1, **metapsychology**), 2) *what* is the unconscious? (chapter 2, **sexuality**), 3) *what* causes mental suffering (chapter 3 **seduction**), and 4) *why* does psychic life develop? (chapter 4, **translation**). Each chapter introduces a new Laplanchian concept – metapsychology, sexuality, seduction, and translation – and establishes a firm basis for future theorization.

The long history of trying and failing to develop a coherent account of affect is exemplary of the challenges psychoanalysis confronts with respect to developing and supporting "new foundations." That is, although scientific breakthroughs over the past several decades have declared this "the age of affect," these findings have not, with minor exceptions (Johnston and Malabou, 2013; Demos, 2019) translated into the call for an overall new model of the mind. Within psychoanalysis, there is tremendous pressure to minimize the challenge posed by external critiques and to harmonize every scientific advance with ideas (supposedly) already latent in Freud. Much as Cooper and Laplanche have observed, it remains preferable to create new terminology within the Freudian template than "reproblematize the whole," meaning that so long as a bridge can be built linking contemporary findings with a passage or footnote in Freud, then an intellectual crisis is averted, and the metapsychology remains intact. Charles Spezzano's large scale attempt to forge a new affect theory for psychoanalysts reflects these intellectual conditions as when he introduces his work by promising that, "the central project of this book is to *extract* a theory of affect from the psychoanalytic literature. This psychoanalytic theory of affect is not a new theory but a new synthesis of existing theory. It does not ask analysts and psychoanalytic therapists to discard the major existing conceptualizations of psychopathology, nor does it suggest that we have been off base in all our previous conceptualizations of treatment" (1993, xi). Spezzano's anxiety is palpable here and aptly captures the familiar apologias required of anyone daring to challenge Freudian doxa.

It is in this context that we can appreciate the stakes and scale of Laplanche's interventions. For what Laplanche offers in his "faithful infidelity" to Freud and his rigorous critique of psychoanalytic foundations is a bold and provocative way forward that is unprecedented in the field's history. In addition to modeling a critical, sober new way of relating to Freud that sustains a deep interest in the field's originator but prioritizes the psychoanalytic discovery over the idiosyncratic ideas of Freud himself, Laplanche also wages a ruthless critique of the field's conceptual foundations that firmly establishes the *link* between its Ptolemaic, auto-centric orientation and the systematic inability to accurately prioritize affect and *enlarged* sexuality. From this perspective, the field's longstanding failure to develop a systematic theory of affect that can reflect its centrality to clinical reality is inextricable from the problems engendered by its deeper Ptolemaic core. What a complex account of affect reveals is, first, that the psyche is governed by a primordial emotionality and second, that this emotionality requires and enables complex relating to others. While affect theorists seldom focus on sexuality and Laplanche's call for a genuinely radical psychoanalysis that centers on sexuality makes no mention of affect, a careful exploration of contemporary science alongside Laplanche's rigorous critique demonstrates that the wrong idea of sexuality is enabled and maintained by the wrong understanding of affectivity. As such, revising our ideas about sexuality along Laplanchian lines requires a more comprehensive reformulation of the mind's basic ontology.

In the interest of utilizing Laplanche's interventions as new pillars of a reformulated psychoanalytic theory, this book also reconfigures how the contemporary psychoanalytic landscape is conceived. Whereas it has become customary for clinicians today to disclaim rigid stratification and work flexibly instead across a range of different schools (Reis, 2019), such an admirable approach has the disadvantage of leaving the underlying theory, with all of its problems and inconsistencies, totally intact. This may be because of the difference between clinical and theoretical work: while it is possible to create a useful working theory by picking and choosing the "good" parts and ignoring the "bad," such an approach is utterly incapable of adjudicating the substantive merits of foundational ideas. We previously saw how the avoidance of direct challenges to psychoanalytic doxa routinely manifests as a general disinclination to adjudicate at all, as if doing so compromises one's fidelity to the field as a whole. But this approach to theory is ultimately incompatible with Laplanche's call for "new foundations" and for this reason, the book strives to draw out the discipline's conceptual underpinnings even if contemporary practitioners say they don't entirely support those underpinnings anyway.

In keeping with its pedagogic purposes, this book is therefore addressed to the two major theoretical orientations at work in Anglo-American psychoanalysis today. Although different psychoanalytic schools commonly identify themselves somewhere on the "drive" vs. "object" divide, this book follows Slavin and Kriegman's view that a range of differences among theoretical models can be shown to coalesce around two major paradigms, and that, "although everyone's map of the field is different, there is a great deal of overlap between several of these broad characterizations of the psychoanalytic landscape" (1992, 19). As an example, although Greenberg and Mitchell use "drive/structure" to label the field, Modell uses "one person" vs. "two person" psychologies and Eagle frames the contrast

between "instinct" vs. "deficit," "roughly speaking, the divergent paradigms typically correspond to the classical and ego psychological traditions on one side and aspects of object relations theory, interpersonal
approaches, and self-psychology on the other" (19). Moreover, "although rarely articulated in their most clearly contrasting form," the
"classical" vs. "object relations" approaches do in fact correspond to a
"major division between what are essentially different psychoanalytic
"world views" (19). Slavin and Kriegman organize these "competing
currents" into two camps with respect to the question of the "psyche-in-
the-world" (20) but because my own project is focused on psychoanalytic foundations (rather than the status of the psyche-
in-the-world), the primary tool for organizing competing theories is
between the "traditionalist" position, on the one hand, and the
"progressive" position, on the other.

This categorization builds on the familiar division between "classical" vs. "object relations" approaches, but instead of differentiating
psychoanalytic models according to their stance with respect to
particular concepts, such as "drive," "intersubjectivity" or "attachment," for example, I focus instead on whether a given psychoanalytic model adheres loyally to Freud's original program or aims to
revise and adapt it. Since most theoretical developments in the field
can be classified as either trying to maintain Freud's original ideas or
trying to revise them, the only meaningful way to assess the quality
and substance of these changes is *not* by merely emphasizing their
continuity or distance from Freud, but by putting them in conversation with Laplanche's comprehensive innovations. Until now,
"traditionalists" derive their credibility from fidelity to Freud and
"progressives" identify as radical by virtue of their flexibility, but
both of these positions define themselves by their relationship to
Freud alone, without identifying in any *substantive* way what makes
their theories logically coherent or theoretically viable. It is in this
way that Laplanche offers a new path forward since rather than
designating his interventions by the familiar appellations – "classical"
or "relational," etc. – or perpetuating stale diatribes for or against
Freud, he rigorously demonstrates instead why a "third way" offers
the best chance of preserving what it essential to psychoanalysis while
reformulating what no longer works. After generations of "holy
wars," Laplanche's unique strategy of "putting to work"

psychoanalytic concepts, offers a sobering and hopeful path for future growth. In one of his many remarks describing his own style, Laplanche writes, "to intervene in a debate is, if possible to cause another voice to be heard – not a conciliatory voice, nor yet a voice that embraces one of the positions against the other, but the voice of a third party" (IDH, 140).

Laplanche's new foundations for psychoanalysis: translation, sexuality, seduction

"There are two facets to the Freudian revolution in the radical decentering it offers," Laplanche explains. "The first is classical: the discovery of the unconscious, in so far as it is precisely *not* our center, as it is an 'excentric' center; the other facet, the seduction theory, is hidden but indispensable to the first for it maintains the unconscious in its alien-ness" (UCR, 62). Seduction, sexuality, and translation are the new pillars of a rigorously Copernican metapsychology and in order to understand how these concepts are inextricably correlated, it will be necessary to integrate scientific findings on affect and human motivation. To briefly preview a central claim that will be developed later, affect is not just a feature of supposedly "higher" motivations, like "libido" or "attachment," but *the* fundamental mechanism for regulation of behavior. This insight compels a new understanding of mental life that puts the mechanics of affect at its center. Synthesizing a broad range of neurobiological findings, Damasio writes: "Emotions are complicated collections of chemical and neural responses, forming a pattern; all emotions have some kind of regulatory role to play, leading in one way or another to the creation of circumstances advantageous to the organism exhibiting the phenomenon; emotions are *about* the life of an organism, its body to be precise, and their role is to assist the organism in maintaining life" (1999, 51). By recognizing the singular role of emotions in homeostasis, researchers have made a tremendous discovery – emotions are not just irrational and mysterious obstacles to cognitive mastery, but *the* primary mechanism of biopsychical functioning. Moreover, emotional regulation constitutes the overarching developmental agenda of the human infant. As many scientists have repeatedly observed, "regulation" is one of the few theoretical concepts utilized by every developmental discipline. In his seminal text on the subject, neurobiologist Allan Schore explains that, "one such finding that appears again and again is the interactive nature of development. Development essentially represents a number of sequential mutually driven infant-caregiver processes that occur in a continuing dialectic between the maturing organism and the changing environment. It now appears that affect is what is actually transacted within the mother-infant dyad, and this highly efficient system of emotional communication is essentially nonverbal. Human development, including its internal neurochemical and neurobiological mechanisms, cannot be understood apart from this affect-transacting relationship" (1994, 7).

Whereas previous research by ethologists and animal researchers focused on the centrality of attachment to human development, the new work done on affect marked a radical departure from previous ways of thinking about affect and human development. Early studies on the mother–infant relationship posited that the child's need for attachment was rooted in an evolutionary demand for protection. This perspective, most often associated with John Bowlby, emphasized the biological necessity of attachment and insisted – directly against psychoanalysis – that attachment was part of a behavioral system which was independent of any so-called "drives." This story was elaborated in the late 1970s by Alan Sroufe and Everet Waters, who expanded attachment to mean "felt security," thereby greatly extending the concept to include older children and experiences beyond the individual caregiver. Later, in the 1990s, work on rodent pups by Myron Hofer further reconceptualized what attachment meant – instead of an end in itself, Hofer discovered that "the evolutionary survival of staying close to and interacting with the mother goes way beyond protection and may be expanded to many pathways available for regulation of the infant's physiological and behavioral system" (Fonagy 2001, 16). This "reformulation of attachment in terms of regulatory processes, hidden but observable within the parent-infant interaction, provides a very different way of explaining the range of phenomena usually discussed under the heading of attachment" such that attachment is now seen in reverse – not as an end goal, but as a "system adapted by evolution to fulfill key ontogenetic physiological and psychological tasks" (16).

Building on these insights, a wealth of research has since observed that the familiar model of attachment is insufficient; the motivation for attachment isn't protection but *development*. The human mind *grows* through its relationship to another human mind and *affect* is the primary mechanism of these mind-to-mind transactions. As such, what's "lost" in a disrupted social bond isn't attachment per se, but "the opportunity to generate a higher order regulatory mechanism: the mechanism for appraisal and reorganization of mental contents. In this context attachment is conceptualized as a process that brings into being complex mental life into being from a multi-faceted and adaptable behavioral system" (17). This broad body of work persuasively shows there is nothing vague or remotely sentimental about the infant's motivation to attach to an adult caregiver; evolution has prepared the human brain to seek a regulatory object who can effectively manage and shape early affect until such processes become increasingly self-regulated. To the extent the implications of this research remain unclear, it is worth specifying that recent findings on affect convincingly invalidate the binary – which has defined psychoanalysis for the past several decades – between drive theory and attachment studies. The argument between whether the human infant is primarily "pleasure seeking" or "object seeking," first advanced by Fairbairn and amplified by Stephen Mitchell, is shown to be distorted and profoundly off-base. The adaptive agenda of the human infant far exceeds any simple understanding of pleasure, attachment or security. Instead, we now understand the infant to be, from the very beginning, actively pursuing the *development of its own mind*, which is a complex regulatory process requiring the input and involvement of *another more developed mind*. As such, the infant is seeking neither discharge nor comfort but mental and physical *growth*, which is a complex socioemotional process that actively and entirely depends upon interchanges with the adult environment. Affect is what is transacted within the adult-infant dyad and can be seen as a "highly efficient system of emotional communication" for it acts as a "psychobiological regulator of the child's immature psychophysiological systems" which in turn "directly influences [the] child's biochemical growth processes" (1994, 7).

Putting affect regulation at the center of psychobiological growth moves us far away from the familiar, crude dichotomies between "pleasure" versus "object-seeking" by elaborating a model of the human infant as intensely active, dependent and agentic. In a bold attempt to bring evolutionary biology to bear on psychoanalytic theory, Slavin and Kriegman argue that "in the movement from Freud's narrowly defined, mechanistic drive conceptions to Mitchell's relational conflict model, a crucial dimension of the *inherent* conflict of interests is lost. "Yes, we are a social species for whom relational attachment is both problematic and of primary importance. Yet this is simply a *description* of the problem… We are motivated to do more with one another than just attach, stay close, and provide mutual support and comfort. We are also designed to *use* one another, and to guard against being used in ways that are dangerous to ourselves, in order to maximize our inclusive fitness … overall, the adaptive problem of the human child is far more complex than has ever been dealt with by attachment theories" (1992, 134). Seen this way, it becomes totally biologically and psychologically incoherent to describe the infant as seeking either basic discharge or security because both of these things, to the extent they are pursued, are only relevant in the context of complex affective interchanges which are geared toward enabling the structural maturation of the infant's brain. Put another way, neither discharge nor security can be said to correspond to the developmental requirements of the infant's psychophysiological regulatory systems, and as such cannot be treated as primary motivations in and of themselves.

Understanding that the human infant has a developmental agenda of its own which depends, for its success, on the availability of an adult other moves us away from the sentimental arguments and metaphors that have dominated the discourse from its inception. What is more, the neurobiological findings on affect regulation and the psyche's primordial affectivity bring together two problems that have always "haunted" psychoanalytic theory: affect and the Other. In fact, what recent breakthroughs in science reveal is that the field's inability to theorize affect coherently, and its Ptolemaic orientation, are *inextricably related*. To explicate this idea further, it is crucial to recount that for Laplanche, psychoanalysis is beset by insurmountable flaws pertaining to the origins and structure of *enlarged* sexuality. After reminding us that *enlarged* sexuality refers to the sexual drive beyond genitality, and that it *cannot* therefore be said to *derive* from biological development, nevertheless, Laplanche shows, psychoanalysis continues to provide an account of sexuality which aligns it with biology rather than psychology. For Laplanche, there are many moments in Freud's thinking when this "going-astray" occurs, but the most decisive and by far most consequential concerns Freud's abandonment of the seduction theory. Laplanche writes that, "the unconscious is only maintained in its radical alterity by the other person: in brief, by seduction" (UCR, 71). Since the radicality of sexuality is dependent upon our understanding it as an unconscious force that irreducible to biology, it is crucial to conceptualize *how* sexuality develops. Where does it come from? What sets it in motion?

For Laplanche, seduction is the linchpin of *enlarged* sexuality because it alone explains can account for the *development* of un-conscious life. Laplanche writes: "when the alterity of the other person is blurred, when it is reintegrated in the form of *my* fantasy of the other, of *my* 'fantasy of seduction,' then the alterity of the unconscious is put at risk... The other person is the other of seduction, the adult who seduces the child" (72). Any formulation which negates or in any way minimizes the role of the *other* person in the development of sexuality "put[s] at risk" the very meaning of the unconscious since without a credible account of how sexuality develops, psychoanalysis invariably resorts to mythological speculations which reproduce, rather than challenge, normative tropes. As Laplanche repeatedly points out, it isn't merely mythological speculation that fills the vacuum created by incoherent metapsychology, but an *auto-centered* ideology that affirms the autarky of the individual. Once the individual is positioned as the originator of his own sexuality, the coherence of the unconscious as distinct from biology completely falls apart – without an *actual other person* to transmit unconscious messages to the infant, there is no *source* for sexuality other than biology alone. Without a logical, ex-plicable source for sexuality, or an explanation for how it develops, psychoanalytic metapsychology becomes both incoherent and re-gressive. Laplanche outlines "new foundations for psychoanalysis" that put the *other* person at the center of *my* sexuality, thereby effecting a genuinely Copernican revolution in metapsychology.

Although Laplanche rarely mentions affect directly, a close reading of his theory in the context of contemporary neurobiology reveals that an *other*-centered metapsychology is not only superior for being more radical or more coherent – it is the only model of the mind that is compatible with current scientific knowledge. The human being's primordial affectivity is what enables a *channel* to be established between the infant and the adult and it is *this* channel – which is, developmentally, a psychophysiological necessity – that explains the emergence of sexuality. By reading affect research alongside Laplanche's rigorous critique, we observe that if we don't currently have a credible account for sexuality's development it is *because* we do not have a coherent affect theory. In a major departure from prevailing ideas, this project demonstrates that the repeated failure to theorize affect is itself a misreading of the underlying problem in psychoanalysis, which isn't that psychoanalysis does not *have* an affect theory but that the only way it *can* conceptualize affect within existing bounds is narrow, flawed and ineffectual. Psychoanalysis *has* an affect theory which consists of the insistence that feeling must be *felt first* in order to eventually *become* unconscious. This idea of the mind *feeling* things *before* repressing them reinforces the auto-centric notion of a mind beset by forces that originate *within*. To the extent it has not challenged these underlying ideas about affectivity, the existing psychoanalytic model of the mind perpetuates the fantasy of individuals as origin and center of their unconscious lives. Scientific developments on affect and Laplanche's discovery of the field's auto-centric core are not discrete and unrelated breakthroughs but two different paths to a single conclusion: psychoanalysis needs new foundations that revolve around the psycho-sexual other.

Notes

1 While "putting to work" echoes certain general features of conventional ideology critique, it is crucial to specify here that whereas immanent critique focuses on exposing the contradictions produced by history upon any positivist or transcendental accounts of "objective" reality, "putting" metapsychology "to work" involves identifying the precise moments in a theoretical formulation when the "exigency" of sexuality is vitiated or obscured. Therefore, whereas immanent critique offers a supremely effective analytic for undermining the totalizing claims of ideology, it is as such ill-suited to appraise the transformation of its own critical maneuvers or measuring the invariable distance of a radical formulation from a conservative outcome. For an incisive account of the differences among Horkheimer, Adorno and Marcuse on the question of ideology critique, see Daniel Held, *Introduction to Critical Theory: Horkheimer to Habermas* (1980).

2 In Joel Whitebook's recent intellectual biography of Freud, a deliberate effort is made to advance Freud scholarship beyond the familiar choice of hagiography or rejection. Whitebook describes the dominant trends in Freud scholarship as divided between attempts to protect Freud or to dismiss him, leaving little space for rigorous scholarship that takes a more nuanced and critical view (Whitebook, 2017).

3 Throughout his many essays, Laplanche provides different explanations of Freud's "going-astray"; he writes, "how can we doubt that Freud was capable of going- and could have gone – further than he did, in so far as that is precisely the ambition of our undertaking? With regard to the reasons for his blockage and then his going-astray, I have put forward on several occasions partial explanations – explanations which, moreover, are correlated: the centering on pathology, when the rejection of a normal unconscious; the inadequate elaboration of the translation theory; and, above all, the absence of the category of the message as a third reality ranking alongside material and psychological reality" (UCR, 80). In an effort to account for this oscillation between "centering" vs. "decentering" Laplanche at various times locates the problem in the lack of certain concepts (as mentioned above) and sometimes in Freud's own personal blockages and vulnerabilities; specifically, Laplanche observes that Freud was propelled by the desire for maximum universality that was often at odds with a certain intellectual rigor. A similar point has been observed by Louis Breger in his biography which discusses Freud's quest for fame, which often at the expense of intellectual honesty or carefulness. As it pertains to the question of Copernican vs. Ptolemaic tendencies, we might see the constant "going-astray" as an effort, on Freud's part, to preserve the shock value of his ideas about sexuality, which were ultimately superficial compared to the more genuinely scandalous theory of *enlarged* sexuality which he repeatedly shied away from in order to turn everything into genital sexuality instead.

4 See Yerushalmi (1991); Richard Bernstein (1998) and Assman (1998) for rigorous explorations on this subject.

5 I think it would be incredibly profitable to elaborate this idea along the lines Yerushalmi suggests in his study, particularly Freud's experience of Judaism as a kind of "negative" commitment whereby he couldn't imagine himself being anything but a Jew, but also couldn't actively subscribe to any Jewish-religious traditions. "Common to all these pronouncements is Freud's stubborn insistence on defining himself *via negationis*, by a series of reductions. He is not a Jews by religion, or in national terms, or through language (though there is evidence, yet to be considered, that he was by no means as linguistically ignorant as he claimed), and yet in some profound sense he remains a Jew" (Yerushalmi, p14).

6 Cooper writes very clearly about these changes, describing how our understanding of human motivation has changed dramatically, and therefore our ideas of analytic intent as well. Cooper writes: "It became apparent to increasing numbers of analysts after Freud's 'Inhibitions, symptoms and anxiety' (1926a) that individuals were motivated at least as much by their needs, whether for dependency, empathic contact, self-esteem, or safety, as they were by inherent sexual or aggressive drives. The infant is clearly motivated by powerful, often relatively conflict-free, desires for stimulation, satisfaction of curiosity, communication, learning, and object-

contact, all resting upon the sense of safety and security that the infant derives from the solid bond to its caretaking object (1985, 56)" cooper notes that "today's analyst is far more interested in tracing conscious and unconscious affects than in finding the source for behavior in drives" (56) and furthermore, that there is an "even more profound change in analytic intent. Where, for Freud, the analytic task of making the unconscious conscious...today's psychoanalyst is likely to view the undoing of the repressed past as a portion, and often only a small portion, of the task of bringing to awareness and to affective experience the nature of the patient's ongoing ways of feeling, perceiving and relating" (58).

7 See Gil Katz, *The Play within the Play* (2013) and Andrew Druck, Carolyn Ellman, Norbert Freedman and Aaron Thaler, Eds. *A New Freudian Synthesis* (2011).

8 One reason for the way Laplanche has been read might have to do with the translation history of his texts which have been sporadic until recently. Jonathan House has written that Laplanche indeed wanted his writing might also be a function of the fact that his early work was mostly translated and in circulation until recently and this often consisted of more dense re-interpretations whereas now the bigger project is more broadly available as a whole in translation – indeed, evidence of his motivation might be that he wanted his work published in reverse order (Jonathan House writes about this in his translations of Laplanche's work). For an excellent introduction to Laplanche's work, see Scarfone (2015).

Bibliography

Aron, Lew (1996). *A Meeting of Minds: Mutuality in Psychoanalysis.* Hillsdale: Analytic Press.

Aron, Lew, Sue Grand and Joyce Slochower, Eds. (2018). *De-Idealizing Relational Theory: A Critique from Within.* New York: Routledge.

Assman, Jan (1998). *Moses the Egyptian: The Memory of Egypt in Western Monotheism.* Cambridge: Harvard UP.

Atlas, Galit (2018). "Don't throw out the baby! External and internal, attachment, and sexuality," *Decentering Relational Theory: A Comparative Critique,* Eds. Lewis Aron, Sue Grand and Joyce Slochower. New York: Routledge.

Benjamin, Jessica (1988). *The Bonds of Love: Psychoanalysis, Feminism and the Problem of Domination.* New York: Pantheon.

Benjamin, Jessica (1995). *Like Subjects, Love Objects: Essays on Recognition and Sexual Difference.* New Haven: Yale UP.

Benjamin, Jessica (2005). From Many into One: Attention, Energy, and the Containing of Multitudes. *Psychoanalytic Dialogues* 15: 185–212.

Bernstein, Richard J. (1998). *Freud and the Legacy of Moses.* Cambridge: Cambridge UP.

Birksted-Breen, Dana, Sara Flanders and Alain Gibeault, Eds. (2010). *Reading French Psychoanalysis.* New York: Routledge.

Boesky, Dale (2005). Psychoanalytic Controversies Contextualized. *Journal of the American Psychoanalytic Association* 53(3): 835–863.

Bollas, Christopher (1987). *The Shadow of the Object: Psychoanalysis of the Unthought Known.* London: Free Association Press.

Bowlby, John (1969). *Attachment and Loss. Vol.1: Attachment.* New York: Basic Books.

Bowlby, John (1973). *Attachment and Loss. Vol.2: Separation, Anxiety, and Anger.* New York: Basic Books.

Bowlby, John (1980). *Attachment and Loss. Vol.3: Loss.* New York: Basic Books.

Bromberg, Phillip (1998). *Standing in the Spaces: Essays on Clinical Process, Trauma and Dissociation.* Hillsdale: Analytic Press.

Cooper, Arnold (2008). American Psychoanalysis Today: A Plurality of Orthodoxies. *Journal of the American Academy of Psychoanalysis and Dynamic Psychiatry* 36 (2): 235–253.

Cooper, Arnold (1983). Psychoanalytic Inquiry and New Knowledge. *The Quiet Revolution in American Psychoanalysis.* New York: Routledge.

Cooper, Arnold (1984). Psychoanalysis at One Hundred: Beginnings of Maturity. *The Quiet Revolution in American Psychoanalysis.* New York: Routledge.

Cooper, Arnold (1986). Psychoanalysis Today: New Wine in Old Bottles or the Hidden Revolution in Psychoanalysis. *The Quiet Revolution in American Psychoanalysis.* New York: Routledge.

Corbett, Ken (2009). *Boyhoods: Rethinking Masculinities.* New Haven: Yale UP.

Crews, Frederick (2018). *Freud: The Making of An Illusion.* New York: Picador.

Damasio, Antonio (1999). *The Feeling of What Happens: Body and Emotions in the Making of Consciousness.* New York: Mariner.

Demos, E. Virginia (2019). *The Affect Theory of Silvan Tomkins for Psychoanalysis and Psychotherapy: Recasting the Essentials.* New York: Routledge.

Division Review: A Quarterly Psychoanalytic Forum. No. 22 (Summer 2020).

Druck, Andrew B., Carolyn S. Ellman, Norbert Freedman, and Aaron Thalers, Eds. (2011). *A New Freudian Synthesis: Clinical Process in the Next Generation.* New York: Routledge.

Fairbairn, W.R.D. (1952). *An Object Relations Theory of Personality* New York: Basic Books.

Fonagy, Peter. (2001). *Attachment Theory and Psychoanalysis* New York: Other Press.

Fletcher, John (1999). "Introduction: Psychoanalysis and the question of the other." *Essays on Otherness: Jean Laplanche*, Ed. John Fletcher. London: Routledge.

Freud, Sigmund (1905). Three Essays on the Theory of Sexuality. J. Strachey (Ed. and Trans). *The Standard Edition of the Complete Psychological Works of Sigmund Freud* (Vol. 7, pp. 225–245). London: Hogarth Press.

Freud, Sigmund (1937). Analysis Terminable and Interminable. J. Strachey (Ed. and Trans). *The Standard Edition of the Complete Psychological Works of Sigmund Freud* (Vol. 23, pp. 209–254). London: Hogarth Press.

Gherovici, Patricia (2017). *Transgender Psychoanalysis: A Lacanian Perspective on Sexual Difference*. New York: Routledge.

Giffney, Noreen and Eve Watson, Eds. (2017). *Clinical Encounters in Sexuality: Psychoanalytic Practice and Queer Theory*. Punctum Books.

Govrin, Aner (2006). The Dilemma of Contemporary Psychoanalysis: Toward a "Knowing" Post-Postmodernism. *Journal of the American Psychoanalytic Association* 54 (2): 507–535.

Greenberg, Jay R. and Stephen A. Mitchell (1983). *Object Relations in Psychoanalytic Theory*. Cambridge: Harvard UP.

Harris, Adrienne (2005). *Gender as Soft Assembly*. Hillsdale: Analytic Press.

Held, Daniel (1980). *Introduction to Critical Theory: Horkheimer to Habermas*. Los Angeles: UCLA, UP.

Jacobs, Theodore (1990). The Corrective Emotional Experience – Its Place in Current Technique. *Psychoanalytic Inquiry* 10 (3): 433–454.

Johnston, Adrian and Catherine Malabou (2013). *Self and Emotional Life: Philosophy, Psychoanalysis, and Neuroscience* New York: Columbia UP.

Katz, Gil (2013). *The Play Within the Play: The Enacted Dimension of Psychoanalysis*. New York: Routledge.

Kernberg, Otto (1976). *Object Relations Theory and Clinical Psychoanalysis*. New York: Jason Aronson.

Klein, Melanie (1940) Mourning and Its Relation to Manic-Depressive States. *International Journal of Psychoanalysis* 21: 125–153.

Lacan, Jacques (1949). The Mirror Stage as Formative of the Function of the I as Revealed in Psychoanalytic Experience. In *Ecrits: A Selection* (pp. 1–6). New York: Norton.

Layton, Lynne (2020). *Toward A Social Psychoanalysis: Culture, Character, and Normative Unconscious Processes*, Ed. Marianna Leavy-Sperounis. New York: Routledge.

Reis, Bruce (2019). *Creative Repetition and Intersubjectivity: Contemporary Explorations of Trauma, Memory, and Clinical Process*. New York: Routledge.

Roustang, Francois (1982). *Dire Mastery: Discipleship from Freud to Lacan*. Trans. Ned Lukacher. APAP.

Rudnytsky, Peter L. (2000). *Psychoanalytic Conversations: Interviews with Clinicians, Commentators, and Critics*. New York: Routledge.

Saketopoulou, Avgi (2014). To Suffer Pleasure: The Shattering of the Ego as the Psychic Labor of Perverse Sexuality. *Studies in Gender and Sexuality* 15 (4): 254–268.

Scarfone, Dominique (2015) *Laplanche: An Introduction*. Trans. Dorothee Bonnigal-Katz. New York: Unconscious in Translation.

Schore, Allan (1994). *Affect Regulation and the Origin of the Self: The Neurobiology of Emotional Development*. New York: Psychology Press.

Silverman, Doris K. (2015). Freud and the Sexual: Essays, 2000-2006. Essays by Jean Laplanche. International Psychoanalytic Books, 2011. *Psychoanalytic Psychology* 32 (4): 678–683.

Slavin, Malcolm O. and Daniel Kriegman (1992). *The Adaptive Design of the Human Psyche: Psychoanalysis, Evolutionary Biology, and the Therapeutic Process*. New York: Guilford Press.

Spezzano, Charles (1993). *Affect in Psychoanalysis: A Clinical Synthesis*. New York: Routledge.

Stein, Ruth (2008). The Otherness of Sexuality: Excess. *Journal of the American Psychoanalytic Association* 56 (1): 43–71.

Sullivan, H.S. (1953). *The Interpersonal Theory of Psychiatry*. New York: W.W. Norton.

Sulloway, Frank J. (1979). *Freud: Biologist of the Mind*. New York: Basic Books.

Tomkins, Silvan (1962). *Affect, Imagery, Consciousness: Vol.1. The Positive Affects*. New York: Springer.

Westen, Drew (2002). The Language of Psychoanalytic Discourse. *Psychoanalytic Dialogues* 12(6):857–898.

Whitebook, Joel. (2017). *Freud: An Intellectual Biography*. Cambridge, Cambridge UP.

Winnicott, D.W. (1958). *Through Paediatrics to Psychoanalysis*. London: Hogarth Press.

Yerushalmi, Yosef Hayim (1991). *Freud's Moses: Judaism Terminable and Interminable*. New Haven: Yale UP.

Chapter 1

Metapsychology – Mytho-symbolic versus metapsychology

My "witch": the history of metapsychology

When Laplanche asks, "New foundations for psychoanalysis? Is it necessary to return to foundations? Furthermore, in what sense could they be new?" (NFP, 3) he is knowingly and deliberately calling attention to the ambiguous status of change, especially with regard to the field's original foundations. In order to build the necessary "new foundations," Laplanche will carefully distinguish what ought to constitute relatively immutable foundations from the range of particular theories which naturally come and go.

But before outlining Laplanche's specific views, it is crucial to evaluate the current state of metapsychology because its notoriously tangled genealogy aptly serves as the first clue to how fraught every attempt at engaging with the field's underlying theoretical assumptions has been. As several critics have observed, Freud himself famously referred to metapsychology as his "witch" (1937, 225) and never seems to have wavered on the centrality of metapsychology even as he struggled to locate its particular place. On the one hand, Freud seems to have believed that "without metapsychological speculation and theorizing ... we shall not get another step forward" (225) and at other moments, metapsychology seems to stand for nothing other than the abstract extrapolations of observed clinical practice. Although these ideas are not necessarily at odds, Joel Kovel has correctly observed that Freud's writing sought to strike a delicate balance between maximizing empirical investigation while preserving a set of theoretical foundations (1978, 22) and that one result of this tension is trying to ascertain which ideas qualify as metapsychological, and whether making changes to metapsychology alters clinical practice or our general theory of mind. Moreover, any debate on metapsychology necessarily encounters a set of complicated questions about the relationship between the "object" of psychoanalysis and the theories elaborated around it.

Derived from the Greek word "*meta*," meaning "beyond" or "behind," metapsychology most typically refers to a level of psychological conceptualization that organizes clinical observations. Because the psychoanalytic method of treatment, the clinical theory and the metapsychology are three parts of a unitary whole, Johann Erikson observes that "Freud himself claims that metapsychology retains a privileged position insofar as it constitutes a theoretical fundament for the other parts of psychoanalytical science. For even if the metapsychological theories are based upon clinical experiences, the ambition of these theories is no less than "to clarify and carry deeper the theoretical assumptions on which a psycho-analytic system could be founded (Freud, 1937, p. 222)" (22). In a seminal paper from 1959 that is largely credited with launching subsequent debates about the role of metapsychology in psychoanalytic theory, David Rapaport and Merton Gill begin by announcing that "at some point in the development of every science, the assumptions on which it is built must be clarified...This justifies our attempt to state explicitly and systematically that body of assumptions which constitute psycho-analytic metapsychology" (1959, 154). Claiming that a rigorous appraisal of metapsychology is aligned with Freud's intentions, Rapaport and Gill argue that a "systematization of metapsychology is necessary, if only because the increasing use of the metapsychological points of view in the literature is often at odds with Freud's definitions, without the authors' justifying this or even indicating an awareness of it" (154). In order to enable such a rigorous theoretical exercise, Rapaport and Gill offer the following definition of metapsychology: "Metapsychology proper thus consists of propositions stating the minimum (both necessary and sufficient) number of independent assumptions upon which the psycho-analytic theory rests. Metapsychology also includes the points of view which guide the metapsychological analysis of psycho-analytic propositions, both observational and theoretical" (155). While they acknowledge that in everyday practice most clinicians are relatively disinterested in parsing the coherence of any particular idea they hold, he ends his paper emphatically arguing for the stakes of this endeavor – "the future development of psycho-analysis as a systematic science may well depend on such continuing efforts to establish the assumptions on which psycho-analytic theory rests" (161).

Written in technical and unsentimental academic prose, Rapaport and Gill's paper can hardly be said to predict hardly anticipates the decades of controversy it engendered. While the call for a study of psychoanalysis' underlying assumptions seemed sensible and straightforward, even a natural next step for a maturing scientific discipline, what ensued was a highly partisan debate about the very status of psychoanalysis as a natural science. On the one side, Rapaport's students called for the totalizing rejection of metapsychology on the grounds that it was merely speculative pseudoscience that failed to substantively deepen clinical experience (Klein, 1976; Schafer 1976; Holt, 1981, 1989; Gill, 1976), while on the other side, ego psychologists defended metapsychology with the view that it was impossible, to separate Freud's metapsychology from his clinical theory, and that discarding the larger claims of psychoanalysis fatally compromised the entire enterprise. Why the role of metapsychology turned into a debate about whether or not psychoanalysis was a natural science is not immediately obvious; after all, Freud was relatively clear about his intentions to ground the study of unconscious processes in available knowledge of the brain and for decades before this debate broke out, metapsychology was more or less easily understood as referring to the study of psychology's underlying principles.

As John Gedo has observed, a confluence of forces arose in the mid-1970s that precipitated the collapse of a metapsychological consensus (1997). Since over time it became fairly evident that "Freud's metapsychological hypothesis did not prove to have clinical relevance or predictive value" (780), they were "amended" in the work of Heinz Hartmann, Ernst Kris and David Rapaport. By 1970, Roy Schafer was the "first simultaneously to pay tribute to the heuristic value of these theoretical contributions while pronouncing them passe" and by 1976 a series of papers was published in a collection entitled "Psychology versus Metapsychology" that took aim at the persistence of metapsychology as an unjustified flight into speculative abstraction and called for psychoanalysis to limit its focus to what it knows best – mental contents as they are expressed and constructed in the clinical encounter (1976). According to this view, expressed succinctly by George Klein, "psychoanalysis does not need a theory to explain a theory, that is, a metapsychology to explain the psychology" (1988, 37). As Gill explains, "those who hold that psychoanalysis is not a natural science but a hermeneutic one believe that Freudian metapsychology employs natural-science dimensions, that these are not the dimensions of clinical theory, and that therefore metapsychology is not a generalization from the clinical theory but rather is in a different universe of discourse... It is important to recognize that this position is not atheoretical but rather holds that the clinical theory suffices" (37). A central feature of this hermeneutic position was its decisive turn away from biological science; "hermeneuticists, of course, accept the necessity for a biological science of man, too," Gill writes, "but argue that psychoanalysis does not have the data required to build such a science" and "while they agree in principle with the idea that psychoanalytic concepts should be consistent with the findings of other sciences, they believe that hermeneutic propositions are in a different realm of discourse from natural science so that the issue of compatibility does not even arise" (43).

From the outset, there were major differences among thinkers on how best to respond to the obvious shrinkage of psychoanalytic theory. Charles Brenner rejected the argument outright, claiming that the widespread use of metapsychology to mean the logical foundations of a clinical theory are completely mistaken and that "Freud meant by 'metapsychology' the psychology of unconscious mental processes. He used the word as essentially synonymous with 'psychoanalytic psychology,' since psychoanalysis began as depth psychology and remains unique in its focus on that aspect of mental life" (1980, 212). Brenner further concluded that since "psychological phenomena are an aspect of brain functioning," psychoanalysis is obviously a branch of natural science (212) and therefore any attempt to distinguish metapsychology from specific clinical theories "makes no sense whatsoever" (198).[1] This view didn't preclude other ego psychologists from trying to take new biology into consideration; most notably, Hartmann actively tried to integrate modern ideas on adaptation with Freud's original conceptualization of the ego (1958). But the emphasis for these thinkers was on integrating this new biology with Freud's original model of the mind, tweaking things here and there while preserving the contours of his metapsychological edifice intact. Others, meanwhile, have sought to eschew biology altogether.

Schafer famously proposed the creation of an entirely new "action language" of psychoanalysis that would be deliberately a-biological and based instead on the structure of language (as developed by the English school of psycholinguistic philosophers such as Wittgenstein, Austin, and Ryle). Wishing to expunge every reference to material science on the grounds that Freud's "mixed physicochemical and evolutionary biological language" obscures more than it reveals, Schafer instead proposes an alternative language that is grounded in "the vantage point of personal actions, and we shall neither work in terms of pre-suppositions about psychoeconomics of a Newtonian cast nor burden ourselves with biological commitment of a Darwinian cast to explain and guarantee the continuity of the species" (1976, 8). Emphasizing the symbolic functioning of human being, Schafer calls for a new me-tapsychology that enables us to "speak about people more plainly" and refrains from speculations "about what is ultimately unutterable in any form nor build elaborate theories on the basis of unfalsifiable propo-sitions concepting mental activity at the very beginning of infancy" (10). Schafer's attempt to rewrite psychoanalytic metapsychology along these lines has encountered extensive and impassioned criticism, much of which focused on Schafer's total eradication of the "unconscious" as a meaningful dimension of pre-verbal experience.

In sharp contrast to Schafer's anti-biologism, another group of thinkers has called for deepening, rather than abandoning, psycho-analysis' reliance on biology. Less constrained by the orthodoxy of first-generation ego psychologists and having arrived onto the clinical scene after the advent of object relations theory – which promised to systematize clinical findings that were not otherwise captured by a drive-based model – these clinicians were interested in solidifying the field's scientific credentials while also remaining acutely sensitive to the theoretical coherence of any metapsychological paradigm. In addition to calling for a metapsychology that was scientifically credible, these thinkers were also concerned with ensuring logical and technical consistency; as Rapaport had observed, while the ordinary clinician can claim to simultaneously believe in the centrality of attachment and "drives," in philosophical terms, these different paradigms are in fact theoretically incoherent (1967). For these thinkers, who include John Gedo, John Holt, Benjamin Rubinstein, and Arnold Modell, the goal of a clinically relevant and conceptually coherent psychoanalysis necessitates scientific upgrades (more recent examples of this endeavor include Mark Solms' "neuropsychoanalysis," which aims to integrate current neurology first names, Michael Slavin and David Kriegman with psychoanalysis, Allan Schore's work on affect regulation and Michael Slavin and David Kriegman's work on evolutionary biology).

According to this view, the choice by some (i.e., hermeneuticists, often referred to as "radicals") "to abandon the biological pretensions of psychoanalysis altogether" not only forfeits the "Freudian ambition of establishing a science of mental functions" but in its exclusive privileging of symbolic communications also fails to elucidate the dimension of experience which is "unconscious" (Gedo 1991, 5). They argue that Freud's efforts to ground psychoanalysis on firm biological principles hit the natural limits of nineteenth-century science; it isn't that Freud, as an individual thinker, made wrong assumptions or built a flawed theory but that he did the best he could with the knowledge he had available to him – knowledge that is, as in any science, bound to evolve over time. This position maintains that "depth psychology" is indisputably a branch of biological science because there is simply no way to theorize human behavior without *some* assumption about "the nature of things." Gedo continues, "any clinical theory in psychoanalysis unavoidably uses some sort of metapsychology, despite the refusal to articulate one" (1997, 782) or in Modell has put it: "Facts ... are prestructured, as it were, out of our theoretical preconceptions, out of our metapsychology. Without metapsychology we cannot begin to think" (1981, 395). For the defenders of metapsychology, it is seen as providing "elements of structure and coherence that enable us to organize the buzzing confusion of immediate clinical experience" (395), and more specifically, as Modell has argued so effectively, "Although psychoanalysis is in a certain sense a linguistic enterprise, words cannot be separated from affects and affects have unquestionably evolutionary, that is, biological significance" (397). As such, any attempt to discard metapsychology is wrong on two counts: it generates practical incoherence for the clinician and renders itself incapable of explaining the deep structure of those biopsychical phenomena it seeks to describe. For many working in this tradition, the major goal of a revised metapsychology is the construction of an updated biological framework to replace Freud's outdated one.

Attempts to revise scientific foundations

George Klein went as far as to argue that insofar as 1950s "ego psychology" maintained Freud's underlying model of the mind, it was only ever "an empty conceptual strategem that tried to patch over the insufficiencies of the drive-discharge model of mentation" (Gedo, 1997, 39). And in a similar vein, Robert Holt has shown that among other impossible presumptions, Freud's conception of the nervous system is completely wrong and that as a result, numerous subsidiary concepts which rely on these principles are similarly flawed and mistaken (such as, stimulus barrier, cathexis, aim inhibition). The fact that Freud's purely quantitative explanations for pleasure and unpleasure have been overthrown by neurochemistry has led many writers to conclude that "Freud's overall power-engineering model of the brain has to be replaced by one based on information science" (1999, 37). In a book that is representative of efforts to bring psychoanalysis in line with contemporary scientific standards, Gedo writes: "it should be remembered that, as late as 1895, Freud made a heroic, albeit unsuccessful, effort to ground psychology scientifically through a description in terms of putative processes in the nervous system. Freud had to abandon this 'Project for a Scientific Psychology' because his understanding of neurophysiology, although completely up-to-date, was far from being equal to the task of undergirding psychology. The subsequent development of psychoanalytic theory on the basis of an entirely speculative metapsychology lacking in empirical referents was a desperate expedient – perhaps more indicative of Freud's need to anchor his thinking within the outward forms expected of a scientific enterprise than it was heuristically useful" (1991, 4). Gedo's description of Freud – as a scientific "hero" who strove to place his model of mental life on scientific grounds but came up against the natural limits of an as-yet underdeveloped neurophysiology – exemplifies a popular strategy among those who seek to preserve Freud's metapsychology by modifying some of the language. These thinkers acknowledge that many of Freud's most basic theoretical assumptions are simply not compatible with our current knowledge of evolutionary processes or the brain, but nevertheless believe that the general outline of unconscious life as Freud portrayed it remains valid and useful.

Working against orthodox interpretations which tried to preserve the literal meaning of Freud's ideas, and against the radical "hermeneuticists" who privileged the present-day construction over any transcendental claims, these aforementioned "pragmatists" acknowledge that Freud's original concepts cannot be credibly maintained and that new scientific upgrades are required to ensure the discipline's legitimacy. On one level, these thinkers express a clear-eyed view of the field's intellectual deficits and even the eagerness to challenge and replace major concepts where necessary. But while this rhetoric promised to undertake an exhaustive review of the field's metapsychological foundations, in practice, this approach takes a *concrete* view of metapsychology, treating the "scientific" underpinnings as arbitrary or isolated principles that were not, in themselves, important expressions of Freud's particular style of thought. For example, even when it is clear that Freud's view of "psychic energy" permeated an array of concepts that cannot be easily excised from "drive" theory without capsizing the whole formulation, the emphasis is repeatedly placed on how to better describe what Freud meant rather than to wonder what Freud's particular "mistakes" reveal about his theoretical imagination. In one of the most rigorous appraisals of Freud's scientific assumptions, Don Swanson's 1977 paper draws on research in physics and biology to demonstrate that "psychic-energy, libido, and related concepts in Freud's drive-discharge theory are either impossible, useless or mistaken", and he challenges the notion, maintained by many writing on this topic, that Freud's "mistaken" ideas can be neatly contained to a particular theoretical concept or discrete writing period (1977, 630).[2] After showing that Freud's wrong ideas about psychic energy were consistently operative in hundreds of papers spanning a 40-year period, Swanson concludes that the necessary revisions will need to be substantive and far-reaching if the goal is to bring psychoanalysis in line with modern scientific understanding.

And yet, despite demands for metapsychology to undertake major scientific revisions, thus far the results of attempts to integrate contemporary findings have been circumspect and predictable: the picture of mental life has acquired more detail and precision but the overall *language* of how the mind is conceptualized has stayed exactly the same. Indeed, even while the conceptual bedrock of psychoanalysis has been systematically deconstructed by contemporary scientific findings, it remains difficult to notice in what particular ways the field's foundational gestalt has changed, if at all. This phenomenon is what Cooper refers to when he observed that, "basic ideas have changed radically in response to our vastly expanded clinical experience as well as to researches in ethology, infant observation, and psychoanalytic process, but little of this is reflected in the ordinary discourse of psychoanalysis. The changes in psychoanalysis are of a magnitude that most fields would consider a major paradigm shift" (1985, 52). The strange and stubborn durability of Freud's language – even in the face of having been disproven and rendered scientifically obsolete – leads Cooper to observe that "it is as if we cannot bring ourselves to talk a language other than the one that Freud taught us" (2008, 241) even after this language has been deemed inaccurate and deficient. How can we explain our continued "clinging" to Freud's original language? Wouldn't those writing at the interface of science and psychoanalysis usher in the biggest changes to our language and conceptual schemata? Given the degree to which contemporary biological knowledge has transformed so many of Freud's foundational preconceptions, wouldn't we expect dramatic changes in how we imaginatively construe mental and interpersonal conflict? If so much has changed in our understanding of mental life, why does our writing continue to rely on terms and tropes from 1895?

This intellectual phenomenon is all the more perplexing today when we consider that major and far-reaching changes in how we understand brain development and neurobiology have nevertheless *not* led to a transformation in the psychoanalytic model of the mind. Much like the "pragmatists" of the 1980s and 90s, recent work by clinicians who are striving for a more scientifically-minded psychoanalysis has sought to improve Freudian ideas, but so far most clinicians who draw on this body of work interpret it as fundamentally *compatible* with existing psychoanalytic ontology. Therefore, rather than extrapolating new models of unconscious life based on the explosion of research in neurobiology and neuroscience in the past several decades, those working at the intersection of these fields repeatedly minimize the tension between new findings and psychoanalytic doxa. In one example of this intellectual phenomenon, Allan Shore's monumental study of neurobiology and emotional development steadily builds a scientific portrait of the infant as a "sensoriaffective rather than sensorimotor being" (1994, 71) whose unusual sensitivity to initial conditions attests to the intricate ways brain development is contingent on the quality of the mother's caregiving. While in his introduction, James Grotstein points out that these findings directly contradict Freud's concept of drive theory such that, "the brain, like the mind, is first and foremost an information-seeking and functioning organ, not primarily a tension-reducing one" (xxiv), in Schore's own description of how affect regulation challenges Freud's model of the mind, the tension between current research and the psychoanalytic tradition is noticeably downplayed as *merely* a scientific elaboration of ideas Freud, more or less, already had. Insisting that he is "expanding Freud's thesis" rather than challenging it, Schore repeatedly reassures the reader that despite the fundamental differences between his own depiction of infantile life and Freud's original descriptions, contemporary neurobiological findings produce a model that somehow "supports Freud's description of the human mind." Citing Freud's 1920 line that, "the unconscious is the infantile mental life," Schore then proceeds to situate the entirety of his cutting-edge findings as humble empirical proof of Freud's astonishing vision. Notably, Schore makes these claims, in spite of the fact that affect regulation, mother–mother interaction and attachment studies do *not* actually confirm the accuracy of Freud's ideas but decisively alter the foundational assumptions of Freud's psychological model.

This dissonance between the findings themselves and Schore's interpretation of them is evident again in his explication of the word "unconscious." While Schore acknowledges that the unconscious was "originally closely tied to the psychoanalytic theory of repression," he

nevertheless claims that current uses of the term are entirely compatible with Freud's ideas even though a new "construct of unconscious is now being used across a number of psychological and
neurobiological disciplines to describe essential implicit, spontaneous, rapid, and involuntary processes that act beneath levels of
conscious awareness," and that this "construct has thus shifted from
an intangible, immaterial, metapsychological abstraction of the mind
to a psychoneurobiological heuristic function of a tangible brain that
has material form" (2019, 2). While for a scientific researcher interested in complex human questions, the strategic appeal of linking
neurobiology to the grand tradition of psychoanalysis should not be
underestimated, Schore's rhetorical moves here are not particular to
him alone but are continuous with the general *harmonizing* tendency
of contemporary psychoanalytic writing. Indeed, reading widely in
this field creates the impression that even among those who believe
that the scientific principles underlying psychoanalytic theory require
major revision, there is a determined effort to minimize and substantially limit the potential impact of these changes on psychoanalytic theory as a whole. Drawing attention to the disappointing
outcomes of so much recent scientifically oriented work, Drew
Westen aptly wonders if there isn't an underlying resistance to innovation on the part of psychoanalysts. In a characterization that
accurately describes what we observed in Schore's work, Westen
writes, "too often psychoanalytic theorists have felt that they must
show that Freud foreshadowed their latest formulation in an obscure
footnote to an obscure paper. In his treatise on affect in psychoanalysis, for example, Spezzano (1993) extracts a series of implicit
propositions about affect, many of them quite valuable, from contemporary clinical writing, but then feels compelled to argue that this
is what Freud meant all along or, at the very least, that the conclusions he reached simply lay 'along the trajectory Freud clearly was
following.' Physics would certainly be in a different place if physicists
had to reconcile all of their contemporary formulations with quotes
from Newton's *Principia*" (1997, 524).

What Westen identifies as a resistance to challenging Freud, my
own project sees as a manifestation of a deeper "Sinai complex" in
which those seeking to remain attached to psychoanalysis forego any
behavior that could be seen as a betrayal. As such, the "clinging" to

Freud's original language that Cooper and Westen observe must be seen as neither arbitrary nor incidental but the product of a deliberate effort on the part of those writing about contemporary science to interpret it in ways that *avoid* a substantive confrontation with Freud. Indeed, instrumental to this defensive stance is a general and en-trenched naïvete with respect to Freud's "scientificity." That is, rather than taking a critical perspective on Freud's theoretical choices, the field (including those who call for scientific revisions) adamantly in-sists on Freud's scientific bona fides, as if whatever limitations psychoanalysis currently has are the unfortunate result of an old-fashioned science rather than the legacy of intentional decisions made by Freud himself. Indeed, a critical assessment of Freud's relation-ship to science will show that the popular trope of Freud as an in-trepid scientist who "heroically" pushed his daring speculations as far as he could go within the limits of available science fundamentally misconstrues the nature of Freud's role in the development of psy-choanalytic theory. More specifically, the oft-repeated claim that Freud "did the best he could with the science that was available" should be seen as a totally *un*-psychoanalytic view insofar as it sug-gests that Freud-the inventor-of-a-field was a passive conduit rather an active agent whose personality and ambition were decisive in de-termining *which* scientific ideas he chose to use and *how* he decided to make use of them.

As Swanson has noted, the common refrain that Freud was led to believe living organisms are closed systems because that was *just what people thought back then*, actually contradicts established history since by the time Freud was writing about the conservation of energy, significant work had already demonstrated important alternatives which Freud deliberately refused to consider (1977, 611). This pattern in which Freud retained certain older ideas long after they have been scientifically discredited persists throughout his career, demon-strating, quite clearly, that Freud was hardly an ideological blank canvas who prioritized scientific accuracy above his own creative formulations. An in-depth exploration of the field's early history will suggest that Freud had a more complicated and less straightforward relationship to science than popular conventions would have us be-lieve. As such, when Freud used certain ideas as the basis for specific formulations it was rarely because there were no available scientific alternatives but because those ideas fit into the larger story of human nature Freud was trying to tell and because science, for him, was something which could be adapted to suit his broader theoretical aims.

Freud's relationship to science

In his recent biography of Freud, Joel Whitebook has expressed hope that new generations of clinicians might develop a "de-idealized" relationship to Freud that can withstand criticism and complexity (2017, 14).[3] While I think the obstacles to this so-called "maturity" are far deeper than Whitebook acknowledges, any wish to develop a more accurate understanding of metapsychology depends, for its success, on a more rigorous appraisal of Freud's behavior with respect to establishing the field's foundations. In Louis Breger's magisterial recent biography, close attention is paid to Freud's interpersonal relationships as a means of circumventing the familiar hagiographies which have until now mostly dominated histories of psychoanalysis. Breger's focus on Freud's relationship to Joseph Breuer and Wilhelm Fliess are especially instructive for our purposes since these friendships take place early in Freud's professional development and are thus inextricably bound up with bigger questions such as the uses of science in psychoanalysis and the direction of a new clinical method. Viewing Freud in relation to his peers provides us with the context necessary for evaluating, if not quite his scientific methodology, then at least his style of relating to science, especially since both men were, like him, scientists and physicians as well.

In the case of Freud's relationship to Breuer, what stands out for Breger is the vast difference between Breuer's caution and intellectual modesty with respect to surmising the causes of Anna O.'s distress versus Freud's forceful eagerness to draw sweeping universal claims from limited clinical data. While the women in Freud and Breuer's *Studies on Hysteria* "suffered sexual molestations, betrayals by intimates and family members, disappointed hopes, loss of love, deaths, disturbed relationships of a variety of kinds, and difficult identity struggles," Freud "assumed sexuality was significant because the patients never mentioned it" (2001, 116). Whereas Breuer gently parted ways with Freud on the prominence of sexuality – "we do not yet see clearly; it remains only for the future, the masses of observations, to bring full clarification to this question" (119) – by 1898, in Freud's "Sexuality in the Aetiology of the Neurosis," his view of sexuality as *the* cause of neurosis hardened into doctrine, even if this meant "ignoring his own case material" (117). As numerous re-readings of these cases have already shown, "Freud collapsed the complex histories and life situations of these women into a single, sweeping principle that cannot be contradicted" because even though hysteria is "not a unitary disease" he was determined to find a "single theoretical principle that would make him famous" (117).

This willingness to privilege one factor over others and condense complicated information into a neat narrative package is no small part of what made Freud such a gifted storyteller and compelling guide on difficult psychological questions but it's also important that not only did Freud emphasize one problem (such as sexuality) over others (like loss, death, family betrayal) but that in doing so, Freud chose a topic that was scandalous without necessarily being *emotionally* threatening. Or, put another way, close readings of Freud's clinical accounts suggest that Freud may have found it considerably easier to treat the patient whom he perceived to be withholding something, lying even, than the young woman who was grieving, confused, or in need of empathy and identification. To momentarily anticipate an idea I will be exploring in greater depth later on, Freud didn't just "cherry pick" clinical data to secure his theoretical claims, but defined his purview as "human nature" while actually privileging a particular aspect of psychic experience which *he* (given his characterological tendencies, professional goals and emotional defenses) was uniquely determined to elaborate. That is, it comes as little surprise to learn from Breger that Freud's aggressive attitude toward scientific data was evident in his therapeutic style as well. "If neurosis was driven by guilt over secret forms of sexual gratification, it followed that patients should be pushed to confess. When they did, they would feel relieved. If, however, they were not conscious of the source of their distress because their symptoms were tied to overwhelming states of fear, pain, and unhappiness, forcing the material into consciousness would be a retraumatization. It came down to whether the therapist was capable of feeling empathy for the patient. While was much that Breuer did not understand about Bertha Pappenheim, he seemed in tune with her painful states and emotions. Freud, in contrast, became increasingly convinced of the correctness of his theories and was insistent that when patients did not confirm his view of things, it was their resistance; it was proof that he was right. As he put it in his 1898 paper: 'We shall in the end conquer every resistance by emphasizing the unshakeable nature of our convictions'" (121).

The relationship to Breuer occurred at a formative moment in Freud's intellectual development. Young, visibly insecure, and determined to burnish his professional credentials, it's not surprising to think that Freud's anxiety about having something to say might cause him to override his mentor's expressions of caution. But rather than a discrete phase of intellectual recklessness and immaturity, Freud actually continues the pattern of seeking scientific validation then debasing it whenever it doesn't accord with his views. After his break with Breuer, Freud initiated an intimate correspondence with Fleiss, whom he saw as possessing many of the characteristics Breuer lacked – charisma, grandiosity, and the capacity for bold and radical thought. Although some contemporaries appreciated Fliess's creativity, to many members of the scientific establishment his wide-ranging biological theories were quackery, beginning "with small possibilities – similarities between nasal and genital tissue, the periodicity of some biological phenomena – and then wildly expanded them" (131). Rather than expressing skepticism, Freud used Fliess as a sounding board for his own wild speculations. Indeed, although in 1897 a stinging appraisal of Fliess' work exposed them as "mystical nonsense" and "disgusting gobbledygook" that "had nothing to do with medicine or natural science" (134), Freud instead "saw these ideas as bold and revolutionary." More importantly, "Fliess's theories seemed to provide a bridge between Freud's old neuroanatomical research and his new involvement in psychology; they dealt with tissues, bones, drugs, numbers, and surgery, rather than ephemeral thoughts, memories, feelings, and psychological therapy. Struggling with the uncertainty of his new psychoanalytic approach, Freud took comfort in the seemingly scientific solidity of Fliess's theories" (134). Drawing on a close reading of their correspondence as well as the scientific norms of the time, Breger concludes that Freud didn't admire Fliess *in spite* of his questionable intellectual rigor but *because* of it. "Fliess's theoretical imperialism was the

principal reason Freud took up with him and dropped the cautious
and scientific Breuer. Fliess seemed like a bold scientific con-
quistador, a 'new Kepler,' which made him a model for Freud, who
would be, in his turn, the new Darwin or Newton of the mind" (135).
Moreover, rather than giving him pause, the disapproval of the scientific community seemed gratifying to Freud, inspiring him to believe that he, like Fliess before him, was being punished for his
prescience. As Breger has observed, "Freud made himself out to be
the misunderstood genius-hero who persevered against a world of
enemies and ultimately triumphed. But none of this was true. He was
not isolated because he was shunned by the medical establishment; in
fact, his early work on hysteria had been received by his medical
colleagues with a mixture of interest, praise, and skepticism. But he
had turned away from them, and even drove the supportive Breuer
away, because they did not completely affirm his theories. Instead of
working within a scientific community of peers, he had chosen to link
up with Fliess in a partnership where each reinforced the other's sense
of grandeur" (148).

What these and other incidents roundly indicate is that Freud
maintained a tense, often antagonistic relationship to science which
predates his own so-called "rejection" the picture that emerges is of a
man who anticipated, and often courted, admonishment by his peers
while at the same time demanding unquestioning fidelity from his
followers. Although the story of Freud-the-intrepid-scientist has been
unquestioningly rehearsed since the field's inception, historical
scholarship does not support this narrative. While Freud was certainly trained by esteemed scientists at reputable institutions and was
heavily invested in the development of scientific understanding, he
also repeatedly bristled at having to conform his speculations to
scientific protocol. His simultaneous admiration and hostility toward
science – whatever its unconscious motivations – is an important
corrective to popular mythology, specifically, insofar as it invalidates
the trope of Freud as a passive scientific vessel whose metapsychological mistakes were merely the natural result of flawed nineteenth-
century science. History suggests that Freud was rarely as passive as
contemporary critics make him seem; as Yerushalmi writes in his
discussion of *Moses and Monotheism*, "though the truly decisive re-
volutions in molecular biology and genetics were not to take place

until after his death, Freud was always aware that Lamarckism was under sharp scientific attack. Nevertheless, and despite the urgent pleas of Ernest Jones that he expunge these embarrassing elements from the Moses book, he held fast" (1991, 31). While Freud's hostility to science is typically excused as the inevitable outcome of his speculative enterprise – brain research was in its infancy then and he couldn't wait for science to confirm his propositions – such an explanation belies his behavior, which was to presume science was the skeptical, withholding enemy of the "truth" he was trying so heroically to impart.

Ignoring the complexity of Freud's relationship to science is not only weak historiography but detrimental to further theoretical development insofar as it renders completely *invisible* the cast of Freud's singular views. A close engagement with history demonstrates that Freud was not exactly a humble and fastidious scientist whose service to the Truth prompted him to build a theory out of whatever scientific principles were available to him, but was, by all accounts, an ambitious and creative thinker who wanted science to corroborate his observations and intuitions but was also willing, if necessary, to proceed headlong without it. One primary advantage of such a critical perspective is that it treats Freud's metapsychology as a unitary and coherent whole and in so doing makes it possible to ask: what vision of mental life was he trying to describe? There have been many harsh critics of Freud who have used his questionable intellectual habits to impugn psychoanalysis in its entirety, but to my mind such a position takes a narrow view of "personal" motivation as something that *interferes* with scientific discovery. Such a false binary – between so-called neutrality and subjectivity – derogates intuition and leaves us with a stringent positivism that drastically constrains our capacity for inventive thought. Besides, what would it even *mean* to accuse Freud of being subjectively motivated? Are we referring to unconscious motivations? To his personality? Saying Freud privileged his own intuitions over and against scientific credulity is certainly relevant but hardly as damning as it is made to sound. For someone as educated, trained, and sophisticated as Freud there is no meaningful or usable distinction between his "scientific" and "personal" self. Freud most certainly had an agenda for his innovation, which included maximizing its longevity and popularity, superceding rival views and producing a theory that was coordinated with clinical technique, but these facts are most profitably applied to sharpening our understanding of the *kind* of theory he invented. We know he never hesitated to expel ideas that challenged his own, or to ignore scientific data which contravened his suppositions, but assuming his autocracy served a higher purpose (of protecting his invention), what, might we ask, was he trying so hard to ensure his new model would show?

There are likely many possible answers to this question – the unconscious, infantile sexuality, the Oedipus complex – and Freud was notoriously vigorous in using "shibboleths" to record his own changing self-assessment of which ideas formed the bedrock without which the entire model would collapse. But hasn't clinical experience taught us well to look upon self-assessment with necessary skepticism? For example, a patient is convinced his mother issues are the reason for his professional paralysis but over time analysis reveals a deeply problematic connection to his father. Likewise in philosophy, we learn more about what holds a theoretical edifice together by observing how it functions over time than by adhering uncritically to authorial intent. As such, we must take our distance from Freud's self-assessments to explore what deeper, often implicit, metapsychological formulations psychoanalysis was built to elaborate. These metapsychological formulations are *not* the same as biological assumptions that can be swapped with other, more updated, scientific findings. Indeed, given what we learned of Freud's theoretical-philosophical process, it seems less plausible to try drawing a direct link between nineteenth-century science and Freud's theoretical speculations than to ask what specific psychic phenomena Freud was *using* science to explain. Or put another way, given that Freud refused to subsume his ideas to scientific dictates but regularly bent and manipulated science to suit his theoretical aims, it is worth being clear about what specific questions Freud was trying to answer rather than necessarily presuming they are the same as our own.

As one example, it's worth remembering that the locus of Freud's interest in hysteria had always been the pathogenic effects of "undischarged or strangulated affect." As Morris Eagle correctly observes, "the constancy principle, undischarged or strangulated affect, isolation of mental contents, and repression, all combined in a logical structure, come into play in accounting for hysteria. As noted, the most fundamental assumptions are that a basic function of mind is to discharge excitation and that the failure to do so, that is, the buildup of excessive excitation, has pathogenic consequences" (2011, 14). From this perspective, it should come as little surprise that Freud would forcefully resist such notions as, say, "unconscious affects," since the very possibility of affects being *un*conscious invalidates the necessity of their being objects of internal conflict and defense. More broadly, we can infer from examples such as these that there is a vital but as yet unexplored difference between the proper object of psychoanalysis – what Laplanche calls its "exigency" – and the particular story about human suffering that Freud, the individual thinker, was trying to tell.

The *exigency* of psychoanalysis

In his essay, "Countercurrent," Laplanche writes, "to go against the current is thus to try to rediscover the first and constant exigency at work in Freud, which is in opposition to those aspects of his work I have sometimes called his 'going astray.' We must try to restore this exigency – which continues is a more or less latent way to drive the practitioners of analysis – as a live force in both theory and practice. This means that the necessity for 'new foundations' remains always present" (FS, 83). For Laplanche, the "exigency" behaves as a force which compels Freud without Freud necessarily knowing it; indeed, it is what "pushes Freud in a single direction, which is constantly at work in him" and "primarily it is the exigency of the *unconscious*, encountered in the practice of analysis" (FS, 270). In sharp contrast to the variety of themes chosen by different psychoanalytic factions as *the* privileged object of psychoanalysis, Laplanche asserts that *enlarged* sexuality is the great psychoanalytic discovery, maintained from beginning to end and difficult to conceptualize – as Freud himself shows when he tries to reflect on the question, for example, in his *Introductory Lectures*. It is infantile, certainly more closely connected to fantasy, governed by the unconscious. (Isn't the unconscious ultimately the *sexual*? One can legitimately ask this question). So for Freud, the '*sexual*' is exterior to, even prior to, the difference of the sexes, even the difference of the genders...

nevertheless, whenever Freud tries to define it he is brought back to the need to put it in relation with what it is not, that is to say with sexed activity or with sex (FS, 162).

Writing elsewhere in a more concise fashion, Laplanche refers to *enlarged* sexuality as "infantile sexuality in the sense of the *Three essays*, that is to say in the sense of what I call the 'sexual' beyond the 'sexed,' beyond the difference between the sexes and beyond even the diversity of genders" (FS, 243). Laplanche is emphatic in his insistence that *enlarged* sexuality alone qualifies as the true discovery of psychoanalysis and that beginning with Freud himself, the field has shown an abiding confusion about *what* exactly constitutes the real object of psychoanalysis. As if to illustrate his point by putting it to test, Laplanche says, "one could give up the whole theory of the drives, but could one give up the sexual unconscious?" (FS, 18). For Laplanche, the answer is a resounding "no" because while other scientific fields track biological or sociological processes, psychoanalysis is a clinical method which is unique for being able to "give an account of the genesis of the psychosexual apparatus of the human being, starting from interhuman relationships and not from biological origins" (FS, 204).

One might ask why – if *enlarged* sexuality is the proper object of psychoanalytic inquiry and technique – is the field perpetually entrenched in existential battles about the legitimate function of metapsychology? What makes it so difficult for psychoanalysis to assert the primacy of *enlarged* sexuality, over and against particular psychoanalytic concepts such as the Oedipus complex, for example, or the castration complex? In other words, why has the field consistently struggled to decide what constitutes the *foundations* of psychoanalysis versus its constituent *parts*? While acknowledging that the subject of *enlarged* sexuality poses distinctive challenge that studying, say, the solar system, does not, Laplanche nevertheless does not put the entirety of the blame on the subject matter itself, demonstrating instead that a major source of the difficulty can be traced back to Freud himself. Consistent with what we observed in the fieldwide "Sinai Complex," Laplanche observes that there is a veritable prohibition against healthy scientific debate out of fear that "if the case really did contradict the theory" *everything* "would collapse" (FS, 240). Wondering why practitioners persist in feeling as if single changes to particular ideas automatically means the "whole of metapsychology [would] come crashing down" (FS, 240), Laplanche notes that in "Freud one sometimes encounters an absolutism that may lead one to believe that 'the throne and the altar' ultimately depend on a certain number of shibboleths, such that the refutation of one small point of the metapsychology might imperil the entire system" (FS, 240). Taking a charitable perspective on this problem, Laplanche suggests that Freud resorts to "absolutism" because he fails to correctly understand the *difference* – which is a categorical one – between metapsychology, on the one hand, and "mytho-symbolic" explanations on the other. "We propose," Laplanche writes, "to rigorously distinguish between two fields:

1. That of myths, narrative schemas, frameworks for symbolization and narration, some but not all of which were 'discovered' by psychoanalysis: ex, the Oedipus. It makes no sense to describe such schemas as being true or false. This doesn't mean (quite the contrary) that they should be considered as *a priori* axioms or that they cannot be studied – studied as to their genesis, their greater or lesser capacity to symbolize, as to what constitutes their core (ex. Does 'thirdness' explain the power of the Oedipus?), or, finally, as to their 'universality.'...
2. Psychoanalytic theory. This is metapsychology; even if it is necessarily articulated with psychology, it makes no claim to encompass or to conquer it.

Metapsychology is not the theory of clinical work. It is the theory of the human being insofar as he is affected by an unconscious. A theory, therefore, of the unconscious, of its nature, its genesis, its returns, its effects etc." (FS, 93). For Laplanche, "one of the major tasks of metapsychology must be to prove its capacity to account for the function of myths and therefore of hermeneutics, as much within the human being as such as in the effects of psychotherapy. A theory that explicitly aims to account for hermeneutics cannot itself be a hermeneutics! It must aim to rationality, that is to say, at articulating truths and refuting errors" (FS, 94). In sharp contrast to those efforts which seek to treat psychoanalysis as offering just one possible interpretation of human development among many, Laplanche contends that one goal of metapsychology is "articulating truths and refuting errors." However, in order to develop accurate, rational, and falsifiable ideas, psychoanalysis *must* be required to distinguish its major and overarching "theory of the unconscious" from those ideas which are actually only "narrative schemas, frameworks for symbolization and narration" that aid the individual in interpreting events but *do not* constitute scientific knowledge as such.

Metapsychology versus the sexual theories of children

Laplanche arrives at the clear demarcation of these two different levels by starting from the doctrine that every individual is fundamentally *driven* to interpret his surroundings. "We maintain," Laplanche asserts, "that the human being is an interpreter by nature: the only originary hermeneut; a hermeneut by virtue of his condition" (FS, 92). The "condition" Laplanche refers to here is the "fundamental anthropological situation" which will be outlined in detail in chapter 3. To describe the "fundamental anthropological situation" briefly here, we can say that it names the universal and non-contingent encounter between the infant, who requires caretaking in order to develop, and the adult, whose caretaking involves elements of his own unconscious sexuality. "The fundamental anthropological situations confronts an adult, who has an unconscious that is sexual but essentially pregenital, with an infant, who has not yet constituted an unconscious nor the opposition unconscious-preconscious, in a dialogue that is both symmetrical at one level and asymmetrical at another. The sexual unconscious of the adult is reactivated in the relation with the small infant. The messages of the adult are conscious-preconscious and are necessarily *compromised* (in the sense of a return of the repressed), but the presence of unconscious scrambling or interference. These messages are therefore *enigmatic*, both for the adult sender and for the infant recipient" (FS, 207). The specific biopsychical mechanisms at work in this encounter will be the subject of the next chapter on affect theory. For now, what is important is Laplanche's overarching contention that when bombarded with overwhelming stimulation in the form of "enigmatic messages," the infant reacts by attempting to "translate" them. Translation is a method of *binding* the overstimulating content; by interpreting what he observes in the form of narrative schemas and symbols, the infant is able to master the affective overload and achieve stability with respect to the "noise" he has been confronted with. There are two major consequences of the infant's reaction: 1) an "urge to translate" – put into action by the confrontation with an adult – becomes a lifelong capacity that operates at all times for the individual and 2) the infant develops his own unconscious, comprised of "messages" in various different stages of translation, successful, partial or failed translation, etc., and while emerging in relation to the adult's unconscious is nevertheless not reducible to it. What this means with regard to the broader questions about metapsychology is that the individual is never *not* an interpretive being and that instead of treating interpretation as a specialized activity that only trained psychoanalysts do, we ought to see interpretation as something that "by virtue of his condition" *everyone* does, and *has been doing*, all the time.

As it specifically bears on the question of theory, and psychoanalytic theory in particular, one major implication of Laplanche's "fundamental anthropological situation" is that since interpretations serve a *binding* function for the individual psyche, they are invariably on the side of "repression" rather than that of the "repressed." Laplanche explains, "contrary to general opinion, and especially to that of Freud who saw the oedipal relation as the 'kernel' of the unconscious, it is necessary to situate such structures *not on the side of the repressed but of the repressing*; not on the side of the sexual but of that which organizes it, and finally desexualizes it in the name of the laws of alliance, of procreation, etc.... There is nothing in the least sexual (in the original sense of the *Three Essays*) in the myth of Oedipus and the tragedy of Sophocles; nothing that speaks to us less of sexual jouissance or of the pursuit of sexual excitation" (FS, 220). Indeed, "the great narrative schemas, transmitted then modified by culture, come to help the human subject to process, that is to bind and to symbolize, or to translate, the messages, both enigmatic and traumatizing, which come to him from the adult other. Very obviously this relation is indispensable for the human being's entry into his humanity" (FS, 220). Given how interpretations function – "to bind and to symbolize" that which is "enigmatic and traumatizing" – it is logically and practically incoherent to then confuse and conflate those interpretations with the original subject of repression. Using Freud's idea of the "castration complex" as "the most conspicuous example" of this confusion, Laplanche writes that rather than repressed psychic material, the "castration complex" is really only "a way for the child to represent for itself in a 'story' or a narration the difference between the genders as communicated by the parental messages that assign gender to the child" (FS, 247). That is, "the castration complex and the Oedipus complex are mythic theories that do not require proof. In Popper's terms, they belong to the level of metaphysics; what I call the 'mytho-symbolic' is presented to the human being largely by his cultural surroundings. Unfortunately, however, Freud ended up regarding the sexual theories of children – the apparatus best suited to repressing the unconscious – as the very kernel of the unconscious" (FS, 247).

For Laplanche, the effects of Freud's conflation of metapsychology with mytho-symbolic explanations has had devastating effects on the field: "there is the attempt to include among the truths that it has effectively discovered (concerning the 'apparatus of the soul' and the intersubjective situation of the adult-infant couple) and which are 'metapsychological' truths, the more or less contingent schemas of narration which enable human beings in a cultural situation to put their destiny into an order, a history. This is very much the case with the Oedipus complex, which, however general it may be (with numerous variations), isn't a universal characteristic of the human, as it is not necessarily present in the fundamental anthropological situation" (FS, 217). Our preceding exploration of the field's abiding struggle with metapsychology attests to the problem Laplanche describes, for rather than treating the Oedipus complex as one possible narrative schema among many, and as a symbolic construction rather than repressed content, psychoanalysis continues to demonstrate that it, like Freud himself, cannot tell the difference between metapsychology and the sexual theories of children. Lest this failure to clearly differentiate between levels of explanation seem abstract or merely academic, Laplanche reminds us that our grasp of psychoanalysis' exigency hinges on our proficiency since without a working understanding of how metapsychology and mytho-symbolic explanations differ, we fetishize certain narrative schemas (the Oedipus complex, the castration complex, thirdness), thereby using them to *repress* sexuality rather than express it. "You see," Laplanche writes, "that the idea of a theory that is ultimately supple and open to re-working, a theory containing on the one hand a relatively dense kernel and on the other hand statement that are not deduced from the general theory, is valid not only for psychoanalysis but for every science. So, a hard kernel, a suppler periphery. What would be the hard kernel of psychoanalysis... No mistake, what causes scandal today, the hard kernel, what's constantly being left to one side, is infantile sexuality, the unconscious and the paths of access to it, and repression" (FS, 241). Returning to where this chapter began by re-flecting on the meaning of "new foundations for psychoanalysis," we can observe how a more rigorous understanding of metapsychology is not merely better (more cogent, more effective) science, but a vital step in working-through the field's abiding conflicts with innovation/ deviation. Rather than treating Freud's entire idiosyncratic corpus as the "hard kernel" of our science, Laplanche enables us to specify *enlarged* sexuality as the privileged object of our field and to see the explanatory frameworks that we develop around it as contingent symbolic schemas which are supple, and available for revision and reformulation. Refusing the choice between orthodox adherence to Freud's text or the totalizing rejection of it, Laplanche's attitude is that of a 'faithful infidelity.' "A fidelity with respect to reading and translation, restoring to Freud what he meant – including his con-tradictions and his turning points; an infidelity with respect to the interpretation of Freud's 'going-astray,' in order to try to find what I call 'New Foundations for Psychoanalysis'" (FS, 285). While gen-erations of psychoanalysts have sought tirelessly to "change the music without changing the tune" (as Cooper put it), Laplanche in-vites us to develop a new relationship to our field in which a genuine appreciation of our object – sexuality – facilitates a new appreciation for everything that *isn't* sexuality, allowing us to use our schemas and speculations in ways that are at once more rigorous and more flexible. In a spirited plea for us to learn from Freud without submitting to him as our master, to take his *interest* as our own rather than his *answers*, Laplanche writes, "Freud remained dominated by the ex-igency of his discovery: 'the unconscious'; let us follow him in this exigency!" (FS, 286).

Notes

1 It is worth noting that this view of metapsychology is the de facto position of French psychoanalysis who treat metapsychology as the theory of psychoanalysis rather than a separate body of assumptions that need to be investigated.
2 Swanson writes: "If they are defined in a mind-body interactionist framework, they are impossible in the sense that they violate energy-conservation laws of physics. If they are defined in any abstract framework, they are useless in that explanations of behavior so based are trivially and incorrigibly circular. If they are defined instead as biological concepts, the implied notions of energy flow in neural networks are mistaken."
3 Whitebook seems to dismiss Breger's biography for being too critical of Freud while at the same time relying on it for much of his own research and rarely contradicting Breger's conclusions even if he does not claim to explicitly share them.

Bibliography

Breger, Louis (2001). *Freud: Darkness in the Midst of Vision*. New York: Wiley.

Brenner, Charles (1980). Metapsychology and Psychoanalytic Theory. *Psychoanalytic Quarterly* 49: 189–214

Eagle, Morris N. (2011). *From Classical to Contemporary Psychoanalysis: A Critique and Integration*. New York: Routledge.

Erikson, Johan (2012). Freud's Metapsychology: The Formal a Priori of Psychoanalytic Experience. *Scandinavian Psychoanaltic Review* 35(1): 21–34.

Freud, Sigmund (1937). *Analysis Terminable and Interminable*. S.E. 23: 209–254.

Gedo, John (1991). *The Biology of Clinical Encounters: Psychoanalysis as a Science of Mind*. Hillsdale: Analytic Press.

Gedo, John (1997). Reflections on Metapsychology, Theoretical Coherence, Hermeneutics, and Biology. *Journal of the American Psychoanalytic Association* 45: 779–806.

Gill, Merton (1988). Metapsychology Revisited. *Annual of Psychoanalysis* 16: 35–48.

Gill, Merton and Philip Holzman, Eds. (1976). *Psychology versus Metapsychology: Psychoanalytic Essays in Memory of George S. Klein*. New York: International UP.

Hartmann, Heinz (1958). *Ego Psychology and the Problem of Adaptation*. New York: International UP.

Holt, Robert (1981). The Death and Transfiguration of Metapsychology. *International Review of Psycho-Analysis* 8: 129–143.

Holt, Robert R. (1989). *Freud Reappraised: A Fresh Look at Psychoanalytic Theory*. New York: Guilford.

Klein, George. (1976). *Two Theories or One? Psychoanalytic Theory* New York: International University Press. pp. 369–403.

Kovel, Joel (1978). Things and Words: Metapsychology and the Historical Point of View. *Psychoanalysis and Contemporary Thought* 1(1): 21–88.

Modell, Arnold H. (1981). Does Metapsychology Still Exist? *International Journal of Psycho-analysis* 62: 391–402.

Rapaport, David and Merton Gill (1959). The Points of View and Assumptions of Metapsychology. *International Journal of Psychoanalysis* 40: 153–162.

Rubinstein, Benjamin B. (1980). On the Psychoanalytic Theory of Unconscious Motivation and the Problem of Its Confirmation. *Psychoanalysis and Contemporary Thought* 3 (1): 3–20.

Schafer, Roy (1976). *A New Language for Psychoanalysis*. New Haven: Yale UP.

Schore, Allan (1994). *Affect Regulation and the Origin of the Self: The Neurobiology of Emotional Development*. New York: Psychology Press.

Schore, Allan (2019). *The Development of the Unconscious Mind*. New York: Norton.

Spezzano, Charles (1993). *Affect in Psychoanalysis: A Clinical Synthesis*. New York: Routledge.

Swanson, Don (1977). A Critique of Psychic Energy as an Explanatory Concept. *Journal of the American Psychoanalytic Association* 25: 603–633.

Westen, Drew (1997). Towards a Clinically and Empirically Sound Theory of Motivation. *International Journal of Psycho-Analysis* 78: 521–548.

Whitebook, Joel (2017). *Freud: An Intellectual Biography*. Cambridge: Cambridge UP.

Yerushalmi, Yosef Hayim (1991). *Freud's Moses: Judaism Terminable and Interminable*. New Haven: Yale UP.

Chapter 2

Sexuality – Laplanche's theory of the unconscious

Atavism vs. dynamism

In a 2012 paper on the evolution of contemporary psychoanalysis, Latin American psychoanalyst Madeleine Baranger writes, "with or without conscious desire or concordance, psychoanalysis involves a conception of human beings and their fate. We would not be analysts without the desire and construction of this concept" (2012, 130). Perhaps nowhere are the stakes of this "conception" more clearly evident than in debates about what we *mean* by the "unconscious." As a century of writing on the topic has shown, our ideas about the unconscious are acutely emblematic of our deeper views about "human beings and their fate" and for this reason, adjudicating what exactly we mean when we use the word "unconscious" is a task of singular urgency and concern. The breakthrough creation of psychoanalysis and an enduring symbol of the individual's psychological essence, the unconscious has always been the privileged object of clinical and theoretical discourse, even as its precise meaning remains a subject of ongoing debate. Indeed, there are many different ways to describe the juxtaposing viewpoints in these debates – such as, fantasy vs. reality, biology vs. sociality – but for Laplanche, the key tension involves the atavism vs. dynamism of the unconscious. According to Laplanche, our current difficulty defining the unconscious in rigorously metapsychological terms derives from the tension between atavism and dynamism, as they are present in Freud's own formulations. As Laplanche writes in "A Short Treatise on the Unconscious," although Freud was vigorous in claiming to have invented a new science, "it is in the way that the unconscious is conceived – how it is situated *topographically* and *genetically* – that the ambiguity emerges in Freud" (STU, 85).

In the "atavistic" version, the unconscious is primordial, biological and phylogenetic – it originates in the instincts, predates consciousness and is transmitted phylogenetically. "There is a constant temptation to situate the unconscious in some genetic lineage, in which it occupies the first, primordial position. Thus, the psychological lineage: 'Everything which is conscious was first unconscious'; the lineage of individual biology: the id is 'the great reservoir of the instincts' and constitutes the non-repressed part of the unconscious, which would open directly onto the body; and finally, the lineage of the species and of phylogenesis: whether by way of the so-called primal fantasies, which are supposed to constitute the kernel of the unconscious, or under the heading of metabiological and metacosmological speculation, which takes the unconscious drives back to an immemorial atavism" (85). This "atavistic" unconscious has romantic, even superstitious connotations, and stands in sharp contrast to the "dynamic" unconscious implied by such concepts as repression. In the "dynamic" version, which Freud stipulates but later abandons, the unconscious is unique to each person, and comprised of sexuality "and the fantasy inseparable from it" (86). While initially present in papers from 1911 and 1915, over time the psychological dynamism of a concept like repression "tends more and more" to be "subordinated" to the atavism of the primordial id. This evolution is most explicit in Freud's increased reliance on vague and simplistic notions of how the unconscious suddenly "emerges" in each psyche, as if spontaneously or supernaturally from some kind of hardwired drives. Whereas repression stipulated a complex interplay between the psyche and its environment, "the notion of *primal repression*, creator of the unconscious as a place, only appears sporadically after 1915; from then on, repression will be essentially secondary, that is, bearing on drives-impulses already present and welling up from the primordial, non-repressed unconscious" (86). Moreover, "the postulating of such an 'id' – biological, primal, necessarily pre-formed – ran directly counter to the originality implied in the notion of the drive, as a sexual process not adapted, in human beings, to a predetermined goal. It flew in the face of Freud's more complex elaboration of the mechanism of repression and its successive stages" (86).

Although Laplanche uses repression in positive terms, associating it with the workings of a dynamic unconscious, among contemporary clinicians repression retains largely negative connotations. Expressing this position from within the progressive tradition, Jody Messler Davies has advocated for the "presumption that the unconscious structure of mind is fundamentally dissociative rather than repressive in nature" (1996, 564) and in their genealogy of the topic, Elizabeth Howell and Sheldon Itzkowitz link the increased attention to dissociative processes with a growing fieldwide appreciation of real world trauma. They write: "even though psychoanalysis began in the study of dissociation, not long after its inception, Freud redefined the data of psychoanalysis, moving the topic of inquiry away from an explicit exploration of trauma and of dissociated experiences and dissociated mental structure. And for the most part psychoanalysts followed suit, like their forefather, all too often ignoring the importance of exogamous traumatic reality" (2016, 7). As this passage makes clear, for many on either side of the traditionalist-progressive divide, repression represents the "drive-defense-fantasy model of Freud" in which symptomatology is "more likely" attributed to "conflict between the drive and the defense than the emergence of dissociated material" (7). As such, for many who reject the field's exclusive focus on repression, the major problem remains that the repressive model of the unconscious "filters out, or minimizes, the contributing factor of reality in general and the reality of early childhood trauma" (7). In the most popular version of this story, repression has dominated our clinical imagination because it remains easier to tolerate than the reality-oriented outcomes of severe trauma and violence. As many clinicians have observed, even the Oedipus complex "can readily and easily be deconstructed in terms of the underlying motifs of the most heinous type of child abuse: infanticide; murder (Ross, 1982). So, the topics of abuse, murder, and dissociation never really went away, they simply became dissociated as an "unseeable" aspect of reality. Especially among the ranks of the intellectual elite, where the classical model, and of the Oedipal complex often prevailed, there has also been inadequate recognition of the power of overwhelming trauma-generated dissociation. Why?

Nobody likes to think about it. To talk about this is unpopular, even stigmatizing" (8).

While in and of itself, the antinomy between repression and dissociation is not entirely new and can be traced to the early days of psychoanalysis (for example, Pierre Janet's work on dissociation has recently been treated as a crucial precursor to Freud, see Howell, 2005), in contemporary thinking, the most prevalent iteration of these debates centers on how repression is equivalent to a drive-defense model that ignores the role of exogamous trauma. But as Malcolm Slavin and Daniel Kriegman have argued in their exploration of repression, "because analytic theorists have been caught up in the defense or critique of the literal meanings of the classical, hydraulic, mechanical system, they have not been free to explore the full range of its meanings as a functional metaphor of relations between parts, or versions, of the self" (1992, 156). According to them, "more broadly defined, the concept of repression is incontestably at the heart of all narratives, classical and relational, within psychoanalytic theory" and is therefore best understood as a "very broad connotation of a universal, innate process of regulating awareness" (156). Accordingly, "if we do not interpret the content of what is repressed as derivative of blind, instinctual, mechanical forces but, rather, as representing aspects of the child's own version of reality (including its own needs and wishes), it can be said that the classical model of repression points to the fact that certain constructions of subjective experience must be regularly and normally "dissociated," sequestered, or compartmentalized separately from others" (157). Slavin and Kriegman's reformulation of repression through a neurobiological lens is one recent attempt to retain repression without accepting the original drive-defense model that comes with it.

Approaching the debate from a slightly different direction, many "modern Freudians" acknowledge the importance of dissociation while also insisting on the need to maintain Freud's ideas about repression. Reflecting this position, Gil Katz writes that, "the different defensive/protective mechanisms emphasized in these two conceptions of mind need not be considered opposed to each other. Dissociation – which may be a motivated defense as well as an automatic protective mechanism – and repression interact in complex ways. The psychological issues we work with are multiply determined, layered mixtures of both (see also Smith, 2000) even when it comes to trauma. Trauma is best understood not simply as an environmental event, but as a particular interaction between a complex psyche and the environment" (2015, 392). For these thinkers, there is nothing inherently wrong with Freud's mechanistic, instinctual model of repression so long as it is thoughtfully combined with a reality-oriented attention to external traumatic events. Therefore, rather than renouncing repression in toto, contemporary traditionalists who wish to retain Freud's conceptualization of the unconscious as a repository of instinctually-driven fantasmatic content make room for the social construction of experience *alongside* drive-defensive processes.

What even the briefest survey of these debates makes clear is that arguments for and against repression are inextricably bound up with broader questions about what, exactly, the entity known as the unconscious is meant to represent. That is, although the acceptance of repression generally corresponds to a more traditionalist orientation, repression, as a concept, is merely a psychic *mechanism* that derives its meaning from how it functions in relation to the unconscious. For this reason, throughout the history of psychoanalytic thought divergent views about the unconscious have mostly fallen to one or another side of the fantasy versus reality debate, with traditionalists defining the unconscious as a storehouse of repressed mental content and progressives insisting on the unconscious as a repository of actual events. The role of external reality has always been at the center of these arguments: is the unconscious the product of hardwired, self-generated wishes and fantasies or the product of implicit and explicit feelings and memories? If the unconscious were a part of the mind we could open and look inside of, would we find a cauldron of raw drives that have been biologically or phylogenetically inherited, or a movie reel of intersubjective experiences that have been, by various means, recorded? Therefore, although in contemporary discourse the choice between repression and dissociation functions to distinguish traditionalists from progressives (and drive theorists from inter-subjectivists), in actuality this dichotomy is only the most recent attempt to settle, once and for all, the enduring problem of how much, and in what form, external reality belongs in the unconscious.

Part I. The fantasy vs. reality debate

Nearly every close reader of Freud has shown that his abandonment of the seduction theory in 1897 marks the decisive turn in his thinking about trauma and exogamous reality. Until then, Freud (like Janet) was interested in the pathogenic effects of traumatic events and studied the role of consciousness in isolating mental content. But whereas Janet argued that unintegrated memories are suppressed by the force of *external* threat, Freud shifted responsibility to *internal* conflict. It was not, as he initially thought, that every hysterical female patient had been traumatized by sexual abuse but that every hysterical female patient harbored complicated sexual wishes and fantasies that she felt compelled to repress. As Morris Eagle has observed, "the shift from the external to the inner, from trauma to conflict, which is at the core of traditional psychoanalytic thinking, is also, of course, reflected in Freud's (1914) substitution of an actual seduction etiological theory with the notion of seduction fantasy, which is embedded in conflictual wishes and desires…it is the consideration of conflicted wishes and desires, the anxiety they elicit, and the defenses against their conscious experience – not external trauma – that is at the core of Freud's development of the theory of psychoanalysis" (2011, 13).

Over the past several decades, significant attention has been paid to this particular moment in the development of psychoanalytic thought. Feminists, historians and clinicians specializing in trauma have vigorously rejected Freud's disavowal of etiological seduction, arguing that Freud merely preferred internal conflict to external trauma because he couldn't confront the painful reality of rampant sexual abuse in what was otherwise a successful and sophisticated bourgeois population. While this critique has taken many forms, a widespread consensus has emerged on the dangers of privileging intrapsychic conflict over interpersonal events. As a result, Freud's model of the unconscious as a "cauldron of seething excitations" (Freud, 1923 p. 73) has been characterized as retrograde, naïve and unethical to the degree it brackets off unconscious content from any of the social conditions which may have caused it. In Anglo-American writing, Freud's intolerance toward material reality has been treated as emblematic of deeper deficiencies in the traditionalist paradigm of unconscious life. As Jay Greenberg and Stephen Mitchell argued in their seminal intervention, *Object Relations and Psychoanalytic Theory* (1983), "Freud does not allow reality to infiltrate the theory of instinctual drive at all; it remains on the "surface," and is seen in terms of introducing contingencies that require the control of impulse rather than as influencing the nature of impulse itself" (53). As such, "although with the introduction of the reality principle the external world regained some of the theoretical status lost when Freud abandoned the seduction theory, its place remains secondary. The infant turns to reality only as the result of frustration at the failure to satisfy internally arising needs" (54). For Greenberg and Mitchell, it was precisely Freud's demotion of external reality to "secondary" status which opened traditional psychoanalysis to even broader critiques, because to the extent Freud treated social reality as merely "an overlay, a veneer superimposed upon the deeper, more "natural" fundaments of the psyche constituted by the drives" then it was "fundamentally wrong in its basic premises concerned human motivated, the nature of experience, and difficulties in living and, therefore, that drive theory provides an inadequate and essentially misleading foundation for psychoanalytic theorizing and clinical technique" (80).

Greenberg and Mitchell's promotion of external reality to primary psychological importance and concomitant concern for the developmental impact of early attachment experiences, has been greatly furthered over the past several decades in a range of clinical work that focuses on infant development, object relations, and interpersonal structures. According to these progressive views, "the very idea of the unconscious as a storehouse of fully formed mental contents of any kind is seen as untenable" (Eagle, 2011, 108) because most of what constitutes unconscious content is comprised of "procedural memory," "procedural knowledge," and "implicit relational knowing" (Lyons-Ruth, 1999). Drawing on cognitive psychology, attachment research and infant observation, the progressive position views the unconscious as a repository of "self, object and interactional *representations* that are closely linked to beliefs, expectations, and affects and that have been acquired early in life in interaction with parental figures. Examples of representation include: Kernberg's (1976) object, self and affect units; Stern's (1985) representation of interactions generalized (RIGs); Beebe, Lachman, and Jaffe's (1997) "interactional structures"; Schachter's (2002) "habitual relationship patterns"; Bowlby's (1973) "internal working model"; the attachment patterns of Ainsworth, Blehar, Waters, and Wall (1978); the "unconscious pathogenic beliefs" of Weiss, Sampson, and the Mount Zion Psychotherapy Research Group (1986) (which are essentially beliefs about the relationship between oneself and parental figures), Mitchell's (1988) "relational configurations"; and Fairbairn's (1952) internalized objects and internalized object relations" (Eagle, 2011, 126). However, as Eagle proceeds to point out, all these major changes to the *content* of the unconscious have fundamentally altered the *nature* of the unconscious as well. "They are," Eagle writes, "unconscious not in the dynamic sense of being repressed but rather in the sense of being implicit" (127). Therefore, whereas for traditionalists, "repressed wishes are recoverable once repression is lifted, insofar as early representations function similarly to procedural knowledge, they are not recoverable in the same way that repressed wishes and memories are... Rather than leading to direct access to representational structures of the repeated early experiences from which they were abstracted, treatment often facilitates recognition of, awareness of, and reflection on the patient's representational structures" (128). These memories belong to the category of "procedural knowledge" rather than "declarative knowledge" (Lyons-Ruth, 1999) and function more like "habits or motor skills (e.g. riding a bicycle) that have been etched into the behavioral procedures in the body" (127).

Given that these ideas about the unconscious have emerged in the context of vigorous arguments about the role of reality in psychic illness, and have often been aimed specifically at correcting the "mistakes" made by Freud's retreat to intrapsychic fantasy, it is hardly surprising to find that the progressive unconscious is "essentially a rational and reality-oriented unconscious" (129). As Eagle observes, "RIGs, interactional structures, and so on, are understood as pretty much accurately reflecting actual events, that is, as abstracted records of actual interactions with the caregiver. Thus, the unconscious representations of the contemporary psychoanalysis, although reflecting the immature cognition of the child (Eagle, 2011), are not based on endogenous fantasies but are rather the result of implicit and explicit parental messages and communications" (129). As Stephen Seligman recently explained, "the infant developmentalists' assertion that relationships were primary, dislocated the instinct model's assumptions about infancy and, correspondingly, about the instinctual-primitive core of human psychology, child development, psychic structure, psychopathology, and clinical technique. The classical "metaphor of the baby" (Mitchell, 1988), then, as passive and driven from within was neither theoretically viable nor sustained as reflecting observed reality (2018, 99). The reality-oriented infant stands in direct contrast to the infant as imagined by Freud and Klein, for whom the primitive unconscious is a bedrock of phantasmatic object relations. Indeed, not only is the traditional infant seen as instinctually driven by destructive and libidinal impulses, but even the experience of actual caregivers is mediated by internally generated fantasies. "The Kleinian *ph* connotes the depth of those instinctual structures that were prior to the encounter with reality" and as such "phantasies are primary in the sense that they are prior to the experience of external reality; they are the first format for mental life" (49).

For this reason, it can be useful to consider how the fantasy vs. reality debate remains at the center of broader arguments about the nature of the unconscious.[1] That is, as Eagle has shown and Seligman confirms, there are major differences in the meaning of the term "unconscious" depending on whether fantasy or reality is the starting point. Eagle writes, "In the Freudian vision, psychopathology is characterized by the continued pursuit of infantile wishes that are unlikely to be gratified in the real world and that are in conflict with both, other aspects of the personality and society, as well as by defenses against the conscious experiences and acknowledgment of these wishes. In the contemporary view, psychopathology is a product of such factors as negative self-representations that produce dysphoric affect, fixed and stereotyped representations of oneself and others that are based in early experiences with parental figures and that make satisfying relationships more difficult, and expectations and pathogenic beliefs regarding the kind of life one must lead if one is to maintain ties to objects" (131).

Although the reality-oriented unconscious was intentionally formulated to counteract the fantasmatic id of traditional psychoanalysis, in recent years, the sharp division between fantasy vs. reality has been the object of increasing scrutiny. Not only have most "modern Freudians" accepted the importance of actual events to the developing psyche (Katz, 2013) but many progressive clinicians express a growing dissatisfaction with how the emphasis on reality has foreclosed meaningful exploration of the unseen and internal. As Galit Atlas has recently argued regarding her own intersubjective orientation, relational psychoanalysis "leaning on infant research, narrowed the scope to the Pragmatic levels in our understanding of the mind. It maintained the split between the internal fantasy world, privileging external reality, trauma and observed interactions... sexuality is often described as derived only from a secondary precipitate of a desire for connection or as part of the mother-infant early sensual attachment, thus depriving sexuality of its mysterious dimension" (2018, 134; Benjamin, 1988, 1995, 2005). Not only has the progressive reorientation to reality conceded to the split between reality vs. fantasy rather than transcending it, but as Atlas correctly observes, the exclusive focus on the unconscious as a repository of internalized relationships, interactional structures and early childhood representations has left the field totally unable to account for the singular importance of sexuality in psychic life. "The relational observed baby seems not to have phantasy, aggression, or sexuality," Atlas writes, because although this baby "responds in highly complex ways to her environment ... her sexuality is often described as derived only from early patterns of attachment or as a secondary precipitate of a desire for connection, as opposed to the infant sexuality of the Freudian baby" (136). Moreover, in privileging actual experience over fantasy, "we too often privilege so-called truth and leave the Enigmatic levels of communication on the periphery" (136). These challenges from within the progressive tradition are part of a growing body of work that finds the unconscious of actual events ultimately unable to account for the depth and range of psycho-sexual experiences (Saketopoulou, 2019; Gonzalez 2017, McGleughlin, 2020).

In a correlated critique, Slavin and Kriegman argue that the major problem with treating the unconscious as a repository of cognitive and implicit events is that it neglects the role of endogenous motivations, that is, motivations which are self-directed and *not* necessarily reducible to relational desires. They argue, "in virtually no theory that we term "relational" is a "genuine clashing" (Goldberg, 1988) of individual aims and goals given a fundamental status as an inherent feature of the basic motives of normal individuals in the good-enough environment" (1992, 24). According to them, "the "drives" are not "outmoded and implausible...phylogenetic vestiges" (Mitchell, 1988, p. 81) for they are seen as filling a crucial, current day function. Indeed, it is possible that classical drive theory has survived as well as it has, despite the manifold, well-documented conceptual and clinical problems associated with it (e.g., Klein, 1976; Holt, 1976) because, at a metaphorical level the theory retains a persuasive power in capturing an aspect of our deep structure that we intuitively sense is a functional necessity for dealing with problems inherent in negotiating development within a biased, conflictual, deception-prone relational world" (164). Although Slavin and Kriegman frequently use the phrase "different drummer" to denote the function of the drives – in contradistinction to the Freudian id, instincts, or pleasure principle – they persuasively demonstrate how the wholesale dismissal of "endogenous" psychic functioning, on the grounds that it leads to a simplistic, mechanistic model of the mind, depletes psychoanalysis of necessary conceptual and explanatory resources.

Rather than superficial integration or some kind of hybrid model, many of these critiques are calling for a reformulation of existing metapsychological coordinates. Whereas the fantasy vs. reality divide has shaped the discourse around the unconscious since the field's inception, a heterogenous range of work has convincingly demonstrated why a more systematic engagement with the underlying terms of these debates is both urgent and necessary. Laplanche's "new foundations" provide an exemplary opportunity for such a radical reformulation because rather than choosing either side of the fantasy-reality divide, his thinking exposes what *they have in common*. Until now, arguments from either the traditional or progressive position have mainly recycled familiar complaints about the limitations of the other side – prioritizing fantasy neglects actual events, and prioritizing actual events ignores fantasy. And while some traditionalists acknowledge the role of reality, and some progressives accept the need to make room for fantasy, the debate remains mostly stuck in the choice of seeing unconscious content as either, hardwired, instinctual and self-generated or cognitive, impressionistic and realistic.

Laplanche's use of the "Ptolemaic"/"Copernican" heuristic as a device for parsing the quality of a given theoretical idea provides a new way of understanding what is missing in *both* traditional and progressive models of the unconscious.

According to Laplanche's astronomic metaphor, there are two totally different versions of the story you could tell about psychosexuality: the first –Ptolemaic version – is that the individual's psychic life is dominated by the repressed sexual wishes he feels but cannot actualize towards his primary objects. The second – Copernican version – is that the individual's psychic life develops in *relation* to the unconscious sexuality of his earliest objects. The Ptolemaic story locates the genesis of sexuality within each individual, and as such runs into considerable incoherence in its attempt to account for the *cause* of sexuality's origins. In sharp contrast, the Copernican reformulation says that in spite of how personal my sexuality *feels* to me, it actually comes at me, first, from another person. With this categorical distinction firmly in place, Laplanche becomes able to identify what constitutes the specifically Copernican discovery – which is the primacy of *otherness*-in-*me* – versus what merely seems revolutionary but is in reality yet another iteration of Ptolemaic ideology. With this distinction in mind, it becomes possible to define *erotophobic* as *the denial of enlarged sexuality that leads to and enforces the belief in psychic self-begetting.* A close examination of traditional and progressive models of the unconscious through this lens will show how both positions on either side of the fantasy vs. reality debate function erotophobically to reassert the primacy of the *self* over and against the discovery of the otherness-in-me.

Part II. Critique of the traditional unconscious

The unconscious as a storehouse of repressed mental content has been vigorously critiqued for its depiction of early psychic life as improbable, extreme, and autarkic. For his part, Laplanche shows less interest in judging the empirical accuracy of the biological-fantasmatic unconscious than in exploring the theoretical repercussions of adhering to this view. Approaching the problem from an unusual direction, Laplanche develops a critique that focuses on the erotophobic implications of the traditional unconscious. Specifically,

Laplanche shows that, "from the moment when the unconscious is assimilated to a primordial id, itself connected not only to the body but to a biologism, even a vitalism, the forces at work there become vital forces, independent, at their origin, of both sexuality and the fantasy inseparable from it" (STU, 86). The major problem, according to Laplanche, is not so much that the *content* is fantasmatic rather than actual, but *how*, if it is in the unconscious, it could have gotten there. "There is no choice, then, but to raise the question of the type of reality which should be attributed to unconscious elements" (90) and a genuinely rigorous account of the unconscious "would set itself the objective of giving precise meaning to the notion of psychical reality, which is constantly put forward by Freud but of which he never truly gave an autonomous definition, or only on rare occasions, while most of the time he reduces it to psychological reality, that is to say in the last analysis to our subjective lived experience" (91). Setting out to define what kind of reality the unconscious is comprised of, Laplanche demonstrates the ways Freud was repeatedly "haunted by the passionate search for a preformation of the sexual, for a sexual that is hereditary in humans" (NFS, 37). Freud's "passion for the phylogenetic" and for the biological were attempts to locate the origin of unconscious fantasies and to show that the conflicts individuals experienced were endogenous to humankind. While the hereditary acquisition of certain traits is indisputable for Laplanche (and for a range of recent neurobiological work, see Slavin and Kriegman, 1992), the problem arises in how instinctual life is used to *generate* the content of unconscious psycho-sexuality.

Laplanche is adamant that he has "no wish to reject biology in the name of psychology, nor even in the name of the mental. To imply as much would come dangerously close to opposing mind to body, or psychology to biology" (TOB, 12). As such, the "issue is not the mind-body relationship but the articulation of sexual with self-preservative functioning, both being inextricably mental and somatic in character" (13). To elucidate what goes wrong in Freud's formulations – and what continues to be wrong with the traditional model of the unconscious – Laplanche meticulously distinguishes "instinct" from "drive" in order to show that despite early efforts to differentiate the two terms, Freud eventually *"instinctualizes"* the unconscious, turning it into a hardwired, mechanistic and demonic psychic entity. Reading across Freud's oeuvre, Laplanche shows how "instinct" "denotes a behavioral mechanism with three features. First, it has a vital biological purpose (*Zweckmassigkeit*) – for instance, the avoidance of danger...A second feature is the invariability, in a single individual or in a given group, of a relatively fixed pattern...third and last, instinct has what may be called quite simply an innate character – that is, it is not acquired by the individual...These three characteristics, adaptiveness, invariability, inheritedness...are completely compatible with present-day accounts" (18). By contrast, "drive" "would not be hereditary, nor necessarily adaptive" (FS, 12) and where instinct seeks the diminution of tension, drive seeks excitation. It follows from this distinction that there are "two radically different models: drive, which seeks excitation at the cost of total exhaustion, and instinct, which seeks relaxation" (14). What a rigorous close reading of Freud reveals is that, in spite of instinct and drive having substantively different economies and characteristics, Freud – and the analytic orientations which follow him – endow the unconscious with the attributes of instinct *rather* than drive. "I am dismayed," Laplanche writes, "that there are still analytic institutes that teach Freud as one would teach the catechism, with an ordered succession of infantile stages of sexuality... It is precisely such a re-inscription of the drive back into the field of instinct that Freud would eventually seek to enforce, setting out, in spite of everything, a kind of pre-programmed course of development in which infantile sexuality is continuous with pubertal and adult sexuality" (20). It is precisely this "re-inscription of the drive back into the field of instinct" that undermines and radical potential of the psycho-sexual unconscious.

Laplanche demonstrates two interrelated problems with the instinctualized unconscious of traditional psychoanalysis. The first is that it becomes impossible to explain *how* and *why* endogenous fantasies develop in the first place. Melanie Klein's formulation of sex and aggression as hardwired biological drives follows this instinctualizing logic to the extreme, arguing that "all development of fantasy, and even its very genesis, are conceived of ... in terms of endogeny" (TOB, 111). As a result of conceptualizing the unconscious this way, there is no developmental account of *how* or *why* the unconscious emerges – "the drives have absolutely always existed" and the "adult-as-object serves above all as a point of purchase for instinctual tendencies that are by their nature endogenous in children" (111). While such a model obviates the need for a developmental account, it is precisely the impossibility of grounding the unconscious in a complex, interpsychic environment that regresses psychoanalytic theory to a pre-sexual idea of the mind. After all, "what ultimately loses any real place with the antagonistic pairing of love and aggression is sexuality. As with the Freudian conception of Eros, the sexual becomes totalizing, synthesizing love" (111). The total absence of sexuality in the instinctualized unconscious deprives psychoanalytic theory of its singular innovation – the discovery of sexuality – and reduces the unconscious to a hardwired, inherited entity that functions according to the laws and motivations of biological instinct. What is lost in conceptualizing the unconscious this way is precisely what makes psychoanalysis a radical metapsychological project to begin with: that it affirms the psychological *primacy of the other*, over and against the tendency to believe *my* psychology begins with *me*.

Indeed, once the unconscious has been assimilated into the laws of ordinary instinctual life, there is no meaningful psychological role for external others; adult objects merely serve as "a point of purchase for instinctual tendencies that are by their nature endogenous in children" (TOB, 111). The problem with this idea is that it turns the unconscious into a fundamentally *auto*centric system. As Laplanche explains, if the Copernican revolution is so hard to maintain it is because "doubtless there are deeper roots to humanity's clinging to the Ptolemaic vision. When Freud speaks of narcissistic wounding in this connection, he is referring to the humiliation of man as *flesh and blood*, as an empirical individual. But one must go further: it is not only that man in his concrete existence is humbled to find himself nowhere, in the midst of the immensity of the universe; the Copernican revolution is perhaps still more radical in that it *suggests* that man, even as subject of knowledge, is not the central reference-point of what he knows" (UCR, 56). According to Laplanche, the difficulty in maintaining a genuinely Copernican orientation can be traced to the challenge of acknowledging "the other thing in us" (UCR, 62). Laplanche continues: "'Internal foreign body,' 'reminiscence': the unconscious as an alien inside me, and even one put inside me by an alien. At his most prophetic, Freud does not hesitate over formulations which go back to the idea of possession, an idea which Charcot, to his credit, took seriously (even if he transposed it into scientific terms). But on the other side of these Copernican advances – always hard to sustain beyond metaphor, *extravagant* in that they presuppose, as it were, the soul's extra-vagation – the dominant tendency is always to relativize the discovery and to re-assimilate and reintegrate the alien, so to speak" (65). It is not only non-psychoanalytic fields which deny the true meaning of the unconscious as "an alien inside me, and even one put inside me by an alien" but psychoanalysis itself which reduces the unconscious to a part of *my* own mind which *I*, alone, created. "Thus the very movement of psychoanalysis would be to deny the alien-ness of the unconscious by offering to reduce it, both in theory and in the practice of treatment. This is the conclusion of the long prosopopoeia psychoanalysis addresses to the ego: 'Turn your eyes inward, look into your own depths, learn first to know yourself' (SE XVII, p. 143). In other words: you do not recognize that which in reality is clearly yourself. It is your own inner core that you fail to recognize; and the unconscious will reveal itself finally as 'something in the depths of man'" (66). This constant temptation to re-assimilate the unconscious to *my* own self, which has been generated by *my* own drives "goes to show that from the moment that the unconscious is reduced from its alien-ness to what one could call, along with theologians and those of a certain faith, an *intimior intimo meo* ['something more inward that my inwardness'] – we can only observe a return to centering: there is something in me which I've split off from, denied, but which I must re-assimilate. Certainly, the ego is not the master of its own house, but it is, after all, at home there nonetheless" (67). From this angle, the problem with the instinctual unconscious is not merely that its origins cannot be logically explained, or that sexuality is foreclosed, but that in functioning like an endogenous extension of hardwired instincts, the unconscious is domesticated into an expression of *au-tocentricity* rather than the place where the *other* lives in me. "To speak of the *fantasy* of seduction, of the *delusion* of persecution, the myth of revelation appears like a reversal of passivity into activity through which an autocentered or re-centered subject claims to be the origin of what, primarily, he has submitted to. One must wonder whether, in referring to their primal passivity, the neurotic, the paranoiac, the religious person are no 'in some way right after all' (Freud): not only with reference to the *content* of fantasies, delusions and beliefs, but also with regard to the centripetal, rather than centrifugal, vector of the intervention of the other" (SPR, 196).

Critique of the progressive unconscious

The absolute rejection of a fantasy-dominated instinctual unconscious has led to a progressive alternative in which the external world plays a leading role in generating the content of unconscious life. On the surface, such a turn toward the social and relational environment offers a welcome antidote to the mythical drama of competing endogenous forces, and in so doing, offers to correct those problems caused by the exclusive focus on self-generated fantasy. Indeed, the progressive tradition has deliberately sought to radicalize psychoanalysis by replacing inborn drives with environmental conditions and mechanistic forces with interpersonal heterogeneity. And yet, a closer engagement with these ideas reveals that, despite its stated appreciation of otherness and celebratory privileging of difference, the progressive model of the unconscious brings us no closer to the Copernican revolution. In fact, if the traditionalists can be said to *instinctualize* the unconscious, then progressives can be shown to *cognitivize* and *subjectivize* it in ways that ultimately undo its radical potential. While traditionalists have always rejected the progressive unconscious on the grounds that it neglects the importance of intrapsychic fantasy, this familiar critique falls short of grasping the deeper problems at work in current popular views. That is, by resorting to longstanding arguments about the privileged importance of endogenous fantasy, traditionalist critiques remain stuck in the stale debate between fantasy vs. reality, unable to grasp the limitations of the progressive unconscious while continuing to defend their own problematic views.

Rather than perpetuate the impasse generated by these familiar debates, Laplanche focuses on the implications, for theory and practice, of transforming the unconscious into a repository of implicit memories and events. Laplanche observes that the temptation to cognitivize the unconscious preceded contemporary efforts and that Freud himself was constantly tempted by archeological metaphors in his descriptions of unconscious content. In this view, the unconscious is comprised of "traces," "reminiscences," and "memories" which may or may not be remembered but nevertheless exert a determinative impact on emotional life. The benefit of such a model is that it prioritizes the role of external reality by suggesting that what is *in* the unconscious, got there from occurrences *outside.* On the surface, such a focus on the actual events of material life acknowledges the importance of real objects and takes seriously that even seemingly minor or benign details can engender major psychic reactions. However, as Laplanche will show, such a reliance on material reality brings with it a whole new set of problems, namely, that it presupposes a veritable 1:1 ratio between unconscious content and objective facts. Although contemporary clinicians are often careful to explain that the patient's subjective account is not the *only* possible Truth, a central characteristic of progressive theories is their conception of the unconscious as comprised of those implicit beliefs, self, object and interactional representations that took shape in early childhood. In popular concepts such as "procedural memory," "procedural knowledge" and "implicit relational knowing" (Lyons-Ruth, 1999) the unconscious is depicted as consisting of representations of repeated interactions with parental figures; indeed, questions about the "objective" veracity of these representations are rendered moot by the simple fact that it is the patient's implicit *biases, tendencies,* and affective *responses* that is the focus of recollection rather than a specific traumatic event. In other words, the focus of this work is less on whether a particular scene took place exactly as one remembers it, than on how the origins of one's current struggles can be reconstructed from memories and perceptions in early childhood.

As an abundance of research in cognitive psychology has persuasively shown, "the RIGs or interactional structures one has formed early in life strongly influence one's expectations and representations regarding significant others, as well as one's corresponding self-concept. For example, if one has experiences repeated rejections, one's concept of the other would be of someone who rejects or does not meet one's needs, and one's concomitant self-concept would be someone who is unworthy and unlovable ... the concept of interactional structure can be seen as an example of Mitchell's (1988) view that mind can be understood as "transactional patterns and internal structures derived from an interactional interpersonal field" (p. 17) (Eagle, 2011, 127). As passages such as these make clear, the focus of treatment is on uncovering increasingly deeper and less verbalized layers of early perceptions in order to delineate the sources of one's current personality and concomitant struggles. Eagle writes: "Whereas, according to traditional theory, repressed wishes are re-coverable one repression is lifted, insofar as early representations function similarly to procedural knowledge, they are not recoverable in the same way that repressed wishes and memories are... The emphasis on representations reflects the reduced importance given to the recovery of repressed memories in contemporary psychoanalysis. Patients can and do remember specific past episodes that often serve as a model or prototype of inferred repeated early experiences that are assumed to have played a formative role in the development of their representational structures. However, from a contemporary perspective, the therapeutic significance of recovering such memories lies less in the direct curative role of recovering memories per se and more in the fact that such memories instantiate the kinds of experiences that constituted the basis for the patient's representational structures" (Eagle 2011, 128).

As Eagle so astutely points out, since the so-called "memory wars" of the 1980s, the definition of material "reality" has undergone significant revision so that what is said to comprise unconscious content is not necessarily a singular, traumatic event, but a diverse panoply of experiences that, taken together, constitute one's general representational structures. Such a shift in how "reality" is used – to denote one's present-day representational structures as opposed to events in the historical past – effectively circumvents the problems encountered in the debates around false memories while nevertheless ascribing to the belief that what is in the unconscious reflects the implicit experience of actual events. And yet, while such a conception of the mind as made of "transactional patterns ... derived from an interactional interpersonal field" (Mitchell, 1988) is, in and of itself, an uncontroversial claim, in the context of metapsychology one major result of defining the unconscious along cognitive lines is that only a certain *kind* of psychological experience is emphasized, namely, those moments that are perceptible, memorized and experienced. While such a range *does* account for a vast array of adult–child interactions, it completely ignores the dimension of inter-affective communication that *supersedes* verbal and cognitive exchanges between the child and its caregiver.

As Laplanche will show with his concept of "translation" (chapter 4), it is the *unconscious* messages of the adult which – because they are unconscious to the *adult* – provide the child with an excess of material demands to be "work on" and digested. "The thing-like presentations which form the kernel of the unconscious are to be conceived as that which eludes the child's first attempts to construct for itself an inter-human world, and so translate into a more or less coherent view the messages coming from adults. The partial but necessary failure of these attempts derives from the fact that these messages are enigmatic for the one who sends them, in other words they are *compromised* by the sender's unconscious. The only emphasis I would add here is to recall that the adult-child relation is eminently suited to re-awaken the conflicts and desires coming from the unconscious" (STU, 93). Understood in affective terms, we could say that in adult-child interactions there is a level of communication that functions *parasitically* in relation to conscious and symbolic content. By parasitic, Laplanche means that *un*worked-through affectivity attaches to words and ideas that *are* worked-through and symbolized, creating *noise* that the child hears but cannot readily make sense of. "What the theory and observations of attachment fail to take into account is the asymmetry on the sexual plane. What is missing is an insistence on the fact that the adult-*infans* dialogue, reciprocal as it may be, is nevertheless *parasited by something else* from the beginning. The adult message is scrambled. On the side of the adult there is a unilateral intervention by the unconscious. Let us even say, an intervention by the *infantile* unconscious of the adult, to the extent that the adult-*infans* situation is a situation that reactivates these unconscious infantile drives" (FS, 205). It is the presence of this *noise* that is attached to an otherwise comprehensible message that forces the child to translate what he hears. "While in normal dialogue (verbal or non-verbal) there exists a common code and there is no need of translation (or it is instantaneous), in the primordial communication the adult message cannot be grasped in its contradictory totality" (FS, 207). That is, the infant is forced to translate messages that he has no other way of understanding because he is being bombarded with unmetabolized content that he needs, for his own self-preservative sake, to mediate and organize.

In this schema, it makes no sense to equate the unconscious with the internalized representational structures of childhood because such cognitive experiences have been neither inaccessible nor repressed. While it is true that the definitive internal structures developed in childhood are mostly implicit and as such benefit greatly from a process of verbal elaboration, they are, structurally speaking, *available* for recollection. In contrast, the kind of dynamic unconscious Laplanche describes is comprised of messages that have eluded complete translation and so sit "like a splinter underneath the skin" propelling the individual forward in ways that are opaque to him. Therefore, while the cognitive unconscious can, at least in theory, be exhaustively elaborated, the kind of unconscious material Laplanche describes is not subject to the same degree of access or expression; internalized representations derive from memories and interactions that *can* be reconstructed whereas *noise* that was parasitically attached to adult-infant dialogue has only ever been noise, meaning it has *never* been accessible to verbal or non-verbal reconstruction. Put another way, while concepts such as "implicit relational knowing" greatly expand how we understand knowledge to be transmitted and recorded, (opening the doors to a vast range of symbolic, gestural and affective communications), the psychological mechanisms described herein remain relatively straightforward and neat: the child is acutely more sensitive than previously appreciated, and as such notices and internalizes immense amounts of what the adult says to him, deriving his own expectations from these experiences. But precisely because we are describing internalized representations, there is a presumptive causality between who the child is now, and what the child remembers of childhood. What is totally absent from this relatively linear picture of early psychic development is all those communications the child did *not* remember or record because they were never discrete psychological events that could be easily localized to someone specific in the external world. Insofar as these messages sounded like *noise*, they demanded that I, the child, work to translate them and in doing so, they became *my own* unconscious content. Whereas I can remember episodes of mistreatment that made me feel unloved, I cannot recollect unconscious messages that I never understood in the first place.

Rewriting the primal scene to demonstrate what he means by a new dimension of unconscious communication, Laplanche explains: "Whenever primal scenes are observed or discussed, two worlds without communication divide, so to speak: on one side, parental *behavior,* the experience and content of which are by definition beyond the subject's grasp; and on the other, the side of the child, a traumatic *spectacle*, more often glimpsed or guessed than seen, suggested by a mere allusion (animal coitus) which the child must then fill out, interpret and symbolize. My point is that between these two worlds something is missing: the supposition (which should have occurred to a psychoanalyst!) that showing sexual intercourse is never simply an objective fact, and that even the letting-see on the part of the parents is always in a sense a making-see, an exhibition. But Freud is never to suspect this idea – that the primal scene only has its impact because it bears a message, a giving-to-see or a giving-to-hear on the part of the parents. There is not only the reality of the other 'in itself,' forever unattainable (the parents and their enjoyment) together with the other 'for me,' existing only in my imagination; there is also – primordially – the other who addresses me, the other who 'wants' something of me, if only by not concealing intercourse" (UCR, 78). As Laplanche repeatedly insists, the content of my unconscious is reducible neither to endogenous instinctual forces nor memories and reminiscences because both of these approaches domesticate the unconscious into yet another extension of my inborn and private psychological mind, totally erasing the fact that what is in my mind got there through my encounter with another person, and that what is mine cannot be neatly disentangled from what is someone else's because from the moment *I* start translating, it is *my* unconscious that has done the work. Indeed, it is my unconscious that has developed *by* being called upon to do the work. Laplanche explains: "II.2 The translation of the enigmatic adult message doesn't happen all at once but *in two moments*. This schema of two moments or times is the same as that of the model of the trauma: in the first moment, the message is simply inscribed or implanted, without being understood. It is as if maintained or held in position under a thin layer of consciousness, or 'under the skin.' In a second moment the message is reactivated from within. It acts like an internal foreign body that must at all costs be mastered and integrated ... II.3 The translation or attempt at translation establishes in the psychical apparatus a *preconscious* level. The preconscious – essentially the ego – corresponds to the way in which the subject is constituted and represents its own history. The translation of message is in essence the production of history, more or less coherent. But because the message is compromised and incoherent, located on two incompatible planes, the translation is always imperfect, with certain *residues* left aside. These are the remainders that constitute *the unconscious in the proper Freudian sense* of the term, in opposition to the preconscious ego. It is clear that the unconscious is marked by the sexual, since it owes its origin to the compromising of the adult message by the sexual. But it is not in any way a copy of the adult unconscious, because of the double 'metabolism' that the sexual has undergone in its trajectory: a distortion in the compromised message on the part of the adult, and a work of translation that revises completely the implanted message on the part of the infant recipient" (FS, 208). In this schema, the unconscious *is* "what has escaped from the construction of meaning that I call translation. It isn't part of the domain of meaning, but is constituted by signifiers deprived of their original context, therefore largely deprived of meaning, and scarcely coordinated among themselves" (209).

We can measure the distance of Laplanche's model from the cognitivized unconscious by observing that everything progressives say comprises the unconscious, Laplanche designates as left outside of it. Implicit relational knowledge and internalized representational structures are capable of translation and therefore become part of the child's "more or less coherent" narrative history. The unconscious, as a particular psychological entity, is *not* made up of messages that have already been adequately translated and understood but of those elements that *cannot* be sufficiently processed and translated. In other words, there is no doubt that the infant is constantly bombarded with parental messages and that a vast range of information is stored and hugely influential; but, for Laplanche, the radicalism of the unconscious depends on it being structurally and functionally distinct from the general operation of preconscious, ego-related activities. In the absence of this distinction, the unconscious is reduced to a series of cognitive processes that fail to account for the role of adult sexuality in the formation of the child's unconscious.

Indeed, one of the signal advantages of Laplanche's formulation is that it takes full account of attachment's centrality while at the same time conceptualizing the distinctive realm of sexuality. According to Laplanche, *enlarged* sexuality refers to sexual life beyond "the limits of the difference between the sexes and beyond sexual reproduction" (FS, 19). At the level of psychic functioning, sexuality can be understood as referring to those elements of the adult's mental life that generate "noise" for the infant, although not for the adult himself. This is the case because every adult has a part of psychic life that has not been worked-on via symbolization and interpretation and is, as such, a powerful but unmediated component of all communicative activity. Indeed, for Laplanche, sexuality is an indelible dimension of any complex psychic apparatus and it operates by a distinctive drive-economy that seeks an increase rather than a diminution of tension. Moreover, it is because *every adult is sexual* that a rigorous metapsychology must strive to account for the transmission of this sexuality to the infant *who is not inherently sexual.* Laplanche will elaborate the mechanics of this transmission in his theory of seduction but as it pertains specifically to the unconscious what matters is that any conceptualization of unconscious content *takes into account* the infant's encounter with adult sexuality. Progressive depictions of the unconscious as a repository of cognitive and subjective experiences completely neglects this dimension of psychic life because it focuses exclusively on what the child perceives, feels and notices at the expense of the vast world of sexuality which *perverts* reciprocal dialogue. Therefore, while cognitive psychologists and infant researchers have persuasively shown that a vast amount of data is communicated *implicitly* between adults and infants, the emphasis on unearthing procedural memories and internalized representational structures re-centers psychoanalysis to the concrete, discrete, and accessible, as if the unconscious could be equated with the sum of these sub-conscious exchanges. Indeed, not only does such a re-centering ignore the operation of sexuality as a perverting "noise" that occurs *beyond* the ordinary circuits of reciprocal dialogue but in so doing assimilates the unconscious into yet another expression of *self*-knowledge and *personal* identity.

While on the surface it may seem as though filling the unconscious with implicit and procedural memories is a benign and un-controversial theoretical development, a Laplanchian critique will show that such an approach inevitably re-centers the individual, and erases the impact of the actual other. Laplanche writes: "If the un-conscious consists of memories which have been unable to lodge in the ego because they are irreconcilable with it, the fact remains that a memory, even if repressed, is historically *my* memory. If it is to be-come mine again, as it is nothing but a part of me from which, at some moment, I have been forced to separate, what could be more natural? Moreover, if the repressed is never anything but part of my stock of memories, the task of psychoanalysis, which is to do away with repression and suppress the unconscious, has rightly no limit: since it was already myself, there is no reason why it should not become, one day or another, me again!" (UCR, 70). In this view, the major problem with turning the unconscious into a storehouse of implicit memories is that it is *still* a storehouse of *my* memories and such, a structure which reaffirms my power as an agent in my own unconscious – *I* perceived, *I* remember, *I* was told, etc., are all for-mulations which put the individual at the center of his psychic life as though nothing could or did happen that he did not actively, and on some implicit level, register. Indeed, while the focus on what other people have done to impact my personality may seem like an ac-knowledgment of radical alterity, in actuality the cognitive un-conscious merely shifts psychological responsibility from the child (and his endogenous fantasies) to the adult (and his problematic behaviors) without in any way recognizing how the child's auto-centricity is maintained equally in both of these models. This is be-cause what progressives have done is invert the arrow of causality from the parents to the child; where Freud can be said to have blamed children for their pathology by tracing conflicts to fantasies that are endogenous to children, progressives can be said to blame parents for their child's pathology by linking all present-day struggles with representational patterns acquired or inherited from parents in early childhood (Kohut is often considered exemplary of this shift). While superficially the focus on external sources of difficulty liberates the individual from the closed circuit of self-generating fantasy, the liberation is only skin deep, so to speak, because the "other" of the parental dyad is always and ever reducible to *my* memories and *my* experiences, putting *me* at the center of my unconscious instead of an actual psychological other who inflicted sexuality upon me that I live with but have never made *my* own.

With this problem in mind, Laplanche asks: "Would it not be possible, then, to maintain that the unconscious has a close link with the past, the past of the individual, *while at the same time abandoning the psychological problematic of memory* with its intentionality aimed at *my* past, but also its retrospective illusions and its ultimately undecidable nature? For Freud neglects here the innovative core of his own initial formulation: hysterics suffer, not from memories, forgotten or not, but from 'reminiscences.' The term could, of course, be reduced to memory – a memory cut off from its context – but it could equally be allowed to bear the value of *extravagance* which is not lacking in Platonic doctrine: something which returns as if from elsewhere, a pseudo-memory perhaps, coming from … the other" (UCR, 71). As Laplanche repeatedly demonstrates, just because it is "my" unconscious does not mean it is the product of *my* memories, because if the adult *is* sexual (as the adult always is) then enigmatic messages are necessarily transmitted to me which I receive but cannot sufficiently translate. Untranslated, these messages sit like a splinter "underneath the skin," compelling me but *not* accessible to cognitive awareness. This is why turning the unconscious into an entity that is functionally synonymous with memory (implicit memory is, after all, still memory) invariably transforms the unconscious into an extension of *my*self rather a structure that is built in relation to *someone else's* sexuality. And it is this assimilation of the unconscious into a part of *my*self that inadvertently transforms the unconscious into something *I* have supreme and subjective access to, thereby converting psychoanalysis into a *self*-affirming hermeneutic exercise.

To be clear, for Laplanche the problem with self-centeredness is not merely the familiar poststructuralist complaint about selfhood as an ideological and linguistic façade that manufactures the authenticity it claims to reflect.[2] Laplanche is not opposed to selfhood, nor is he promoting, as some thinkers in the French philosophical tradition have, the annihilation of subjectivity as a cure for mental suffering that is socio-culturally induced.[3] Instead, what Laplance rigorously demonstrates is that the constant tendency to re-center psychology on the individual rather than the "other" is an enduring and pernicious defense against acknowledging the role of other people in the development of one's private psychic life. In one sense, this is a natural consequence of becoming speaking subjects – we speak from our experience and in so doing orient the world according to our personal perspective. But in another sense, our constant re-centering is hardly so innocent since putting ourselves at the center can also been seen as a successful maneuver to deny the degree to which our deepest needs and fantasies are inhabited by other people. In what is often considered the most recent prominent attempt to recognize the impact of external others, the progressive tradition has emphasized the mind's social constructedness, often going so far as to claim that there is no stable core of inner traits or tendencies. As Eagle notes, while "most would agree that one would not develop what we would normally call a human mind without being immersed in repeated human interactions ... the claim that mind is socially constructed has been extended to include the more radical assertion that in its adult function – beyond infancy and childhood – mind is a product of ongoing and often varying social (intersubjective) interactions. In this view, mind is conceptualized not as a relatively stable inner structure but rather as fluid and ever-shifting responses to social influences and interactions" (2011, 132). But while acknowledging the impact of human interactions is a considerable improvement from an earlier view in which all fantasies were seen as more or less pregiven and inborn, the preceding critique has endeavored to show how the blanket affirmation of sociality actually gets us no closer to an account of the specific, structural role others play in the development of psychosexual life. Indeed, according to Laplanche, we will continue to circle indefinitely around otherness without really understanding what it means for the unconscious, until we can recognize the fundamental deficiencies of *both* positions on the fantasy vs. reality debate. *Both* the instinctual id and the cognitive unconscious evade a rigorous reformulation of psychoanalytic theory by failing to observe how genuine alterity requires the construction of a new category – *psychical reality* – in which neither hardwired fantasy nor naïve realism prevails.

Part III. The realism of the unconscious: a third way

In 1959, Laplanche and Leclaire put forward their report to the Bonneval conference in which they introduced the "realism of the unconscious." As Laplanche explains, "a realism of the unconscious would set itself the objective of giving a precise meaning to the notion of psychical reality, which is constantly put forward by Freud but of which he never truly gave an autonomous definition, or only on rare occasions, while most of the time he reduces it to psychological reality, that is to say in the last analysis to our subjective lived experience" (STU, 91). *Psychical reality* is intended to add a third option to the two orders of reality that psychoanalysis (following Freud) predominantly relies on – external, material reality on the one hand, and psychological reality on the other. This third category is meant to refer to the "reality of the message" as it is transmitted from the adult to the child. In an effort to distinguish psychical reality from the more familiar analytic registers, Laplanche insists that it alone affirms "*Das Andere*, the other thing in us: this is the unconscious as it is discovered before 1897 and as it will re-emerge at numerous points in Freud's work" (UCR, 62). Laplanche is emphatic in his insistence that psychical reality must maintain the fundamental *alien-ness* of the unconscious. Explaining what Laplanche means by this "alien-ness," the translators write: "[*etrangerete*: 'strangeness' translated as 'alien-ness.' Laplanche's description of the unconscious as a neologism connecting the other thing in us, *Das Andere*, back to *Der Andere,* the other person (*l'etranger*, the stranger/foreigner) who takes part in the seduction scene. The English 'strange' has a subjective dimension that is relative and reducible. Strangeness is in the eye of the beholder: the 'stranger' can become over time familiar, whereas 'alien' denotes an irreducible strangeness, the result of an *external* origin. While the foreigner may lose his effect of 'strangeness' over time, he never becomes a 'native' but remains a 'resident alien' however 'naturalised.' The hyphenated form 'alien-ness' allows the reader to hear the noun in Laplanche's neologism – etrangerete – and distinguishes it from the usual abstraction 'alienness' – *etrangete*.]" (UCR, 62). As this explanation makes clear, maintaining the fundamental "alien-ness" of the unconscious is a central concern for Laplanche because as soon as this "alien-ness" is compromised – that is, assimilated into a more benign and ordinary "strangeness" – then the very structure of the unconscious loses its radical force. To this end, Laplanche rejects accepted ideas of the unconscious as derived from either fantasies (in the traditional paradigm) or memories (in the progressive paradigm) and postulates instead a model in which a "dynamic unconscious" is comprised of "messages," "a third reality ranking alongside material and psychological reality" (UCR, 80). What are these messages and how do they form an unconscious?

Introducing the distinctive register of psychical reality, Laplanche writes, "let us state the problem from the outset: the existence, the postulate, of a third domain, which is not material, factual, perceptual reality, but which is also not subjectivity" (IDH, 153). Freud introduces the term psychical reality but "was never able to fulfill what he describes," instead constantly reducing psychical reality to psychological reality or else to a crude understanding of factual history. "My objection," Laplanche writes, "is not that, as has been demonstrated to excess, 'human facts are not things' and, in the most general sense, that they 'have a meaning,' but that *infantile scenes – the ones with which psychoanalysis is concerned – are first and foremost messages*" (IDH, 155). To particularize the distinction between "messages" and the familiar categories of memories or facts, Laplanche explains that the "term 'message' insists on the fact that the signifier represents someone to another" (IDH, 158). While the mother feeding her baby is the prototypical example of the ordinary transmission of 'enigmatic messages,' Laplanche uses the example of Freud's paper "A Child in Being Beaten" (1919) in order to demonstrate the specific ways in which what both Freud and his subsequent critics have missed is the role of the 'message' as it has been communicated from the father to the child. For Laplanche, this paper is "exemplary in demonstrating that the memory is very different from the unconscious fantasy that has arisen from it, and, incidentally, from the conscious fantasy derived from the former" (IDH, 154). In his close reading of this paper, Laplanche begins by highlighting the "three formulations proposed by Freud" to account for the patient's experience.

1. My father is beating a child (a little brother-or-sister).
2. I am being beaten by my father.
3. A child is being beaten.

Laplanche concentrates on Stages 1 and 2 since Freud "sometimes describes them as two stages of one and the same fantasy, but, if we look at them closely, how can the same type of reality be attributed to each? Stage 2 is really what we call an unconscious fantasy. It has a fixed and stereotyped character of such a fantasy; and being in-accessible to any reshaping, it is all the more fixed and stereotyped because it can never become conscious. It is constructed only by the analysis... On the other hand, Freud hesitates openly about the first phase and inclines towards deeming it real" (155). Working through the different possibilities, Laplanche then observes that Freud himself suggests there is an "original phantasy" at work in Stage 2 which "competes with an even invalidates the conception of 'primal fanta-sies' of phylogenetic origin, formulated two or three years earlier" (156). In other words, Freud concedes that there may be such a thing as an unconscious fantasy which is "'original' without ceasing to be the product of an individual process and without any need to refer to the archetypal and the unconscious of the species" (156). But if this type of unconscious fantasy exists, then how and where does it originate?

Laplanche announces that "it is time to attempt a different de-scription of the process." This reinterpretation of the sequence begins with the idea that in the first stage, "the real events that have taken place between the family protagonists are something quite different from mere material sequences. It seems to me obvious that, in one way or another, they are *presented* to the child. If a little brother-or-sister is beaten in the presence of the child, it is not like beating an egg white in the kitchen" (156). While it might seem "obvious" that beating a child is not the same as "beating an egg white in the kitchen," the way unconscious fantasy is typically understood ignores precisely this *performative* aspect of the adult-child scene. That is, "the fact that the father is addressing himself to the spectator of the scene is illustrated in Freud in his addition to the initial formulation: 'My father is beating the child [brother-or-sister]/whom I hate.' This 'whom I hate' is not a factual, perceptual component of the scene. It is a *contextual* component. It does not belong to one or other of the protagonists, but is their secrete or common possession. If I hate the little brother-or-sister and, knowing this, my father beats him or her in front of me, this confirms that he is addressing a message to me" (157). Another way to say this would be that the scene of a father beating one child in front of another is hardly *communicatively* neutral. The scene has a *performative* aspect that derives from the father's un-conscious communication to the child; in this particular instance, the child interprets the communication to mean, "'My father is beating [in front of me] the child [little brother-or-sister] whom I hate.' 'It means [*das heisst*]: "My father does not love this other child, he loves only me."'" (Freud, 1914a, p. 187) Laplanche is careful to point out that the child's interpretation of the event is *not* a "copy of the conscious scene" (156), nor is it a straightforward account of what the father *meant* to say or show. In fact, we can assume that the father "means to say, for example: 'Disobedient children must be punished to teach them how to behave" and therefore "barely" knows that he "*says* more than he consciously means" and that "he is saying a whole lot of other things, such as: 'Loving means beating, sexually assaulting, and having intercourse, as, for example, I do with your mother....and furthermore, not only genitally but also anally – for how else could one assault a little 'brother-or-sister,' etc." (158). In beating one child in front of another, the "father has no idea at all that he is saying a whole lot of other things" and for this reason, the child is not only impacted by the spectacle of watching his sibling being punished but by the "enigmatic message" which is transmitted from the father and "compromised by any number of unconscious resurgences" (158). What does the child do in this scenario? The child "translates it as best as he can, with the language at his disposal. This translation coincides precisely with the words that are spoken/lived/felt: 'My father does not love this other child, he loves only me'" (159).

To specify how his reinterpretation of Freud's paper challenges existing ideas about the unconscious, Laplanche suggests that "alongside perceptual reality and psychological reality ... we should place a third reality, that of the message, i.e., of the signifier in so far as it is addressed by someone to someone. If we say that this category is practically absent from Freud's thought, we are also saying that the other, the human other, is also absent from it, as a source of messages. The other – particular the parental other – is barely present at all, and then only as an abstract protagonist of a scene or a support for projections" (159). For Laplanche, the major weakness of the fantasy vs. reality debate is that it leads to two equally impossible positions; either fantasies are endogenous, instinctual and self-generated in which case they are products of the child's self-enclosed imagination, or else they are memories of historical events in which case they are the cognitive products of factual encounters. What both of these possibilities completely obscure is how the adult-other is a separate source of psychic content that is *not* reducible to either factual reality or endogenous fantasy because it is *unconscious* to the adult, meaning it is neither in the actual behavior of the adult nor in the child's own imagination but in the 'message' that gets transmitted *from* the adult's unconscious *to* the child.

Unconscious content

Having worked out a new, third category called *psychical reality,* Laplanche speculates about the nature of unconscious content. Since it is not derived from memories or fantasies, what *is* unconscious content comprised of? To answer this question, Laplanche relies on the translation model discussed in the fourth chapter in which the pressure exerted by the 'enigmatic message' propels the child toward a process of translation. Once the general outlines of the translation sequence are firmly in place, Laplanche is able to demonstrate that "the thing-like presentations which form the kernel of the un-conscious are to be conceived as that which eludes the child's first attempts to construct for itself an interhuman world, and so translate into a more or less coherent view the messages coming from adults" (STU, 93). According to this schema, the child is compelled to translate the affective *noise* that perverts the communication from the adult and does so, by making use of the linguistic codes that are available to him. However, during this translation process, there are elements of the "enigmatic message" that the child naturally *fails* to translate. Laplanche explains: "the translation of the enigmatic adult message doesn't happen all at once but *in two moments.* This schema of two moments or times is the same as that of the model of the trauma: in the first moment, the message is simply inscribed or im-planted, without being understood. It is as if maintained or held in position under a thin layer of consciousness, or 'under the skin.' In the second moment the message is reactivated from within. It acts like an internal foreign body that must at all costs be mastered and in-tegrated" (FS, 208). Because this is a two-step process, it is important to map out how each step works: in the first step, the "message" is received without being translated or understood but the very *attempt* to translate or understand the adult's "enigmatic messages" "establishes in the psychical apparatus a *preconscious* level. The preconscious – essentially the ego – corresponds to the way in which the subject is constituted and represents its own history. The translation of messages is in essence the production of a history, more or less coherent" while in the second step, the fragments of untranslated 'messages' are reactivated in such a way that propels the individual toward further mastery and translation. What is more, "because the message is compromised and incoherent, located on two incompatible planes, the translation is always imperfect, with certain *residues* left aside. These are the remainders that constitute *the unconscious is the proper Freudian sense* of the term, in opposition to the preconscious ego" (FS, 208). What this means is that Laplanche's new model of the unconscious is comprised of those failed translations, the "residues" of imperfect translations which then become a part of the *child's* unconscious even as they derive from the unconscious of the *other* person. Indeed, it is precisely because this model treats the adult-other as a real source of the child's psychic content that Laplanche can say it is a model which genuinely affirms the status of an actual "other" in metapsychology.

To further elaborate the characteristics of the unconscious, Laplanche describes three major features: "(1) *the absence of time* in the unconscious, since it is what escapes, the process of repression, from the constitution of the domain of the temporal that is the flowering and enrichment of the preconscious personality; (2) the absence of coordination and of negation, since it is precisely what escapes from coordination that is indispensable to the process of translation; (3) *the realism of the unconscious*, corresponding to Freud's 'psychical reality,' is repudiated as scandalous by a large number of modern interpretation. This realism opposes the idea that the unconscious is *a second meaning* subjacent to the 'official' and preconscious meaning proposed by the subject. On the contrary, the unconscious is what has escaped from that construction of meaning that I call translation. It isn't part of the domain of meaning, but is constituted by signifiers deprived of their original context, therefore largely deprived of meaning, and scarcely coordinated among themselves" (FS, 209). Laplanche emphasizes that the inevitable and partial failures of translation account for the "'classical' normal-neurotic unconscious" whereas more radical failures of translation result in more extreme psychological disturbance. In these scenarios, "nothing is translated, the original remains as such in the psychical apparatus, whether implanted or intromitted. It thus constitutes what one might call an 'inserted'/'enclosed' unconscious" (FS, 210). Laplanche acknowledges that, as yet, this is a new and unfamiliar "line of investigation" and that the "conditions are probably multiple" in which such a "radical failure of translation" might occur (FS, 211). That said, he speculates that the intergenerational transmission of trauma might be a leading cause of such failures of translation since in those instances the trauma of one generation is not at all "metabolized" and thus more likely to be transmitted to the infant without the aid of symbolization or working-through. The recent popularity of intergenerational trauma attests to the diagnostic importance of this concept even though most current endeavors to think through its impact dissociate trauma from sexuality. Laplanche observes that "confronted more and more in their practice with cases deviating from this model (limit cases, psychoses, mental illnesses, perversions) a large number of theoreticians have *put to one side* the Freudian conception, founded on repression and the unconscious, as being relevant only to a small number of cases. They have then constructed other models *alongside* the Freudian edifice ... these models are, most of the time, desexualized, and they scarcely make use of the notion of the unconscious" (FS, 212). But while sidestepping the "normal-neurotic" unconscious has immediate advantages (namely, resetting the debate to focus on severe pathology), the separation of pathology from *enlarged* sexuality and unconscious processes hinders the development of a comprehensive metapsychology which can account, equally thoroughly, for normal and disturbing outcomes.

As such, Laplanche establishes a paradigm of unconscious life in which *enlarged* sexuality compromises and perverts the adult "message" – bringing "noise" to what may otherwise *seem* to be a straightforward, interactional exchange – and prompting the child's efforts at translation. In this model, sexuality is a major feature of the "enigmatic message" and propels translation accordingly, but there is a vital difference between the sexuality that makes a given message "enigmatic" and, in other situations, the pathology that *prevents* a message from being translated. Often distinguishing between "implantation" and "intromission," Laplanche suggests that "implantation" refers to the fundamental situation in which "signifiers brought by the adult are fixed, as onto a surface, in the psychophysiological 'skin' of a subject" whereas "intromission" refers to a "violent variant" of this sequence in which a process "blocks this, short-circuits the differentiation of the agencies in the process of their formation, and puts into the interior an element resistant to all metabolization" (II, 136).[4] Therefore, whereas implantation is "a process which is common, everyday, normal or neurotic," intromission provides a way of describing how this ordinary process can be sabotaged, leaving the child with a stock of messages that are resistant to translation. These translation-resistant messages are distinct from the "*stock of untranslated messages*" that exist "not only in the infant but in all human beings" (FS, 212). That is, since "translation can only be got under way by a reactivation, a reactualization" then there is no guarantee *which* "messages" will get translated versus which will remain stagnant, under the psychophysiological skin, in a "kind of 'purgatory' of messages in waiting" (FS, 213). According to Laplanche, the role of psychoanalytic treatment is precisely in relation to these messages: "analysis is first and foremost a method of deconstruction (ana-lysis), with the aim of clearing the way for a new construction, which is the task of the analysand" (IDH, 165).

Viewed in relation to prevailing views of the unconscious as either a storehouse of repressed wishes or a repository of memories, it becomes possible to observe how Laplanche establishes a separate and distinctive register of unconscious life by particularizing the structure and content of unconscious material. That is, from within Laplanche's model it becomes clear that the implicit knowledge progressives trace to the cognitive unconscious *does* exist, just not in the *dynamic* unconscious. The kinds of interpretations and translations the child conducts on the material he encounters is a vital and indispensable dimension of psychic experience; Laplanche confirms that "the translation of messages is in essence the production of a history, more or less coherent" (FS, 208) and since these translations are constitutive of the individual's personal history, they are an active part of the "ego," even if particular memories or ideas are implicit and internalized rather than conscious and explicit. However, the dynamic unconscious stands in sharp contrast to the ego and it's translated messages because it is only the "residues" and failed translations that "escape the construction of meaning" and ultimately end up in the unconscious. It follows from this description that the memories and implicit representational structures that are called unconscious in contemporary progressive theory, in actuality correspond more directly with the pre-conscious and ego-based ideas that are a part of every functional psyche. Put another way, just because implicit relational knowledge is not at the foreground of conscious awareness, does not mean it is in the enclave of the unconscious either. To wit, it is only dynamically unconscious contents which are at the "origin of the *drives*" insofar as *they* are what impose "'the demand for work'" on the body and the mind (FS, 209). The "drives" are *not*, as Freud often insisted and his followers have maintained, the origin of unconscious content because that would require them to be instinctual and hardwired, but they *are* the product of the actual adult-infant interaction. Laplanche's bold inversion of the standard relationship between the unconscious and the "drives" offers a remarkable new picture of psycho-sexual life in which the individual is *driven* by alien forces as set in motion by the child's early and unavoidable encounter with an actual alien-other. For Laplanche, the particulars of "drive theory" can be taken or left but the universal, ineluctable fact of the adult-infant encounter lie at the center of any rigorous metapsychological investigation. To date, the field remains, as Freud did, "the prisoner of the antithesis of *factual reality* and a purely subjective interpretation close to *fantasy*. He lacks a third category, that of the *message* whose meaning is immanent, in particular taking the form of the mostly non-verbal sexual messages conveyed by the adult to the small child" (IDH, 165). Laplanche's refusal to domesticate the "alien-ness" of the unconscious by assimilating it to instinctual biology or individual pathology results in a model of the unconscious that is genuinely de-centered insofar as it puts the adult-other at the origin of an unconscious which is only ever, somewhat, *mine*.

Notes

1 Andre Green writes a powerful critique of infant observation (1995).
2 The attack on the "self" as an identity category that merely serves as a mechanism for ideological.
3 Deleuze and Guattari's Anti-Oedipus and Schizoanalysis are exemplary of this line of thought.

4 At various different moments in his discussion of intromission, Laplanche wonders if the superego forms in this kind of process since it operates like "a foreign body that cannot be metabolized" (II, 136).

Bibliography

Atlas, Galit (2018). "Don't throw out the baby! External and internal, attachment, and sexuality," *Decentering Relational Theory: A Comparative Critique*, Eds. Lewis Aron, Sue Grand and Joyce Slochower, New York: Routledge.

Baranger, Madeleine (2012). The Intrapsychic and the Intersubjective in Contemporary Psychoanalysis. *International Forum of Psychoanalysis* 21(3): 130–135.

Benjamin, Jessica (1988). *The Bonds of Love: Psychoanalysis, Feminism and the Problem of Domination*. New York: Pantheon.

Benjamin, Jessica (1995). *Like Subjects, Love Objects: Essays on Recognition and Sexual Difference*. New Haven: Yale UP.

Benjamin, Jessica (2005). From Many into One: Attention, Energy, and the Containing of Multitudes. *Psychoanalytic Dialogues* 15: 185–212.

Davies, Judy Messler (1996). Linking the "Pre-Analytic" with the Post-Classical: Integration, Dissociation, and the Multiplicity of Unconscious Process. *Contemporary Psychoanalysis* 32: 553–576.

Eagle, Morris N. (2011). *From Classical to Contemporary Psychoanalysis: A Critique and Integration*. New York: Routledge.

Freud, Sigmund (1895). "Beyond the pleasure principle," J. Strachey (Ed. and Trans). *The Standard Edition of the Complete Psychological Works of Sigmund Freud* (Vol. 20, pp. 75–156). London: Hogarth Press.

Freud, Sigmund (1895). "Project for a Scientific Psychology," J. Strachey (Ed. and Trans). *The Standard Edition of the Complete Psychological Works of Sigmund Freud* (Vol. 1, pp. 283–294). London: Hogarth Press.

Freud, Sigmund (1911). "Formulations regarding the two principles of mental functioning," J. Strachey (Ed. and Trans). *The Standard Edition of the Complete Psychological Works of Sigmund Freud* (Vol. 12, pp. 213–226). London: Hogarth Press.

Freud, Sigmund (1914). "On Narcissism: An Introduction," J. Strachey (Ed. and Trans). *The Standard Edition of the Complete Psychological Works of Sigmund Freud* (Vol. 14, pp. 73–102). London: Hogarth Press.

Freud, Sigmund (1923)."The Ego and the Id" J. Strachey (Ed. and Trans). *The Standard Edition of the Complete Psychological Works of Sigmund Freud* (Vol. 19, pp. 12–59). London: Hogarth Press.

Freud, Sigmund (1926). "Inhibitions, Symptoms, and Anxiety," J.Strachey (Ed. and Trans). *The Standard Edition of the Complete Psychological Works of Sigmund Freud* (Vol. 19, pp. 1–66). London: Hogarth Press.

Gonzalez, Francisco (2017). The Edge is a Horizon: Commentary on Hansbury. *Journal of the American Psychoanalytic Association* 65 (6): 1061–1073.

Green, Andre (1995). Has Sexuality Anything to Do with Psychoanalysis? *International Journal of Psycho-Analysis* 76: 871–883.

Greenberg, Jay R. and Stephen A. Mitchell (1983). *Object Relations in Psychoanalytic Theory.* Cambridge: Harvard UP.

Holt, Robert. (1981). The Death and Transfiguration of Metapsychology. *International Review of Psycho-Analysis* 8:129–143.

Howell, Elizabeth F. (2005). *The Dissociative Mind.* New York: Routledge.

Howell, Elizabeth F. and Sheldon Itzkowitz, Eds. (2016). *The Dissociative Mind in Psychoanalysis: Understanding and Working with Trauma.* New York: Routledge.

Katz, Gil (2013). *The Play Within the Play: The Enacted Dimension of Psychoanalysis.* New York: Routledge.

Klein, George. (1976).*Two Theories or One? Psychoanalytic Theory.* New York: International University Press. (pp. 369–403).

Lyons-Ruth, Ruth K. (1999). The Two-Person Unconscious: Intersubjective Dialogue, Enactive Relational Representation, and the Emergence of New Forms of Relational Organization. *Psychoanalytic Inquiry* 19 (4): 576–617.

McGleughlin, Jade (2020). The Analyst's Necessary Nonsovereignty and the Generative Power of the Negative. *Psychoanalytic Dialogues* 30 (2): 123–138.

Mitchell, Stephen (1988). The Intrapsychic and the Interpersonal: Different Domains of Historical Artifacts? *Psychoanalytic Inquiry* 8 (4): 472–496.

Saketopoulou, Avgi (2019). The Draw to Overwhelm: Consent, Risk, and the Retranslation of Enigma. *Journal of the American Psychoanalytic Association* 67 (1): 133–167.

Seligman, Stephen (2018). *Relationships in Development: Infancy, Intersubjectivity, and Attachment.* New York: Routledge.

Slavin, Malcolm O. and Daniel Kriegman (1992). *The Adaptive Design of the Human Psyche: Psychoanalysis, Evolutionary Biology, and the Therapeutic Process.* New York: Guilford Press.

Chapter 3

Seduction – Laplanche's theory of psychic structure

Pathogenesis and psychic structure

As a science of psychological illness and a treatment methodology, psychoanalysis relies on a presumptive theory of what *causes* mental suffering, whether it acknowledges those operational assumptions explicitly or not. Indeed, as the field has changed dramatically over the past several decades, so too have the stories we tell about pathogenesis. Whereas earlier generations of psychoanalysis focused on establishing a credible link between the force of a patient's endogenous drives and the defensive conflicts that ensued, the rise of alternative psychoanalytic paradigms – namely, attachment theory, object relations, self-psychology, and the relational school – challenged the putative role of the patient's internal life in generating internal conflict by focusing instead on how conditions in the external environment can be shown to provoke the defenses that cause disease. Although the different positions in this debate are often caricatured in simplistic terms – as blaming the patient or blaming the parent – they are actually consistent with, and contingent upon, a complex set of ideas about the psyche-social matrix. This is to say that although a story of what causes suffering is an essential component of any coherent metapsychology, pathogenesis is rarely treated as a separate or discrete concern because how one views the origin of illness turns out to follow pretty consistently from how one understands the development of psychic structure. In what Slavin and Kriegman call different psychoanalytic "worldviews," there are major divisions over the "*nature of the mind*" as well as the "fundamental *character of the relational world*" (1992, 20). According to them, "the most fundamental issue around which the major psychoanalytic traditions clash" continues to be the "developmental story of the psychological operations used by children and adolescents within the family and then, through a series of transformations, in the larger, adult relational world" (20).

Organizing the field into the "classical" and "relational" narrative,[1] Slavin and Kriegman explore how different paradigms of what causes mental suffering can be traced to divergent views on psychic structure: while the "classical" theorist "would see the mind as intrapsychically structured by the vicissitudes of endogenous motives," the "relational" theorist would see the mind "as understandable only within a particular relational context, and interactionally structured from the vicissitudes of prior and current relationships" (25). As it pertains to psychic suffering, the distance between these positions can be measured by the different ways they each conceptualize the emergence of unconscious content. In the "classical" narrative, conflict is generated in the unconscious as an inevitable consequence of the clash between normal, individual aims and the limits of other people in reality, whereas in the "relational" narrative, internalized representations, perceptions and beliefs are stored in the unconscious as an "unfortunate by-product of complexity, human limitations, and pathology" (25). While this contrast is rudimentary, it nevertheless makes clear that there is no universal agreed-upon definition of the unconscious – each narrative defines the unconscious to suit its metapsychological vision – *and* the definition of the unconscious is inextricable from broader debates about the structure of the mind. This is why debates about pathogenesis are always bound up with questions of psychic structure, and why seemingly technical debates about psychic structure are at the heart of bigger questions about the cause and origin of psychic suffering.

In addition to grasping the major theoretical differences among competing factions, Slavin and Kriegman's juxtaposition of the "classical" and "relational" positions is helpful for reflecting the state of the field as it exists today, that is, caught between divergent views that each in their own way generate theoretical and technical problems they are insufficiently equipped to solve. A close reading of how traditional and progressive models conceptualize psychic structure will clearly demonstrate that both sides fail to account – in a rigorous and meaningful way – for the psychological effects of the encounter *between* the infant and the adult caregiver. Although Laplanche did not intervene in these debates directly, he wages a vigorous critique of any idea that obscures the role of the actual adult-other in the development of psychic structure. Laplanche focuses specifically on how the unconscious can be said to emerge; what sets the unconscious, as an entity, in motion? What factors contribute to its emergence? Is it present at birth or does it develop over time? What are the conditions which facilitate its normative development? Since all sides can agree that the unconscious is the source of psychic content – even if what is meant by "unconscious" and "content" differs dramatically among divergent schools – this chapter focuses on delineating the different ways each model theorizes the development of the unconscious.

What this exercise in critical close reading will show is that one's theory of what causes psychic suffering follows directly from one's views on how the unconscious, as a psychic structure, develops. Therefore, rather than challenging prevailing paradigms of pathogenesis, this chapter will explore the *source* of the problem – the different theories of psychic structure themselves – and demonstrate the ways both traditional and progressive models fail to integrate the *actual* adult-other into the process of unconscious development. This failure to account for the impact of the actual other results in models of psychic structure that are incoherent and simplistic, and which ultimately bring us no closer to grasping psycho-sexual life in all of its singular complexity and alien-ness.

In a powerful essay entitled, "Interpretation between Determinism and Hermeneutics," Laplanche sets out to explore the field's major divergence with respect to clinical aims and methodology. Starting backwards, Laplanche endeavors to show how different views of psychic structure manifest clinically in fierce debates about the goals of treatment. Although the particular terms of these debates differ widely depending on the specific national-cultural context in which they appear – French and English authors each characterize their positions using different philosophical language – "ultimately, however, although the various protagonists' starting points and philosophico-epistemological foundations differ, we are left with two positions, nicely summed up by the antithetical terms of *reconstruction* and *construction*" (139). The "first," Laplanche explains, is a "'realistic' standpoint, which claims that neurosis is a 'disease of memory' and that only the recovery of the subject's *real* history (whether by a lifting of infantile amnesia or by a reconstruction) can allow the ego to detach itself from blind mechanisms and achieve some degree of freedom." This "realistic" standpoint views the *reconstruction* of repressed or dissociated childhood memories as the primary goal of analytic treatment and can be said to correspond to the progressive paradigm of treatment in which implicit knowledge and cognitive representations are stored in the unconscious and need to be reconstructed in order to facilitate the patient's agency and self-awareness. The "second position is a 'creative hermeneutic' one, taking cognizance of the fact that every object is *constructed* by my aim and that the historical object cannot escape this relativism. The psychoanalytic approach to an individual's past cannot constitute an exception to this rule: there are no crude facts: 'there is no experience but that which is inquired into'" (139). From this "hermeneutic" standpoint, the goal of treatment is to produce interpretations which are "sovereign" with respect to historical reality because what matters most is what the patient, in the present, does with his experience rather than anything which can be said to have actually occurred. Insofar as this approach prioritizes the patient's subjective experience over and against any concern with actual events, it can be seen to correspond to the traditional paradigm of treatment in which unconscious content is derived from one's internal reactions to endogenous conflicts while the external world, and the events that transpire within it, are props for these projections without any substantive structural role in their own right.

As if often the case with Laplanche's meticulous close readings, he traces the coordinates of this debate back to the origin of psychoanalysis, pointing out that "both of these voices are equally entitled to claim kinship in one way or another with Freud. They are, for example, the two alternating attitudes that lie behind the successive versions, the second thoughts, of the case-history of the 'Wolf Man.' One is the search for factual, detailed, chronological truth about the primal scene, while the other, at a stroke wholeheartedly embracing Jung's objections and abandoning almost all of the reality so painstakingly reconstructed, admits that all this may be nothing but retroactive fantasy, with only a few clues, if that, as foundation" (140). If both of these positions "appear equally Freudian," then how "are we to proceed?" Laplanche asks, since "we are confronted with two positions" which can lay claim to being equally authoritative. To put pressure on this impasse, Laplanche reminds his readers that "putting Freud to work" does *not* mean "trying to find a lesson in him – still less an orthodoxy. Nor is it a matter of choosing one Freud against another, or of 'fishing' here and there for a formulation which suits me. Putting Freud to work means demonstrating in him what I call an *exigency*, the exigency of a discovery which impels him without always showing him the way, and which may therefore lead him into dead ends or goings-astray. It means following in his footsteps, accompanying him but also criticizing him, seeking other ways – but impelled by an exigency similar to his" (147). And what is this exigency exactly? "My answer, my proposition, is this: *it is not history*. Or, to be less provocative, it is something that has nothing to do with the history of the historiographers" (147). What, then, kind of history does Laplanche have in mind? Toward the end of this paper he will outline a "kind of history of the unconscious, or rather of its genesis" (148) in which the contents of repressed psycho-sexual life are "*eigentlich*: 'actually' or 'in actual fact' – what Freud is seeking 'in actual fact' is not what 'actually happened,' in the sense of the crude event" (149).

Although the specific definition of this new paradigm of the unconscious will be elaborated in more depth later in this chapter, for our current purposes it is important to observe that, according to Laplanche, we arrive at the *wrong* understanding of unconscious content if we simply follow in Freud's footsteps because his oscillation between factual history and subjective fantasy are *both* wrong insofar as they each, in different ways, collapse the delicate tension between determinism and hermeneutics. Referring again to the clinical manifestation of this problem, Laplanche writes, "interpretation therefore finds itself trapped in the unresolvable dualism of pure factuality on the one hand and a creative imagination on the other: in the one case, it patiently reconstitutes 'facts' which it hopes will prove to be the source of a determinism, explaining the present by the past... In the second case, the interpretation notes that human facts always have 'a sense,' but it adds too quickly that this sense is imposed on an inert datum by the individual – an infantile subject, and then the subject of the treatment, conceived as a kind of collective interpreting entity" (160). Both of these problematic outcomes are the direct result of the field's flawed models of psychic structure. That is, we volley interminably between interpretation as either *construction* or *reconstruction* because the story we tell about *how* the unconscious develops remains stubbornly oblivious to the impact of the "other – in particular, the parental other" (159) on the genesis of unconscious processes. What would it look like to challenge these views, entrenched as they are not only in contemporary approaches but even within Freud himself? To start, we need to go back to the beginning, specifically, to the beginning of unconscious life, and ascertain what role the adult-other currently occupies in the development of psychic structure. Is the parental-other incidental or fundamental to the process of setting psycho-sexuality in motion? As Laplanche will persuasively show, both the traditional and progressive paradigms of psychic structure rely on developmental teleologies that trivialize, if not outright ignore, the impact on the child's mind of its encounter with the adult psyche.

Drive vs. attachment

The antinomy between attachment and drive theory has long been at the center of debates about psychic structure. As Peter Fonagy observed in his comprehensive account of this difficult history, "there is bad blood between psychoanalysis and attachment theory. As with many family feuds, it is hard to identify where the problem began" (2001, 1). But while it may be difficult to ascertain an accurate portrait of these divisions, each side of the "family feud" has nevertheless sought to provide competing explanations of where the problems began. For pro-drive theorists, "attachment theory was criticized as mechanistic, nondynamic, and explicated according to thorough misunderstandings of psychoanalytic theory" (A. Freud 1960, Schur 1960, Spitz 1960)" (2001, 1), while for attachment theorists, "the psychoanalytic model of personality development is regarded as a single-track rail along which stops can occur. Adult pathological states are considered as due to fixations at, or regressions to, early phases of normal development" (2). While the original contours of these arguments have become more nuanced and flexible over the past several decades with many drive theorists increasingly acknowledging the role of object relations and attachment theorists incorporating ideas about disposition and conflict into their work, an abiding tension between attachment and drive theory continues to organize the field. In their seminal inauguration of relational theory, Greenberg and Mitchell drew a sharp line between drive theory and other models which put relationships at the center, arguing that in the "drive/structure model, psychic structure is a product of drive discharge and regulation" whereas in an alternative system, "the self is organized around relational configurations" (1983, 103). In a later essay on the topic of drives, Mitchell strives to go even further in his rejection of drives by claiming that it is logically and clinically unfeasible ascribe to *both* attachment and drive theory. Mitchell writes, "to argue that we need a concept of drive to describe what the individual seeks in interactions with other people presumes that the individual qua individual is the most appropriate unit of study. It assumes that the individual, in his or her natural state, is essentially alone and then drawn into interaction for some purpose or need. I believe that Fairbairn (like Sullivan) was struggling toward a different way of understanding the nature of human beings as fundamentally social, not as *drawn* into interaction, but as *embedded* in an interaction matrix with others as their natural state" (1998, 117). For this reason, those attempts by clinicians to combine attachment with drive theory are, "while admirable in its inclusiveness," fundamentally "misunderstanding of what Fairbairn was up to" since we only need a "hybrid" model because our "one-person" model already "empties out the individual persons from the two-person model and then claims that we need a one-person/two-person hybrid to bring them back" (119).

Mitchell's hardline rejection of drive theory has been extraordinarily effective at transforming the choice between traditional and progressive models of the mind into a referendum on the value of relationality. But as Laplanche remarks in a tour de force essay on the relationship between attachment and metapsychology, "for years a certain, predominantly Anglo-Saxon tradition continued to wrestle with the myth of the originary monad, or with the false problem raised by Fairbairn of the pleasure-seeking drive and the object-seeking drive, and without taking account of the fact the double opposition between self-preservation and sexuality on the one hand, and drive and instinct on the other, would perhaps open onto new perspectives" (FS, 35). While there is currently no doubt that Mahler's idea that "every child passes through an autistic phase and then through a phase of symbiosis with the mother before acquiring its 'separation-individuation'" is totally wrong – and has "in fact been swept away on the international level by all the data of child observation, which can currently be gathered together under the general heading of 'attachment theory' – the solution remains deeply problematic insofar as intersubjectivity *inevitably* comes at the expense of infantile sexuality" (FS, 36). "We should add," Laplanche concludes, "that the same disaster could well cause the disappearance of the Freudian unconscious, along with the major function of fantasy" (36). According to Laplanche, the major problem with the current configuration of the field into a drive versus attachment antinomy is that it reduces the complex problem of sexuality's relationship to self-preservation, and instinct's relationship to drive, into a simplistic, and ultimately incoherent choice between pleasure and object-relating.[2] What makes this choice a false and flawed one is that it remains based on the myth of the "originary monad" which in turn requires a supposedly primary intersubjectivity to correct, all without recognizing that "intersubjectivity effected under the sign of a motivated-based monism (in this case, attachment; in Balint, it was love)" always effaces the role of "infantile *sexuality*, in the Freudian sense of the term" (FS, 36).

As things currently stand, neither the traditionalist nor progressive model of the mind provides a logically consistent way to explain how the two different registers of sexuality and self-preservation relate to each other in the development of psychic structure. As a result of this metapsychological deficit, the field continues to resort to a range of conceptual maneuvers for explaining the interplay between sexuality and self-preservation that nevertheless fail to address the *source* of the problem, which remains the underlying inability – within current terminology and theory – to understand *how* and *where* sexuality originates. Laplanche addresses this problem directly and extensively throughout his career, focusing specifically on the stories we tell about the genesis of psychic structure. What he finds in this meticulous process of close reading is a remarkable discovery that he will come to label the "leaning-on" hypothesis. A translation of *Anlehnung* which James Strachey translated in a problematic way as "anaclisis/anaclitic," "leaning-on" was introduced and used "sporadically by Freud" but "never given a systematic exposition" (FS, 32). And yet, what Laplanche discovers is that it is precisely the problem of sexuality's relation to self-preservation that the word was introduced to explain. Before exploring the concept in depth, Laplanche observes that "leaning-on" describes the "notion of *a genesis, in which the sexual drive leans for support upon self-preservative instinctual functioning*" and as such, "the very notion of leaning-on presupposes the distinction between an instinctual mode of functioning that is self-preservative and oriented towards the object, and an erotic mode of functioning that begins by deriving support from the former and then detaches itself and 'becomes autoerotic'" (FS, 33). The fact that "leaning-on" presupposes the distinction between an erotic mode, on the one hand, and a self-preservative one on the other, is so important for Laplanche because it contradicts the prevailing tendency to conflate sexuality and self-preservation into a single, biologistic drive that emerges spontaneously and endogenously as part of the human psyche's phylogenetic hardware. Instead, "leaning-on" has the potential to explain how, and why, and under what sociobiological conditions, sexuality develops as a vital but distinctive modality of psychological life.

The "leaning-on" hypothesis

As Laplanche carefully shows, "the notion of *leaning-on* remains indispensable" for showing how "attachment and sexuality seem to coexist" (FS, 44). "Having developed and examined this notion for a long time, we shall recall what is at stake in just a few words. Infantile sexuality first emerges in the exercise of the great functions, in the satisfaction of the great needs of self-preservation. Initially conjoint with the satisfaction of need (feeding, defecation, etc.) sexual pleasure detaches itself secondarily, becoming autonomous with autoerotism and its relation to fantasy. This process, which is barely outlined by Freud, requires interpretation. We have proposed to distinguish three versions of it:

1. An impoverished interpretation that proposes a mechanistic parallelism;
2. An interpretation that makes it into a process of emergence;
3. A contrary interpretation, made in terms of seduction" (FS, 45).

Laplanche systematically works through 1) possibilities and 2) in order to show that despite how intuitive these first two explanations often seem, they are beset by internal contradictions which cannot survive sustained scrutiny and elaboration. Eventually, Laplanche will introduce "3) a contrary interpretation, made in terms of seduction" and successfully demonstrate why this is the only viable way to explain how sexuality develops *in relation* to self-preservation. Although Laplanche's third and "contrary interpretation" will be the major focus of this chapter, it is important to begin by understanding the other explanations – 1 and 2 – as they predominate the field, beginning with Freud himself. Indeed, as Laplanche remarks about the provenance of "leaning-on": Is it even "a "Freudian concept?" (TOB, 29). "What we have in this case," Laplanche decides, "may be described as a concept never identified as such by Freud, who never wrote – and would never have dreamt of writing – an article on *Anlehnung.* Furthermore, for many years it has no specific entry into indexes, even in those to German editions of Freud's work" (29). For Laplanche, the concept's near-total obscurity does not detract from its power; on the contrary, the field-wide neglect of this term is entirely consistent with those impasses in metapsychology that continue to haunt contemporary debates. For this reason, Laplanche seeks to investigate the possible meanings of "leaning-on" in order to establish a plausible "account for the very first appearance of sexuality or, in other words, for *infantile* sexuality" (TOB, 35).

Laplanche begins his in-depth investigation by recapitulating how "leaning-on" is an effort, on Freud's part and in subsequent post-Freudian theory, to account for how sexuality emerges in relation to early experiences of self-preservation. According to him, there are three choices for understanding the relationship between these two modalities (sexuality and self-preservation): "(1) a poor, parallelist interpretation; (2) an interpretation that is rich in the sense that it encompasses an emergence, but contradictory, so that its dialectic opens the door to (3) an inverted interpretation of leaning-on" (TOB, 47). Crucially, each of these three interpretations are working on a common scene which Laplanche refers to as the "celebrated parable of origins" (TOB, 51) in which "the birth of the wish, which is of the human order" comes "out of need and its satisfaction, which are of the vital order" (UCR, 75). According to Freud's earliest outlines in *A Project for a Scientific Psychology* and later *The Interpretation of Dreams*, it is the infant's *first* "experience of satisfaction" (*Befriedigungserlebnis*) that functions to inaugurate the infant's *later* sexual desires. "The first moment is indicated as the infant's *Hilflosigkeit*, in other words its incapacity to help itself, its 'helplessness.' Unable to provide on its own for its needs, the nursling organism is faced with an unbearable build-up of tension, comparable to the rising level of a reservoir, to which it can respond in only two ways: either by letting the reservoir overflow (an action Freud considers 'non-specific,' inadequate because it does not prevent the reservoir from remaining full); or, alternatively, in a 'specific' way, in a series of actions which allow the tension to be discharged for a certain period. What characterizes helplessness is precisely the infant's inability to undertake for itself the action which could empty the reservoir in a lasting way. All it can do is cry, and its cries are themselves, moreover, nothing but the purely mechanical expression of a non-specific overflowing. It is the cries which arouse 'foreign aid,' the mother's activity, which first of all consists of the offering of nourishment. What then follows is a specific sequence of satisfaction: a series of feeding leading to a prolonged relaxation. But just as important as this, according to Freud, are the mnemic traces, the inscribed images, of which there are three kinds: the memory of satisfaction and two sorts of sign – signs linked to the object (an image of the food) and internal images which correspond to a memory of the feeding sequence. At this point it is worth pausing over the description in The *Interpretation of Dreams*:

> A hungry baby screams or kicks helplessly. But the situation remains unaltered, for the excitation arising from an internal source is not due to a force producing a *momentary* impact but to one which is in continuous operation. A change can only come about if ... (through outside help) an *experience of satisfaction* can be achieved which puts an end to the internal stimulus [here is the

turning-point: we move to eh level of representation]. An essential component of this experience of satisfaction is a particular perception (that of nourishment, in our example) the mnemic trace of which remains associated thenceforward with the memory-trace of the excitation produced by the need. As a result of the link that has thus been established, next time the need arises a psychical impulse will at once emerge which will seek to re-cathect the mnemic image of the perception and to re-evoke the perception itself, that is to say, to re-establish the situation of the original satisfaction. An impulse of this kind is what we call a wish; the re-appearance of the perception is the fulfillment of the wish; and the shortest path to the fulfillment of the wish is a path leading directly from the excitation produced by the need to a complete cathexis of the perception. Nothing prevents us from assuming that there was a primitive state of the psychical apparatus in which this path was actually traversed, that is, in which wishing ended in halluci-nating." (GW III, p. 571) (UCR, 76)

This passage of Freud's is quoted at length because for Laplanche this description is "both extraordinary and abortive. Extraordinary because it tries to bring about the birth of one thing (the wish) from another (need). Abortive because, of course, nothing can be born from satisfaction of need but an hallucinatory reproduction of the satisfaction of need. The wish, whose 'genesis' we are given in this description, is the wish for food, nothing more" (UCR, 77). Indeed, studying this passage closely demonstrates for Laplanche that "it is clear that this Freudian alchemy, this attempt to make the base metal of the alimentary give birth of the gold of sexuality, has failed" (UCR, 77) and that in order to understand *how* this alchemical at-tempt fails, it will be necessary to deconstruct the different conceptual moves that are made. This deconstructive reading exposes the three choices Laplanche outlined above – 1) parallelist interpretation, 2) emergence of sexuality and 3) inversion of "leaning-on" – and Laplanche works through the first two choices before outlining his radical alternative.

In the first "parallelist" conception of "leaning-on," sexuality and self-preservation are treated as genetically parallel processes. In this view, the "self-preservative function – nourishment in this case – is seen as the *occasion* of a stimulation of the erotogenic zone, which in this instance is the lips. (It is….easy to guess the occasions on which the child had his first experiences of the pleasure which he is now striving to renew.) Such stimulation is destined to be repeated in an endogenous mode. This implies that there is a kind of disconnect at the source, between the source of self-preservation (hardly the lips: how could the lips be described as the source of hunger?), which is to say the somatic process at the root of hunger, and a sexual source identified by Freud as the mucous membrane of the lips. As for *aim*, what are we told here? Nothing concrete, nothing really specific. The aim of the self-preservative drive is ingestion in the case of nourishment, excretion in the case of excretory zones. No such aim can be found in autoerotic activity" (TOB, 48). Therefore, while "there is naturally no denying that self-preservation can point the way in the search for a sexual object" the kind of sexuality that can be found in this way "involves no fantasy, so that there can be no relationship of *symbolization* between one object and another: it is simply that one object is *replaced* by another within the body. The thumb being 'sucked' replaces nourishment, but in a completely mechanical and non-signifying way" (TOB, 49). Drawing out the reasoning behind this "parallelist" conceptualization demonstrates why such a view "is destructive from every standpoint," and damages our understanding of both self-preservation and sexuality (TOB, 49). That is, the kind of self-preservation Freud was describing could not be said to be originating "in the lips nor even in the stomach, but rather in a whole set of highly complicated homeostatic regulatory processes" and therefore, while Freud was referring to the experience of alimentary needs, it makes little sense to imagine that Freud was interested in mechanisms that "are well described in the physiology of intestinal peristalsis" (TOB, 49). Correlatively, as far as sexuality in concerned, the "parallelist view also impoverishes the concept" since it reduces all of sexuality to the "model of sucking" (TOB, 49). But, Laplanche argues, "if sexuality were reducible to organ-pleasure, it would suffice to assign different measures of sex hormone to different so-called erotogenic zones and other parts of the body – which I defy anyone to do" (TOB, 49). This is not to say, "that no bodily zones are more sensitive than others, but simply that the realm of potential sensitivity must be extended to the entire skin surface, and even to more complex mechanisms, anchored in the body but more complex, such as vision or muscular activity, which Freud invoked in connection with 'indirect sources' of sexuality" (TOB, 49). Laplanche repeatedly opposes this "parallelist" conception of self-preservation and sexuality on the grounds that it treats *both* of these modalities as endogenous to the infant without being able to explain how two distinctive modes can be understood to derive from a single source. "A single source for two instincts? And what source? What parallel aims? What 'object' common to both?" (FS, 45).

Laplanche's thorough and emphatic rejection of the "parallelist" explanation leads him to next consider the idea that sexuality somehow *emerges* out of self-preservation. According to this interpretation, the "*object* of self-preservation is milk while that of sexuality is the breast" (TOB, 50) and as such, "leaning-on" has two phases: "first a functioning in tandem, then a distancing and divergence" (TOB, 50). That is, "at first sexuality obtains satisfaction at the same time as feeding; then it splits off to become autoerotic. Thus, the emergence of autoerotism means a sharp change of direction – not a founding moment but a moment of becoming" (TOB, 50). In this sequence of things, there is a "'metonymisation' of the object at the same time as a turning around within fantasy. For its part, the aim undergoes 'metaphorization' in passing from the domain of self-preservation to the sexual – anal expulsion or projection, for example, being the metaphorization of the excretion of *feces*" (FS, 46). The infant in this scenario transforms self-preservative activity *into* sexuality by "making it pass into fantasy" (FS, 46). Laplanche often refers to this view as the "'creativist' and 'illusionist' conception of human sexuality" because it is characterized by "a veritable sleight of hand: if the sexual is not present *within* the original, *real experience* it will never be rediscovered in the fantasmatic reproduction or the symbolic elaboration of that experience" (FS, 46). That is, "the first real satisfaction can only be the satisfaction of a *need* (an alimentary need in the Freudian example); and *its reproduction* – be it within a memory, a fantasy or even an hallucination – can only be the reproduction of an *alimentary* satisfaction" (FS, 46). For this reason, it becomes totally impossible to suggest that sexuality 'magically' derives from the behaviors associated with self-preservation. Such a view relies on the infant's creativity which Laplanche repeatedly insists cannot "go so far as to create sexuality" (FS, 47). As Laplanche will show in his elaboration of primal seduction, the only viable way to understand the infant's creativity is in relation to sexuality that *already* exists in the intersubjective exchange. Without denying the "active role of the infant in terms of symbolization and the creation of fantasy" it is nevertheless the case that "this activity is brought to bear upon messages that are *already* compromised by the sexual on the part of the adult other" (FS, 47). In other words, "by means of some sort of conjuring trick the sexual is then produced – or, more portentously is said to 'emerge' – from self-preservation, even if it is clear that someone must have put it there in the first place" (TOB, 52).

In addition to the logical incoherence of this view, Laplanche further observes that if "milk" is the object of the infant's self-preservation, it is worth considering that milk "is never designated by Freud as the object of feeding per se. What *is* the object of early alimentary behavior? Probably not milk alone. Does milk in its purely material nature really say much to any young animal, human or otherwise? If you put milk in a jar, not many animals will be tempted to lap it up; even a kitten needs you to stick its nose more or less in the saucer. In short, milk as such is not closely associated with a particular kind of behavior" (TOB, 60). In reality, "the food is only part of an object that is a complex whole encompassing warm milk, the warm breast, and the mother" (TOB, 60) and therefore, insofar as Freud claimed that the breast is the object of the oral drive, he was "clearly mistaken and the proposition incomplete. The breast is sucked not ingested" (TOB, 60), which is to say that from the beginning, the infant is open to the outside world in ways that refute the solipsism of Freud's self-preservation = sexuality sequence. "Not to put too fine a point on it," Laplanche writes, but "the idea of individualized self-preservative drives is perfectly illusory. On the one hand there are appetitive behaviors, immediately open to dialogue with the other person, the adult partner or parent; on the other hand there are needs, something very different: physiological mechanisms that in the first instance do not involve the other person, or even an "object"" (TOB, 63). Demarcating these differences enables Laplanche to conclude that the major problem with viewing sexuality as *emerging* out of self-preservation is that it leaves psychoanalysis in an irresolvable dilemma: "either to assume that sexuality is given from the beginning, which explains nothing (this was to be the Kleinian position); or else to say that sexuality is absent at the beginning, in which case he [Freud] has no adequate way to explain its advent" (TOB, 51). In other words, the interpretation of sexuality's spontaneous *emergence* ultimately reasserts its endogenous origins when it was precisely the *problem of endogeny* that this second interpretation was introduced to solve. The failure of interpretations 1 and 2 prompts Laplanche to develop a third explanation, the "inversion of 'leaning-on'" which he will refer to as primal seduction. Before introducing this new idea – which Laplanche affirms is tantamount to "new foundations for psychoanalysis" – it is crucial to interrogate the ways existing paradigms of psychic structure rely on variations of the "parallelist" or "emergence" conceptualization of "leaning-on." A close engagement with traditional and progressive models will demonstrate that neither framework provides a coherent account for the development of psychic structure because the actual adult-other remains fundamentally obscured in both theoretical models.

Traditional model of psychic structure

Hewing closely to Freud's conceptualization of the drives, traditional models of the mind contend that "psychic structure is patterned and regulated by the vicissitudes of the discharge of instinctual bodily drives" (Slavin and Kriegman 1992, 23). According to this view, instinctual wishes and impulses constitute the main threat to the infant's nervous system and conflicts and defenses are therefore constructed in an effort to cope with such threatening levels of stimulation. Importantly, these wishes and impulses are rooted in our psychobiological nature which means that they are endogenous to the human being as such. "Were our desires and wishes not a fundamental aspect of our human nature and were they, therefore, not pressing for gratification and discharge, repressing and isolating them would not require a constant expenditure of energy, nor would they divide the personality" (Eagle 2011, 17). Moreover, and in sharp contrast to external traumatic events, "instinctual desires and wishes are internally generated, have an aim and require an object for gratification and discharge" (17). Understood developmentally, the unconscious is constructed as a result of "internally generated" instinctual wishes and desires, irrespective of events or conditions in the external world. While many contemporary traditionalists acknowledge the impact of actual traumatic events in childhood, such an acknowledgement does not change the fact that the *origin* of the unconscious remains endogenous to the infant, hardwired from birth as an essential component of human nature. Eagle helpfully links the disparate ideas of classical theory in order to show that underlying the debate about drives is a more fundamental argument about how the mind is organized, whereby "the mind is an apparatus for the discharge of excitation" and as such, "the primary function of mind or the mental apparatus is to discharge excitation or at least to keep 'the quantity of excitation present....as low as possible or at least to keep it constant'" (Eagle, 21). Since this idea "predated drive theory by many years," it is not reducible to drive theory; on the contrary, "when, so to speak, joined to the later drive theory, to say that the primary function of mind is to discharge excitation becomes equivalent to saying that the primary function of mind is drive gratification or drive discharge, insofar as drives constitute the major source of internally generated excitation. As Freud (1920) puts it, 'the most abundant sources of ... internal excitation are what are described as the organism's instincts' (p. 34)" (21). In this model, the unconscious becomes a repository of internally generated desires and wishes, a "cauldron full of seething excitations" (Freud, 1923/1933, p. 73) that is as indelible a feature of the human being as biology itself.

Seen through the lens of Laplanche's critique, we can observe the degree to which the traditional model of the mind relies on a conceptualization of the unconscious, and sexuality in particular, as originating *in* the infant qua biological entity, irrespective of the external environment. Indeed, according to the sequence established by Freud and perpetuated by his followers, the human infant is fundamentally solipsistic – not in the strict Mahlerian sense of an original "autistic" phase – but insofar as *no adult is required* for the development of psychic structure. This is not to say that contemporary clinicians working in the traditional mode deny the existence or importance of early object relationships but rather that the impact of such early relationships are fundamentally circumscribed; they serve as "props" for the infant's projections and fantasies but not as veritable *sources* of the fantasy themselves. Reproducing the incoherence of Freud's original formulations, the traditional paradigm asks us to believe that sexuality develops, *spontaneously,* out of the infant's self-preservative experience even though such a sequence utterly fails to explain how, or why, the experience of eating could – *on its own* – morph into a rich fantasy life. For Laplanche, it is not enough to merely assert the creativity of the infant as if "early psychic creativity" or the capacity to confer meaning is enough to explain the origin of sexuality (FS, 46); as he repeatedly reminds us, 'creativity' cannot "go so far as to creative sexuality" *ex nihilo* (FS, 47). For sexuality to be created it must be "introduced from the earliest subjective experience, and introduced by the activity of the adult rather than the infant" (FS, 47). Treating the unconscious as endogenous to the infant is therefore not only logically and conceptually incoherent, but compatible with our abiding resistance to acknowledging the degree of our dependence on others, and of the "alien-ness" in us, as a result. After all, for Laplanche it is hardly coincidental that traditional metapsychology falters precisely at the place where a true recognition of otherness is required. As we see in the scene of the infant's earliest satisfaction, the adult is relevant "only at the initial stage of the process. The introduction of food simply triggers off the whole activity. Thereafter, the entire mode of functioning is solipsistic. There is no longer any trace of the alien in what is to take place, either in the object or in the aim of the drive" (UCR, 77). In hypothesizing about the origins of psychic structure, traditionalists seem to prefer believing in the infant's magical powers, over and against the actuality of its dependence on a psycho-sexual adult.

Progressive model of psychic structure

As we observed in great detail in the previous chapter, the progressive model of the unconscious "is a very different construct from the Freudian unconscious" (Eagle 2011, 130). Rather than a storehouse of infantile wishes that are endogenous and pressing for discharge, the progressive unconscious is conceptualized as a repository of "beliefs, self, object and interactional representations, and implicit assumptions and expectations regarding how significant others will behave" (130). In addition to storing affect-laden representations of object relationships, the progressive unconscious is also comprised of memories which have been acquired in early childhood but rendered unavailable to ordinary awareness. According to this view, the un-conscious is structured around psychic content which is either dis-sociative or procedural in nature. In the first instance, feelings and thoughts which are threatening to consciousness are split-off and dissociated, ending up in the unconscious as a result of being ban-ished and rendered unacceptable to ordinary awareness. In the case of procedural memories, representations of early experiences with parental caregivers are abstracted and generalized, forming a basis of knowledge that is implicit and unconscious rather than conscious and explicit. These ideas conduce to a very different model of psychic structure than the one maintained by traditional metapsychology. Here, the unconscious is neither endogenous nor the reservoir of repressed wishes but either the unfortunate result of environmental failure or the inevitable consequences of cognitive operations. In both of these scenarios, the unconscious has been radically transformed from being a place of repressed mental content to becoming a subset of memory (in the case of implicit knowledge) or a pathological aberration (in the case of dissociated material). While on the surface these two different versions of the unconscious can seem in-compatible – that is, how can the unconscious be ordinary and uni-versal in the case of procedural knowledge but also the idiosyncratic result of parental pathology on the other? – what they have in common is a view of psychic structure in which sexuality is absent.

In the progressive view, the unconscious is thought to develop alongside ordinary cognitive processes, or in response to environ-mental failure, neither of which ever *leads* to the creation of psycho-sexuality. Indeed, as a mark of the distance progressive ideas have taken from traditional formulations, the very question of sexuality's origins which was such a major preoccupation for Freud and his followers is rendered practically moot for progressive theorists. That is, while traditionalists who believe in the singular importance of sexuality must struggle to account for its origins, progressives who treat the unconscious as a structure that develops irrespective of sexuality have little need to demonstrate where, or under what conditions, sexuality arises. On the surface, the benefits of the progressive approach are legion, especially considering the irresolvable problems that continue to haunt traditional approaches. For example, without having to demonstrate how sexuality originates as a vital component of psychic structure, metapsychology is momentarily released from the impasses which have dogged it for so long. But, as Galit Atlas astutely observes, the circumvention of sexuality's origins is only possible because the entire register of unconscious fantasy life has been systematically obliterated by the field's totalizing reconceptualization of the infant along cognitive-attachment theory lines. In fact, Atlas writes, insofar as "the relational baby is an agent and a participant in the bidirectional co-creation of the interaction" it "doesn't have phantasy life and functions on the procedural level of interaction" (2018, 133). Moreover, in emphasizing the importance of trauma, attachment theory and infant research, "big and small T traumas often become the royal roads to the exploration of mental health situations, and sexuality is seen as another way of expressing residues of early intersubjective exchanges between mother and infant. As mentioned, the relational observed baby seems not to have phantasy, aggression, or sexuality. This is a baby that responds in highly complex ways to her environment, and the implication for adult life is that her sexuality is often described as derived only from early patterns of attachment or as a secondary precipitate of a desire for connection" (136) (Caruth, 1995).

What becomes clear from a critical engagement with contemporary views is that the progressive unconscious does *not* include sexuality; instead of comprising a distinctive realm of psychic experience, sexuality becomes just "another way of expressing residues of early intersubjective exchanges between mother and infant." While the coalition of infant researchers, attachment theorists and trauma therapists that developed the progressive approach actively sought to challenge Freud's views on infantile sexuality, the result is the loss of sexuality *tout court*. As Atlas argues, while infant-adult interactions play a major and decisive role in the foundation of experience, "the mother-baby physical tie then is only one aspect of sexuality… sexuality has its own existence, as a discrete phenomenon that connects us through the body with that which is Enigmatic and beyond our conscious knowledge of ourselves" (138). It is precisely this feature of sexuality as a "discrete phenomenon" that the progressive model comprehensively vitiates in its assimilation of sexuality into yet "another way of expressing" the attachment relationship. Using the terms Laplanche provides, we could say that the progressive model resolves the problem posed by the two registers – sexuality and self-preservation – by simply reducing all of sexuality to the operation of self-preservative needs. While this maneuver seems initially to solve the problem of how to integrate a sexual drive into the infant's self-preservative world, it does so only by eradicating sexuality as a distinctive structural and experiential psychic register. And although progressive clinicians may be on the whole unbothered by the absence of a coherent account of sexuality's origins (especially if sexuality is not seen as a particularly interesting psychic realm in its own right), at stake in these formulations is far more than merely a circumscribed debate about the relative importance of sexuality. For as Laplanche persuasively shows, sexuality is not just another word for genitality or reproduction but *the* exemplary term for a distinctive category of psychic phenomena that exceeds, and often contravenes, the register of self-preservative needs. As such, not only is the distinctiveness of sexuality totally erased by the reduction of everything to "attachment" (self-preservation) but the very conceptualization of attachment itself suffers from sexuality's exclusion. After all, and as Laplanche will point out in his elaboration of seduction, what kind of attachment can we be said to be celebrating if our understanding of the parent-child interaction all but ignores the *psychology of the adult*?

In a provocative articulation of this point, Laplanche writes, "in my view even with an overt act of sexual abuse, such as that performed by an adult against a child – let us say rape – the only psychoanalytic trace that remains is an enigmatic one. An adult may subject a child to the worst outrage, yet the only place where even such a crude and overt act can be fantasized is always, and despite everything, somewhere beyond it" (TOB, 67). For Laplanche, there is no such thing as the adult's "behavior" devoid of unconscious content, and our attempts to reduce parental activity to the things they *did*, or we *remember*, fundamentally precludes a more sophisticated and expansive understanding of the adult-other's role in the child's psychic development. For this reason, the progressive model of the unconscious as a repository of procedural knowledge and dissociated memories – while claiming to counter the solipsism of Freud's endogenous sexuality – invariably recreates its own version of a solipsistic psyche since the so-called other person in the attachment dyad is really no "other" at all, but just an external provider of either "good" or "bad" parenting. As Slavin and Kriegman explain, in the literature on infant research, "harmonious scenes are a result of healthy parental functioning and the disharmony is a result of parental psychopathology or failure" and although contemporary clinicians "clearly attempt to avoid blaming the parent ... the implication that environmental failure is the source of pathology is unavoidable" (131). Indeed, "the assumption that the healthy parent-child relationship is essentially free of significant conflict is implicit in the discourse of most (non-Kleinian) relational theorists from Fairbairn to Guntrip to Sullivan and (after large societal change takes place) Fromm. Healthy parents will respond helpfully, and without substantial conflict, to the child's developmental needs. Minor failures (nontraumatic, nonpathogenic) will inevitably occur. But, failures that produce pathology, or produce an inherently conflicted inner experience (with significant repressions or disavowals), are a result of parental pathology, generally pathology in the narcissistic sphere. Healthy parents are in tune with their child. Unhealthy parents have significant conflicts with their offspring" (132). From an attachment perspective, focusing on the quality of parental attunement is understandable, especially since it offers one of the few opportunities for empirical measurement by outside observers. But within the context of a broader metapsychology, treating the adult as reducible to the quality of attachment alone *instrumentalizes* the adult into a mere extension of "my" individual needs. What ends up lost in this scenario is a view of the adult's complex psychological autonomy and with it, an appreciation of how *necessary* the adult's complex psychology is to the child's developing mind.

In effect, the progressive narrative conduces to a view of psychic development in which the child is technically equipped to survive and flourish in a biosocial environment, and the adult is required to be sufficiently attuned to the child's heterogeneous needs. This can seem like a reasonable demand – the parental equivalent of "do no harm" – but it treats the adult as merely a technical supplier of the child's self-preservative needs. Within this narrative, it is the parent's pathology which interferes with the steady flow of attachment-goods, and thus the adult is responsible for being healthy enough to prevent environmental failures. But what kind of adult is sufficiently able to transcend every internal conflict, and what kind of infant is naturally equipped to flourish with minimal adult intervention? In the progressive story about the origins of psychic structure, the unconscious is either a vital cognitive function that results automatically from the infant's exposure to nonverbal communication, or the necessary container that is built to store the mind's traumatized and dissociated content. In both of these scenarios, the *adult's* psychology is incidental to the child's development; the adult is a supplier of attachment-goods, a source of pathology and implicit knowledge, but never someone who plays a necessary role in the development of psychic structure. Put differently, since the unconscious is seen as either a natural counterpart to memory or an aberrant consequence of distress, the only "good" adult is the psychologically neutral one, the one who gets out of the way enough to enable the infant's natural development. But doesn't such a view amount to saying that the infant *already* has what it needs to survive and develop as a psychological being? Or that the adult should dutifully supply the infant's self-preservative needs but otherwise refrain from generating conflict?

The problem here isn't only, as many have already noted, that such a standard for parental behavior disproportionately pathologizes mothers or invariably creates impossible goals for the ordinary adult, but that is positions unconscious communication as a *burden* on development rather than a *prerequisite* for it. As Laplanche persuasively demonstrates, "it is precisely by virtue of this enigmatic aspect of the adult message that the child is stimulated to develop an unusual activity of 'translation.'... The child's creativity ... is kindled by the 'drive to translate,' which comes to the child from the adult message 'to be translated' – an enigmatic messages since it is compromised by the sexuality of the adult" (FS, 47). According to Laplanche, the development of the unconscious is neither automatic nor pathological but the particular effect of the child's encounter with the adult's unconscious. Moreover, "it is only because the adult's messages are compromised by his sexual unconscious that, secondarily, the child's attempt at symbolization are set in motion, where the child actively works on material that is *already* sexual" (FS, 47). From this perspective, the adult's unconscious material *is*, in fact, a significant problem for the infant but it is a necessary and productive one, since it is precisely this encounter which sets the infant's psychic structuration in motion. The technical aspects of this will be explained in greater detail in the context of affect theory and neurobiology (chapter four). For present purposes, what matters is how thoroughly Laplanche has reoriented our understanding of psychic structure from being something which happens irrespective of the adult to something which is created *because* the adult is neither conflict-free nor purely functional. Indeed, putting the adult's otherness – his psychology, sexuality, unconscious – at the center of mental development leads Laplanche to totally reformulate the "leaning-on" hypothesis along the lines of seduction. Having demonstrated the problems with 1) the parallelist conception and 2) the explanation by emergence, Laplanche introduces a third interpretation in which the concept of "leaning-on" is subverted by means of seduction.

General theory of seduction

In one of his introductions to the concept of seduction, Laplanche writes, "we have reached the point which I consider is the essence of the Copernican revolution begun by Freud; the decentering, in reality, is double: the other thing (*das Andere*) that is the unconscious is only maintained in its radical alterity by the other person (*der Andere*): in brief, by seduction. When the alterity of the other person is blurred, when it is reintegrated in the form of *my* fantasy of the other, of *my* 'fantasy of seduction,' then the alterity of the unconscious is put at risk" (UCR, 71). Recapitulating the field's longstanding difficulty ascertaining the role of the adult-other, Laplanche writes: "the other person is the other of seduction, the adult who seduces the child. Now, from the moment when he formulates the seduction hypothesis and for a long time afterwards, Freud vacillates between two equally inadequate positions. On one side, what could be termed a subjectivist, 'internal' conception – reducing the other to the subject's perception of the other …And then alongside this, from time to time, a philosophically more naïve gesture, consisting in… going to look for the other in the neighboring room … In the concrete situation of the treatment, Freud allows himself to make suggestions, as if to locate the other behind the patient's words: go and ask your servant or your mother; look in the family archives to see whether such-and-such a person was alive when you were a child, whether it is possible you could remember so-and-so" (UCR, 73). In Laplanche's view, both of these possibilities are flawed because they "share the same presupposition: that the other never manifests himself except in the subjective representation of brute reality" (UCR, 73). In other words, neither of these positions recognize the adult other's "alien-ness," by which he means, the actual adult's unconscious. Returning to the scene of the child's early satisfaction, Laplanche writes: "it is the adult who brings the breast, and not the milk, into the foreground – and does so due to her own desire, conscious and above all unconscious. For the breast is not only an organ for feeding children but a sexual organ, something which is *utterly overlooked by Freud and has been since Freud.* Not a single text, not even a single remark of Freud's takes account of the fact that the female breast is excitable, not only in feeding, but simply in the woman's sexual life" (UCR, 78).

Returning to the problem of sexuality's relationship to self-preservation, Laplanche asks, "if infantile sexuality does not have an innate endogenous mechanism, how can it emerge conjointly with self-preservation? And if it corresponds to a simple representation in fantasy of bodily attachment and self-preservative function, by what miracle would this fantasmatization alone confer a sexual character upon somatic functions? As I have pointed out on several occasions, in Freud the putative 'experience of satisfaction' and the putative 'hallucinatory satisfaction of desire' are successful exercises in prestidigitation. They make the sexual emerge from the lack of satisfaction of the self-preservative instinct in the same way that that rabbit emerges from the magician's hat. But the trick depends precisely on the fact that there is someone who has put the rabbit in the hat – and it is certainly the adult who put it there" (FS, 21). What this means, according to Laplanche, is that the only plausible explanation for the emergence of the unconscious involves seeing the *adult* as the *source* of self-preservation *and* sexuality. That is, we already know the adult is responsible for meeting the infant's attachment needs but what we refuse to acknowledge is that *in meeting those attachment needs*, the adult's own *sexuality is provoked*. We must, Laplanche asserts, *"re-fuse to believe in the illusion that Freud proposes*. From the hat of hunger, from a self-preservative instinct, Freud the illusionist claims to produce the rabbit of sexuality, as if by magic. This is only possible if sexuality has been hidden somewhere from the start. The image of the breast can easily be derived from the image of milk by associa-tion. But such a breast would be purely instrumental, the means and the symbol of alimentary satisfaction and nothing else. The experi-ence of satisfaction cannot split apart and open onto sexuality unless there is something sexual that is there from the start. That is, unless from the very beginning the experience of satisfaction was double, ambiguous, and in a word, enigmatic" (FS, 69). It is for this reason that Laplanche insists on seduction as the only possible "truth" of "leaning-on"; "yes, this experience does initially take place in the realm of self-preservation. However, it is an experience that is much more complex, much more intensely charged with meaning and affect" (FS, 69). That is, the realm of self-preservation is undoubtedly central to the child's early development and the adult provides a vital function *but* this experience – while con-cerned with basic "alimentary" needs – also, invariably, initiates the development of sexuality because the adult who feeds and changes the baby inevitably *has* a sexual unconscious. Furthermore, it is by virtue of the infant's dependence on the sexual adult for the satisfaction of self-preservative needs that the infant encounters "enigmatic messages" re-quiring translation. And it is this process of translating "enigmatic messages" – those aspects of parental communication which are com-promised by unconscious "noise" – that prompts the development of the infant's own separate and particular unconscious.

Central to Laplanche's reformulation of "leaning-on" is the re-cognition that sexuality is never endogenous to the infant or an au-tomatic consequence of physical development. The kind of sexuality Laplanche has in mind – *enlarged* sexuality, which is non-reproductive, not contingent on any bodily zones and not interested in the relaxation of tension or orgasm – can only come into being through an encounter with adult sexuality. As Laplanche's compre-hensive critique of predominant explanations makes clear, there is simply no plausible way for *enlarged* sexuality to emerge otherwise.

As Laplanche repeatedly emphasizes, even among those who claim to accept infantile sexuality, "it is usually places under the rubric of genitality, or in other words ascribed to a precocious arousal of the genital organs. And as proof of this spontaneity, the occurrence of erections in the little boy, for instance, is continually cited – as though it was essentially what Freud had in mind. In point of fact, what Freud meant by infantile sexuality was only genital in the most contingent way; the epithet "polymorphous" applied not only to the type of activity but also to the zones excited in the child, which Freud thought multiple, and indeed ultimately to include the entire body" (TOB, 24). By contrast, the kind of *enlarged* sexuality Laplanche has in mind – since it is *not* reducible to genitality or bodily zones – *cannot* be located in any hardwired biological process. "For me, there is no question of denying the notion of a general excitability (*Reizbarkeit*) in every living being, especially at the level of the cutaneous envelope, and in particular with respect to the body's places of entry and exit. How can we deny in the child that which exists for every organism, even a monocellular ball of protoplasm? But the assimilation of this general *Reizbarkeit* to a *Verfuhrbarkeit* (seducibility) risks being misleading, insofar as it implies the prior presence of sexuality within the organism. Yet we know that precisely in the child, the little human being, the hormonal conditions of sexuality that we find at the pubertal period are practically absent" (FS, 258). That is why Laplanche emphatically distinguishes *enlarged* sexuality from endogenous instincts and why it is impossible to rely on biology for the development of *enlarged* sexuality. Laplanche argues that, "in our view, the properly sexual character of the "sexual life of the child" remains impossible to define on a purely physiological basis. It is inseparable from the appearance of the sexual fantasy, which is itself correlative to the intervention of the other (the sexual adult)" (FS, 258). Since *enlarged* sexuality is not a "purely physiological" process nor separable "from the appearance of the sexual fantasy," an urgent conceptual question revolves around the genesis of the infant's fantasmatic life: if fantasy is not inborn, then what prompts its sudden arrival? And if the infant's only early experiences involve basic self-preservation, then what conditions could trigger the spontaneous onset of fantasy life?

In his essay, "The Fundamental Anthropological Situation," Laplanche endeavors to establish the outlines of his general theory of seduction by demonstrating that it offers the only plausible account of how and why the unconscious develops, and what biosocial realities makes this development universal. Noting that "self-preservation now has made a return with the notion of attachment," Laplanche nevertheless explains that "what is lacking, both in attachment theory and attachment observation, is a consideration of the asymmetry on the unconscious level. What is lacking in all the observations, among even the best observers, is an insistence on the fact that the adult-*infans* dialogue, as reciprocal as it may be, is nevertheless parasite by something else, from the beginning" (FS, 103). In fact, not only is the adult message "scrambled" by his own unconscious elements, but the very fact of attending to the infant's helplessness ensures the adult's own unconscious will be provoked. As such, just as there is no such thing as an adult devoid of an unconscious, there is no such thing as an adult-infant interaction without an unconscious dimension. The inescapability of this scenario enables Laplanche to claim: "seduction is not a relation that is contingent, pathological (even though it can be) and episodic. It is grounded in a situation from which no human being is exempt: the 'fundamental anthropological situation,' as I call it. This fundamental anthropological situation is the adult-*infans* relation. It consists of the *adult*, who has an unconscious that is essentially made up of infantile residues, an unconscious that is perverse in the sense defined in the *Three Essays*; and the *infant*, who is not equipped with any genetic sexual organization of any hormonal activators of sexuality. The idea of an endogenous infantile sexuality has been profoundly criticized, and not only be me... The major danger, of course, is moving from a critique of *endogenous* infantile sexuality to a denial of infantile sexuality as such. As we know, infantile sexuality is what is most easily denied and Freud even made this point one of its characteristics: the fact that the adult does not want to see it. Might this be because it derives from the adult himself?" (FS, 102).

According the Laplanche, the field's continued inability to fully grasp the radical implications of infantile sexuality can be traced to a general refusal to acknowledge the infant's vulnerability. This refusal may have multiple causes but Laplanche suggests that, at some level, we simply prefer to believe that the unconscious is like an "id" –

inborn, self-generated and instinctual – because it restores the infant's agency as against seduction, which starts from the basic supposition that even though no infant is born with an unconscious, every adult ends up having one. "Thus," Laplanche says, "as regards infantile sexuality, it is the primacy of heredity that I oppose. I say *sexuality* and *infantile,* by which I mean that there is certainly something innate in what is not sexual, and also something innate in the sexuality that is not infantile. To my mind there exists a fundamental difference between the sexual drive of childhood and what surfaces at the moment of adolescence, which is effectively the emergence of the sexual instinct" (FS, 105). This rejection of "heredity" is meant to oppose what he considers to be among Freud's gravest mistakes; "when Freud abandons the theory of seduction in the famous letter, he does not say: "I am returning to the biological," but "I am returning to the innate, to the hereditary" (FS, 105). For Laplanche, it is precisely this replacement of seduction (which involves the other person) with hereditary (which does not) that systematically undermines any coherent account of the psycho-sexual unconscious. It is as though the inborn "id" – implausible and mythological as it may seem – is *still* preferable to the idea that a loving parent transmits elements of her own perverse sexuality to the infant who depends on her care. This is why Laplanche considers Ferenczi's essay title "The confusion of tongues between Adults and the child" (1949), "a stroke of genius" for it "dared to use the formulation: 'between adults and the child'" (FS, 154). It is only by insisting on what transpires *between* adults and the child that our theory begins to admit the full range of what occurs by virtue of the innocent infant's dependence on an already-sexual adult. Efforts to deny the truth of this universal situation involve either transforming *enlarged* sexuality into something that is endogenous to the infant, or pretending that the adult who provides attachment can turn off his own unconscious. Neither solution is metapsychologically cogent and both perpetuate simplistic myths about the origin of psychic structure.

Between determinism and hermeneutics

At the outset, this chapter observed how differences in conceptualizations of psychic structure have led to major differences with respect to how pathology and treatment are conceived. We noted that a model of psychic structure in which the unconscious is seen as biologically hardwired and endogenous leads to the idea that conflict and defense are subjective and internally generated, that the subjective responses to basic conflicts are representative of an individual's fantasy life, and that these fantasies are the proper subject of analytic treatment since events in external reality, even when injurious, are most profitably understood as props rather than sources of internal struggle. Alternatively, if the unconscious is understood as developing in response to traumatic events, and as a container for either procedural memories or dissociated mental material, then pathology can be said to arise in reaction to assaults sustained in the outside world as they primarily occur in relation to other people, and efforts to reconstruct the memories and feelings associated with these events are at the center of analytic treatment. Contemporary discourse has various ways of labeling these differences but when Laplanche describes the antinomy as between "determinism and hermeneutics" it is because this formulation aptly captures the effects of this divergence on our ideas about psychopathology and treatment. As Laplanche explains, "interpretation therefore finds itself trapped in the unresolvable dualism of pure factuality on the one hand and a creative imagination on the other: in the one case, it patiently reconstitutes 'facts' which it hopes will prove to be the source of a determinism, explaining the present by the past. It is an explanation that will always fall into the famous parody of psychoanalysis, brilliantly anticipated by Moliere: 'And that is why your daughter is dumb.' In the second case, the interpretation notes that human facts always have 'a sense,' but it adds too quickly that this sense is imposed on an inert datum by the individual – an infantile subject, and then the subject of the treatment, conceived as a kind of collective interpreting entity" (IDH, 160). Attempting to intervene in this stale and familiar dualism, Laplanche asks what is *between* determinism and hermeneutics, and specifically, whether a reformulation of psychic structure introduces a new option for understanding how pathology develops. To answer this question, Laplanche offers "a third reality, that of the message" in which 'psychical reality' is distinct from factual reality, on the one hand, and psychological reality on the other. "If we say that this category is practically absent from Freud's thought, we are also saying that the other, the human other, is also absent from it, as a source of messages. The other – in particular, the parental other – is barely present at all, and then only as an abstract protagonist of a scene or a support for projections; this is the case with Freud, but also, and to an even greater extent, with Klein" (IDH, 159).

In an effort to decisively interrupt this enduring stalemate, Laplanche transforms the adult-other into a psychologically real character in her own right. Rejecting the familiar tendency to treat the adult as a mere "abstract protagonist" or "support for projections," Laplanche insists that the adult who meets the infant's self-preservative needs is *also* an adult with a sexual unconscious. As such, there is never a scenario in which the adult offers purely alimentary supplies alone because the very activity of providing for the infant provokes, in the adult, a recrudescence of his own affectively-charged needs. The feelings and fantasies that get evoked in the adult remain *unconscious* to the adult, and as such, are less mediated, worked-through and accessible to him. But what makes them inaccessible to the adult also makes them powerful to the fact because it is in picking up on this "noise" that the infant is propelled to work on the material he encounters, which involves constructing interpretations of his own to bind the energy that is overwhelming. But as Laplanche demonstrates, there is no longer a straight line linking the parent's behavior with the child's ensuing conflicts (as in the deterministic position) because, "with the concept of *enigma*, a break in determinism appears: to the extent that the child possesses only inadequate and imperfect ways to configure or theorize about what is communicated to him, there can be no linear causality between the parental unconscious and discourse on the one hand and what the child does with these on the other. All the Lacanian formulae on the unconscious as 'discourse of the Other,' or the child as 'symptom of the parents,' disregard the break, the profound reshaping, which occurs between the two, and which may be likened to a metabolism that breaks down food into its constituent parts and reassembled them into a completely different entity" (IDH, 160). In fact, not only is the deterministic position shown to be implausible but so too is the hermeneutic notion that the child's later struggles originate in autoerotic fantasies that arise irrespective of the material put before him *by* the other person.

Laplanche's radical reformulation challenges the longstanding debate about whether psychic suffering is the result of subjective fantasy or events in factual reality. By putting seduction as the origin of psychic structure, Laplanche affirms the complex interplay between the quality of the adult's unconscious messages and the infant's interpretive capacities. In other words, it is simply no longer plausible to speak in terms of what the adult "did" or "didn't do" because no amount of remembering parental behavior could ever include those elements of communication which were unconscious, and all the more powerful for being so. Nor could it be possible any longer to trace internal conflicts to subjective fantasy alone, since there is no such thing as an infant who generates, *by himself,* the contents or his own unconscious. Therefore, just as the individual's unconscious is both a product of his own interpretations and a response to the unconscious of the other, so too "the work of the analysand in the analysis is both determined and free. It is *determined* first by the force which moves it: this driving force (*Triebkraft*) which impels the subject to translate has its origin in the forcible entry of the other and in the need to bind this forcible entry: the other (*der Andere*) of the enigmatic message in infancy, and then that internal 'other thing' (*das Andere*) that is the unconscious, and finally, the representative of the other that is the analyst. However, it is *free* in that the other's messages, being enigmatic, will never yield up all in their sense in a 're-velation' sufficient unto itself" (IDH, 164). The picture of analysis that emerges from this view is one in which old translations are carefully approached and systematically deconstructed "with the aim of clearing the way for a new construction, which is the task of the analysand" (IDH, 165). There is no simple explanation for what causes mental suffering, nor is there any straightforward solution, but in forcing metapsychology to see the adult-other as psycho-sexually real, Laplanche demands from psychoanalysis a courageous acknowledgment of our discipline's limitations, and its possibilities.

Notes

1 Slavin and Kriegman acknowledge that these classifications are not exhaustive and may not account for certain factions which do not fall neatly into either one of these categories. Nevertheless, they argue that in the broadest sense, most if not all schools of psychoanalytic thought can be grouped under one or the other of these headings.

2 Later in the essay, Laplanche explains that "the real opposition is not that between 'object-seeking' and 'pleasure-seeking.' Freud clearly demonstrates that these two searches are strictly correlated: the good-enough *object* is procured by means of the specific action ('aim') and leads to a lasting relaxation of tension ('pleasure'). But these are a matter of behaviors that we encompass with the broad term 'instinct.' However, what is opposed to this *joint* pursuit of the object and of satisfaction is most certainly the drive-based quest, which, for its part, is the *pursuit of excitation* to the point of exhaustion, regardless of both the real object and the relaxation of tension" (FS, 40).

Bibliography

Atlas, Galit (2018). "Don't throw out the baby! External and internal, attachment, and sexuality," *Decentering Relational Theory: A Comparative Critique*, Eds. Lewis Aron, Sue Grand and Joyce Slochower. New York: Routledge.

Caruth, Cathy, Ed. (1995). *Trauma: Explorations in Memory*. Baltimore: Johns Hopkins UP.

Eagle, Morris N. (2011). *From Classical to Contemporary Psychoanalysis: A Critique and Integration*. New York: Routledge.

Ferenczi, Sandor (1949). Confusion of the Tongues Between the Adult and the Child – The Language of Tenderness and of Passion. *International Journal of Psycho-Analysis* 30: 225–230.

Fonagy, Peter (2001). *Attachment Theory and Psychoanalysis*. New York: Other Press.

Freud, Sigmund. (1920). Beyond The Pleasure Principle. J. Strachey (Trans and Ed.) *Standard Edition The Complete Psychological Works of Sigmund Freud* (Vol. 18, pp. 7–64). London: Hogarth Press.

Freud, Sigmund. (1923). "The Ego and the Id" J. Strachey (Ed. and Trans). *The Standard Edition of the Complete Psychological Works of Sigmund Freud* (Vol. 19, pp. 12–59). London: Hogarth Press.

Greenberg, Jay R. and Stephen A. Mitchell (1983). *Object Relations in Psychoanalytic Theory*. Cambridge: Harvard UP.

Laplanche, Jean (1999). *Essays on Otherness: Jean Laplanche*, Ed. John Fletcher. London: Routledge.

Laplanche, Jean (2011). *Freud and the Sexual: Essays 2000-2006*. Trans. John Fletcher, Jonathan House, and Nicholas Ray. New York: Unconscious in Translation.

Laplanche, Jean (2015). *The Temptation of Biology: Freud's Theories of Sexuality*. Trans. Donald Nicholson-Smith. New York: Unconscious in Translation.

Mitchell, Stephen (1998) "Fairbairn's object-seeking: Between paradigms," *Fairbairn, Then and Now*, Eds. Neil J. Skolnick and David E. Scharff. New York: Analytic Press.

Slavin, Malcolm O. and Daniel Kriegman (1992). *The Adaptive Design of the Human Psyche: Psychoanalysis, Evolutionary Biology, and the Therapeutic Process*. New York: Guilford Press.

Translation – Laplanche's theory of motivation

The need for "new foundations"

Since every theory of mind depends, at least implicitly, on *some* idea about how the mind is organized, and since every formulation of mental organization requires that motivation be, at least *somewhat,* conceptualized, there is virtually no way to talk in depth about psychic life without inventing or applying *some* version of motivation theory. And yet, precisely because ideas about motivation are inextricably bound up with a host or correlated concerns, some of the most animated field-wide debates about theory of mind are entangled in other, often tangential, arguments about such things as the definition of metapsychology, the usefulness of science and the role of brain research in psychoanalytic theory. As a result, not only is there no "development without breaks" in psychoanalytic theory (NFP, 5), but there is practically no way for theoretical development to occur without first analyzing the manifold obstacles to progress that, for one reason or another, continue to stand in the way. This chapter proceeds from the observation that psychoanalysis has a "motivation" problem, and an "affect" problem, and that these two problems are related. First, we will explore the genealogy of these two topics in psychoanalytic theory in order to understand why they continue to be enduring issues in the field. Second, we will examine the status of both motivation theory and affect theory in traditionalist and progressive schemas, and then assess the limitations of how each faction negotiates these crucial topics. Lastly, we will outline a new role for affect in psychoanalysis that fundamentally rewrites key foundations of metapsychology. These "new foundations" will draw on Laplanche's concept of "translation" in order to show that a rigorous metapsychology is both clinically and scientifically urgent.

Drew Westen has observed that, "the theory of motivation has always been both the heart and the Achilles' heel of psychoanalysis ... theorists from nearly every school generally agree that Freud's dual-instinct model requires substantial modification (e.g., Brenner, 1982; Holt, 1976; Kernberg, 1992; Kohut, 1977; Lichtenberg, 1989; Sandler, 1985; White, 1960). The reasons are many, and familiar to most readers: the nineteenth-century scientific assumptions embedded in it, the unlikely hypothesis of a death instinct ... the ambiguous place of affect, the failure to capture adequately the motives for relatedness that bring people together, and the absence of several motives that seem important in humans, such as the desires for mastery and knowledge, self-esteem, safety and meaning in life. Although the diagnosis seems clear, an adequate prescription for the problem has not been forthcoming" (1997, 522). Indeed, although two decades have passed since Westen's assessment, it remains the case today that our working theory of motivation has not moved much beyond the "object vs. drive" dichotomy; even if the hardline divisions have softened over time, the binary has hardly been transcended or replaced with a new overall theory of mind. Moreover, much as in the previous chapter we observed how the misrepresentation of Freud's scientificity is one prominent manifestation of the field's "Sinai complex," and how, as a result of this dilemma, clinicians who try to bring psychoanalysis in line with contemporary science invariably minimize the discord between new research and Freud's original language, so too in this chapter we'll observe that another powerful demonstration of the field's anxiety about innovation involves its resistance to using science as a necessary component of motivation theory.

To wit, it's worth observing that it has become an almost unquestioned refrain among psychoanalysts that the "psyche" of unconscious life cannot be conflated with the "brain" of neurobiology. Implicit in this popular trope is the idea that where psychoanalysis offers a supple and sophisticated framework for mental experience, biology, by contrast, is crude, technical and ill-equipped to grasp the nuances of complex human desires and needs. As such, even when neurobiology is seen as relevant and possibly useful, there is residual skepticism about how *much* science can be called upon to do. But as the philosopher Adrian Johnston has observed, "nowadays, it simply isn't true that one has to sell one's philosophical or psychoanalytic soul in its entirety in order to dance with the neurobiological devil. In fact, over the past half century, scientific matters concerning neuroplasticity, mirror neurons, epigenetics, and newly proposed revisions to Darwinian depictions of evolution, among other topics, have destroyed the caricature of biological approaches to subjectivity upon which the ever-more-hollow excuses of a tired old antinaturalism rely, caricatures depicting such approaches as essentially deterministic and reductive" (2013, xi). Not only does the evolution of science invalidate psychoanalysis' wholesale dismissal of it on the grounds it is insufficiently nuanced, but the past several decades of research and discovery has convincingly shown that the familiar dichotomy between brain and mind, or psyche and mentation, is wholly unsupported by contemporary findings. In fact, taking a more comprehensive view of the problem, it might be worth wondering whether anxiety about how *much* science to use isn't a displacement of deeper anxiety about how *much* innovation is permissible. After all, the investigative culture of testing hypotheses and discarding flawed notions (common to science as well as philosophy) fundamentally clashes with the particular psychoanalytic valuation of loyalty, tradition, and adherence. That is, for psychoanalysis to seriously engage with the findings of neighboring disciplines requires a genuine receptivity to being changed by new ideas but as the self-identification with "orthodoxy" suggests, for many clinicians practicing today the flagrant disregard of scientific development remains a reasonable professional and intellectual stance. While the relationship to science fares better among those who value theoretical flexibility, the default stance among psychoanalysts nevertheless seems to be that science is an "outside" discipline that psychoanalysis can utilize or disregard, at its own discretion. Here, the unstated presumption seems to be that conceptualizing psychic life does not actually *require* a firm biological base, and that the pursuit of one is futile or quixotic, at best.

This situation might persist indefinitely were it not for the fact that over the past 30 years, the life sciences have made the kinds of breakthroughs that are impossible for any serious metapsychology to ignore.

Moreover, and partly as a result of the constitutive interdisciplinarity of this research, there has been a tremendous eruption of scientific thought that has focused precisely on the questions at the heart of psychoanalytic inquiry – what motivates individuals? how does the mind grow? what enables biopsychical flourishing? – and it has arrived at conclusions that directly *contradict* several basic tenets of psychoanalytic theory. Indeed, the past several decades of scientific discovery not only shed light on questions that are central to psychoanalysis but provide precisely what psychoanalysis has been systematically lacking – a comprehensive theory of motivation that puts *affect* at the center. Regularly hailed as the "age of affect," current findings in cognitive neuroscience, neurobiology, and developmental psychology persuasively and repeatedly show that contrary to longstanding assumptions about the primacy of human cognition, it is *emotionality* which is primordial and predominant in human development and functioning. Overturning centuries of scientific thought that treated affect as untheorizable, irrational, impossible to study empirically and secondary to cognition, new studies across a range of disciplines have consistently demonstrated that "the primal conscious 'state' of mammals is intrinsically affective" (Panskepp and Biven, 2012, 163–4; Demos, 2019, 118) and that "emotions are part of the bioregulatory devices with which we come equipped to survive" (Damasio, 1999, 51). As human beings, we are first and foremost emotional. As Antonio Damasio, one of neurobiology's preeminent theorists, writes, "In brief, those whom the gods wanted to save they first made smart, or so it would seem. Long before living beings had anything like creative intelligence, even before they had brains, it is as if nature decided that life was both very precious and very precarious. We know that nature does not operate by design and does not decide in the way artists and engineers do, but this image gets the point across. All living organisms from the humble amoeba to the human are born with devices designed to solve *automatically*, no proper reasoning required, the basic problems of life" (2003, 30).

A deep engagement with the particular implications of this research involves reading and synthesizing a range of work in affect theory and situating these findings in the context of psychoanalytic theories of motivation, ultimately demonstrating that a scientifically rigorous theory of mental life poses fundamental challenges to the existing psychoanalytic model of the mind. Therefore, whereas the conventions of psychoanalytic discourse typically require a smooth harmonization of science with Freudian/post-Freudian ideas, this chapter demonstrates why such an approach – while standard among psychoanalysts – functions to effectively neutralize any meaningful critique before it even begins. Instead, the ensuing analysis will show that the abundance of recent scientific attention to affect *inversely* corresponds to the total deficit of theorizations on this topic within psychoanalysis, and that psychoanalysis' longstanding inability to integrate affect into its core conceptualizations signals a deeper, more protracted, conflict between psychoanalytic models of the mind and the findings of contemporary research. A close engagement with affect theory will show that there is a strong correlation between psychoanalysis' stubborn neglect of affect and its inability to develop a scientifically plausible model of unconscious life. From this perspective, the neglect of affect and the hostility to science are mutually reinforcing maneuvers that are neither innocent nor incidental, but function to protect Freud's theory of mental life from radical and comprehensive revision.

Affect in psychoanalysis: a history of the problem

Writing a book on the topic of affect in 1991, Ruth Stein wondered why a "coherent and updated affect theory has been conspicuously lacking in psychoanalysis" given that "clinical work has never proceeded and cannot conceivably take place without them" (1). Stein opens her account with a complaint about the lack of an affect theory even though, already in 1953, David Rapaport's famous paper on affect began by announcing that "we do not possess a systematic statement of the psycho-analytic theory of affects" (1952, 177). Indeed, as early as 1937, Marjorie Brierley observed that "whatever differences of opinion exist as to principles of technique, no analyst fails to pay attention to his patient's feelings. Diagnosis, prognosis, and criteria of cure all involve some estimation of affectivity. Indeed, patients themselves leave us in no doubt here. With few exceptions, they one and all complain of some disorder of feeling and tend to estimate their own progress by changes in their feelings and in their ability to cope with them. In practice we find our way only by following the Ariadne thread of transference affect and go astray if we lose contact with this. It is time that we restored affects to a place in theory more consonant with their importance in practice" (257). Stating the problem in his own pithy way, Bion, in an unpublished address to the British Society, is reported to have said that, "feelings are the few things which analysts have the luxury of being able to regard as facts."[1] And yet, in spite of enthusiastic testimonies of affect's centrality, affect remains "one of the most difficult, problematic, and haunting areas in psychoanalysis" (1991, 1). Why?

According to Leo Rangell's classic 1967 paper on the topic, affect was once at the center of early psychoanalytic theories, especially those initial investigations of Breuer and Freud; in the earliest studies on hysteria, suppressed affect was seen as the problem, and the therapeutic method consisted of emotional catharsis and abreaction. However, Rangell writes, "successive historical developmental phases on our science in the epoch-making years that followed ... moved from affects to instincts, from loculated pockets to intrapsychic conflicts, and from abreaction to interpretation. The latter underwent increasing elaboration and refinement paralleling our increasing knowledge of the nature of the internal conflicting forces. I would like to submit the thesis that affects, the original center, in giving way to subsequent developments have become, wrongly, 'the forgotten man.' In spite of their ubiquity clinically, they have in a sense been bypassed, or at least minimized out of proportion, and receive a good deal less of systematic attention than they deserve in our total theoretical metapsychological system" (183). This so-called "forgotten man" hypothesis can be found in most engagements of the topic; that is, for the vast majority of psychoanalytic theorists, there is no inherent tension between affect and psychoanalytic theory, rather the persistent absence of any systematic account is merely a result of the field having been diverted by other concerns. Although Rangell believes the field has made some progress on the topic since Freud, he nevertheless admits that in a fundamental way "we do not yet have a full or complete theory of affects" because – and notwithstanding the worthy contributions of Rapaport, Glover, Jacobsen, Fenichel, and Brierley – "a 'secretory or motor instinctual discharge into the interior' does not sufficiently differentiate affects from other such internal discharges, nor does it separate one affect from another" (194).

Pushing back against this "forgotten man" hypothesis, Westen sees the field's difficulty developing a theory of affects as symptomatic of deeper problems that have to do with theorizing motivation. In a probing analysis of the relationship between affect and motivation, Westen has argued that the field's struggle to develop a coherent and systematic account of affect follows from the abiding resistance, on the part of psychoanalysts, to challenge the underlying "drive model" of Freudian theory and that "attempted revisions of Freud's theories of affect and motivation have too long reflected a compromise between the desire for fidelity to the data of clinical observation and the fear of infidelity to Freud" (1997, 524). Moreover, while this drama over loyalty pertains to revisions of any kind, Rapaport correctly recognized that the repercussions of disputing Freud on the question of affect represents a unique challenge to the entire Freudian corpus, and that "tugging on the loose threads of Freud's affect theory threatens to unravel his drive theory" because, for example, "sexual pleasure is recognized as *one* form of pleasure, then libido in the erotic sense is one of many human motives mediated by affect and no longer has a privileged place in psychoanalysis" (524). According to Westen, contemporary clinicians have found it nearly impossible to replace Freud's incoherent ideas about affect with rigorous and scientifically sound formulations because they insist on preserving Freud's motivational theory over and against the demands of clinical observation and scientific progress. While this account provides an explanation of the field's current dilemma, it abstains from showing why there should *be* such an enduring difficulty with affects, to begin with. After all, if, as countless analysts of various persuasions have repeatedly said, every version of therapeutic practice depends on *some* idea of affective change, then how do we explain the original disconnect between a highly organized and persuasive theory of motivation, on the one hand, and on the other, a conceptually incoherent and clinically impoverished understanding of affect?

The intransigence of the problem, and the fact that urgent calls for a theory of affect have been made without any meaningful success, casts serious doubt on the persuasiveness of the "forgotten man" hypothesis. While the relevance of affect to psychoanalytic work is indisputable, it's worth wondering whether there isn't something endemic to the psychoanalytic model of the mind which militates against a robust theory of affect? In other words, is there something about the idea of a dynamic unconscious that *contravenes* a precise and rigorous conceptualization of affect? While Westen is certainly correct in noticing that throughout the field's history clinicians manifest a deep-seated resistance to appearing in any way "un-faithful" to Freud, and that this obsession with "fidelity" has debil-itating consequences on the discipline's scientific growth, Westen's focus on the field's discursive culture, while accurate, sidesteps an account of what specifically it is about the discipline's foundational tenets that render affect *such* a difficult object of study. After all, it isn't merely that "Freud struggled with the problem of affect all his life" (Demos, 2019, 100) and that his followers have passively in-herited this struggle, but that all subsequent efforts to accord affect a more "cardinal"[2] position within psychoanalysis have done so by either shying away from the full implications of a primary "affec-tivity" or avoiding a direct confrontation with the limits of certain Freudian concepts, thereby blunting the force of a powerful new model that puts affect at its center. The fact that, despite multiple calls for a serious engagement with affect, no substantial recalibra-tions have taken place, suggests that the tension – between Freud's version of a dynamic unconscious and the view of affect as central – is deeply embedded in the psychoanalytic view of human subjectivity.

Andre Green's landmark study on affect sought to address the problem of its neglected status by arguing that it was absent from Freudian metapsychology owing to (1) the difficulty of con-ceptualizing affect and (2) the fact that Freud's original ideas on affect were drawn exclusively from his work with neurosis and this is a necessarily limited perspective.[3] Green is steadfast in his belief that the deficiencies of Freud's model on affect are circumscribed and can be systematically corrected; as such, he outlines a complex theory of affects as intrapsychic and on equal footing with other unconscious processes and aims to show that, while on the one hand Freud made certain erroneous assumption about affect, the real problem is not with Freud himself, but with the field's misreading of him. According to Green, who was a French contemporary of Lacan, it is precisely the latter's idea that the "unconscious is structured like a language" that amplifies the biggest flaws in psychoanalytic theory by following Freud's mistakes rather than the true spirit of what he meant.

Fiercely differentiating himself from the linguistic structuralism of Lacan, and drawing on research in psychosomatic disorders, Green believed in a revision that maintains Freud's original formulations while elaborating a working definition of affects and their relation to the unconscious.[4] Green acknowledges that the absence of any systematic theory of affect is a direct result of how Freud conceived of emotionality – namely, that *affect needed to be perceived in order to be represented* and only content which was representable could be included in the unconscious – but he nevertheless affirms that an affect-friendly version of psychoanalysis can be achieved.

In her recent review of this history, affect theorist Virginia Demos arrives at a decisively less conciliatory interpretation of the relationship between affect theory and psychoanalysis. While she appreciates Green's methodical attempts to salvage Freud's model of the mind, Demos argues that the real problem isn't that Lacan misread Freud or even that Freud made a few flawed assumptions about affects being representable, but that Freud's structural model and dual instinct theory view motivation in ways that are profoundly at odds with an approach that prioritizes affect. Although Demos is careful to show that Freud's ideas on affect underwent considerable modifications throughout his career, it nevertheless remains the case that despite these many permutations, affect maintained a strange status at the periphery of psychoanalytic theorizing. Demos suggests that while there is considerable temptation to merely incorporate new ideas on affect into existing psychoanalytic theory, recent findings in neural sciences compel a more comprehensive replacement of drive theory with affects as a unifying model for human motivation. After tracing the various attempts by different analytic schools to modify psychoanalytic theory in accordance with a greater appreciation for affect, Demos concludes that, "while nearly all the revisions of Freud's dual instinct theory agree that the vicissitudes of affects comprise the most clinically relevant phenomena for understanding our patients' motivations, yet none of these revisions clarify what any theory of motivation needs to provide, namely a clear understanding of how affects are activated and function and how they relate to drives and to cognition … *what would it mean to accept a comprehensive affect theory as a viable replacement of Freud's dual instinct theory, as the primary motivational factor in psychological organization?*" (2019, 113).

In her call for a "comprehensive" new theory which functions as a "viable replacement" of Freud's original model, Demos is aware of being in the minority among psychoanalytic thinkers. The field-wide tendency to continue modifying Freud's original model of the mind rather than decisively replacing it is evident in the way new analytic schools correct a particular, local, element of psychoanalytic theory but generally refrain from providing a unifying alternative. What's more, these gestures typically rely on interpretations of Freud which minimize his limitations and emphasize his courage, or minimize his intellectual rigidity and emphasize the deficiencies of nineteenth-century science. As such, the question of whether new scientific research on affect requires that Freud's model be comprehensively "replaced" is neither abstract nor incidental but follows logically from how one understands the field's problem with affect in the first place. That is, if one believes that Freud's difficulty conceptualizing affect in any kind of philosophically coherent or clinically useful way is merely an isolated issue that does not threaten to undo basic tenets of his theory as a whole, then calls for replacing Freud's model likely sound reactive or extreme. If, however, one believes that prioritizing affect runs into trouble because something about the Freudian unconscious actively prevents it from taking center stage, then it becomes necessary to locate the true source of this powerful tension.

Demos agrees with many thinkers before her that the major cause of this tension is the field's continued commitment to drive theory. According to Demos, "instincts and drives as opposed to affects can no longer stand as a major source of motivation" (96), and that a new and revitalized paradigm of the mind would once and for all replace drives with "affects as the primary motivational source" (97). Demos draws on the argument, advanced eloquently by Joseph Sandler, that Freud's later theory of signal anxiety effectively moved away from his earlier drive theory, but instead of building out the implications of anxiety as a signal, he kept both ideas in place, never reconciling the two theories because they were ultimately and inherently contradictory (1985; see also, Modell, 1973, 1980). According to this interpretation, there is (in Freud's ideas on anxiety as a signal) the earliest beginning of his thinking about affect and the task of contemporary research is to develop this thought further. Many theoreticians who subscribe to this interpretation of Freud cite the work of Otto Kernberg as an example of a "gifted clinician and clear thinker, who accepts basic dual drive theory" while nevertheless acknowledging that affects play a decisive role in the formation of unconscious conflicts (Demos, 2019, 108). And yet, as many have also frequently observed, the fundamental tension between the nature of drives and operation of affects remain ultimately unresolved in Kernberg's model, a fact that, for Demos and Westen, proves the limited range of theories which insist on achieving a compromise between "fidelity to the data of clinical observation and the fear of infidelity to Freud" (Westen, 1997, 524). As Westen has aptly observed, the problem today is that "the grammar of our discourse is filled with constructions we do not believe anymore" (2002, 861).

Affect vs. unconscious: a genealogy of the problem

A different lesson from the field's long history of failed attempts to integrate affect might have to do with how the problem has been predominantly conceptualized until now. According to most popular interpretations, what holds psychoanalysis back is an outdated and deeply flawed drive theory which is (even though many clinicians might not notice it) incommensurable with a theory of primary affectivity. The problem with this view is that it generally neglects what's *underneath* drive theory, which is a model of the mind that "knows its own feelings." As this chapter will show, it isn't drive theory that prevents psychoanalysis from developing a theory of affect but drive theory that reinforces the deeper psychoanalytic belief that all affect is *felt* by the conscious/unconscious mind. Adrian Johnston has astutely observed that "starting with the founder of psychoanalysis, the question of how to situate the unconscious and affective life vis-à-vis each other consistently has been a controversial matter provoking an array of disparate, and often clashing, responses within and beyond analytic circles" (2013, 75). Noting that "for analysis, the ramifications of this riddle are both metapsychological and clinical" (76), Johnston distinguishes his reading from the standard scholarly stories by drawing out the connection between Freud's understanding of unconscious processes and conceptualization of affect. For Johnston, the disconnect that "haunts" the field is neither mysterious nor incidental but directly follows from Freud's intensive efforts to *oppose* affects to the unconscious by insisting that *there's no such thing as unconscious feelings*. For Freud, "unconscious affects" are a conceptual and factual impossibility: since repression and other defensive maneuvers act upon mental contents, it is logically required that in order for a feeling to be repressed it had to be *felt*, on some level, in the first place. Although Johnston argues that Freud was potentially more ambivalent about this question than he explicitly seemed,[5] it nevertheless remains the case that even when Freud *does* begin to consider the possibilities of unconscious feelings, "he quickly shuts down these promising metaphysical avenues, promptly reverting to a theory according to which unconscious affect is, strictly speaking, a contradiction in terms" (108).

For Johnston, the question of whether Freud is right or wrong on the question of whether affects can be "unconscious" is rendered moot by breakthroughs in the life sciences over the past several decades which clearly and consistently demonstrate that affects *do* exist unconsciously, and the psyche must therefore be redefined according to this "primordial emotionality." As Johnston writes: "the most striking affirmations of contemporary neurobiologists like Damasio or LeDoux concern the importance of the emotional brain. All the cognitive operations closely depend on it. Affects function initially at a primitive biological and cerebral level that does not involve consciousness. There therefore exists nonconscious affects, and the brain is their place of origin. This is why it is important, for the neurobiologists, to redefine the psyche according to this primordial emotionality. What challenges do such affirmations throw at psychoanalysis and philosophy?" (211). To begin answering this question, we may recall that in Freud's model of the mind, suffering is the result of desires, wishes, and needs that have been defensively repressed. Insofar as the mind is organized by the "principle of constancy," then a "primary function of the nervous system or mental apparatus is to rid the organism of excessive stimulation. The failure to do so has pathogenic consequences, including the development of symptomatology" (Eagle, 2011, 4). Carefully delineating how the "constancy principle" undergirds every major Freudian formulation (including drive theory, the pleasure principle, instinct theory, etc.), Morris Eagle shows that the "single most continuous and central idea running from the pre-psychoanalytic formulations of Jean-Martin

Charcot, Pierre Janet, and Alfred Binet through the psychoanalytic theorizing of Freud to contemporary psychoanalysis is that mental contents that are isolated and unintegrated into one's personality or self-organization constitute pathogens that bring about various forms of pathological symptoms" (5). The "distinctive psychoanalytic stamp" Freud adds to this idea is that it isn't *external trauma* alone which is subject to mental isolation because an equally powerful and (significantly more universal) source of anxiety is internal conflict and the defenses they elicit. By moving the focus from external events to internal wishes and desires, Freud distinguishes psychoanalysis from previous psychological theories by this emphasis on repression, which is the "purposeful banishment- an act of will-of unacceptable mental contents from consciousness" (15). Whereas drive theory, which comes later, has historically been the locus of controversy, Eagle astutely points out that drive theory fits neatly into, rather than generates, the model of affective discharge Freud initially lays out. That is, the "entire structure of Freudian ideas discussed thus far required no reference to drive theory. The key ideas and concepts of the constancy principle, the quota of affect, strangulated affect, re-pression, and the pathogenic significance of isolation of mental contents were articulated by Freud long before he formulated his drive theory and do not rest on the logic of drive theory. However, the above ideas fit neatly into drive theory once it is formulated. Thus, it is now instinctual wishes and impulses that constitute the main sources of potentially excessive increases in the sum of excita-tion and therefore the main threat to the integrity of the nervous system (or the mental apparatus)" (16). As such, the dynamic un-conscious as Freud articulates it is an unconscious "of desires and wishes pressing for representation in consciousness and for discharge and prevented from achieving conscious representation and discharge by counter-forces (ex. repression)" (19).

If we situate this definition of the unconscious in the context of recent breakthroughs on the mind's "primordial emotionality," we begin to observe that a situation which Freud conceives of as im-possible, is, according to recent scientific findings, actually inevitable: namely, that feelings *can* (and do) exert a powerful influence on mental functioning without ever having been represented or re-pressed. Taking a step back, we can see that in order for Freud to be able to claim that the unconscious is comprised of repressed emotions, he needs to insist on a two-part sequence whereby emotions are perceived by some part of the mind, and then purposefully banished from ordinary consciousness. But what happens if emotions are *not* perceived by some part of the mind? According to Freud, if they are not perceived then they cannot be defensively repressed, hence no such thing as "unconscious affects." While this view is reflexive within psychoanalysis, it means that clinicians of practically any persuasion find it impossible to treat emotional disorders that do not have *some* form of repression at their origin. In order to understand how affect theory radically transforms our model of the unconscious, it is necessary to explore how affect is currently conceptualized within traditionalist and progressive schemas.

Motivation and drive: critique of the traditionalist view

In the history of the field, vigorous debates have mainly converged around the legitimacy of "drive" theory; progressives mainly discarding it in its entirety, while traditionalists insist on maintaining it through an integration with object relations and attachment frameworks. What Eagle's close reading ably shows is that while "drive" theory may seem like *the* antiquated problem that an updated theory needs to solve, in actuality, "drives" only make sense in the context of the constancy principle, repression and endogenous anxiety so that efforts to sidestep "drives" – while successfully altering the discourse – nevertheless leave the underlying model of the mind intact. As Eagle notes, in Freud's distinction between the "descriptive unconscious" and the "dynamic unconscious" (1915b), the "descriptive unconscious" mainly refers to computational cognitive processes that go on outside awareness, while the "dynamic unconscious" "is conceptualized as a repository of repressed wishes and impulses, as a "cauldron full of seething excitations" (Freud, 1923/1933, p. 73) It is called dynamic because these wishes and impulses are always striving for expression in consciousness and in motor action and are prevented from doing so by counterforce of defense. There is always a dynamic tension between these two sets of forces. From this perspective, mental life, including conscious experience, is always the product of compromises between these forces" (2011, 39). As Eagle demonstrates, Freud's focus on the "dynamic unconscious" went hand in hand with his belief that the a "primary function of the nervous system or mental apparatus is to rid the organism of excessive stimulation. The failure to do so has pathogenic consequences, including the development of symptomatology" (4). As Freud develops his ideas, he begins to argue that since repressed wishes continue to press for discharge, repression must be ongoing. Therefore, not only are the causes of anxiety endogenous rather than external, but the work of repression is constant throughout a lifespan rather than acute. Eagle notes, "the constancy principle, undischarged or strangulated affect, isolation of mental contents, and repression, all combined in a logical structure, come into play in accounting for hysteria. As noted, the most fundamental assumptions are that a basic function of mind is to discharge excitation and that the failure to do so, that is, the buildup of excessive excitation, has pathogenic consequences... Given the role of associative isolation and failure to discharge affect in the development of pathology, it follows that treatment should address both factors, the former through bringing isolated or repressed thoughts to consciousness (via hypnosis) and the latter through abreaction of undischarged or strangulated affect. This is the model or logical structure that Freud formulates to account for pathology and to guide treatment. Further, it is essentially this model that is adapted to later developments, including the formulation of drive theory and the structural model" (15).

As Eagle skillfully points out, "the entire structure of Freudian ideas discussed thus far required no reference to drive theory. The key ideas and concepts of the constancy principle, the quota of affect, strangulated affect, repression, and the pathogenic significance of isolation of mental contents were articulated by Freud long before he formulated his drive theory. However, the above ideas fit neatly into drive theory once it is formulated. Thus, it is now instinctual wishes and impulses that constitute the main sources of potentially excessive increases in the sum of excitation and therefore the main threat to the integrity of the nervous system (or the mental apparatus)" (16). As such, "drive" theory is not a discrete biopsychical concept that can be added or subtracted, accepted or rejected at will, because to the degree "drives" operate in coordination with the mind's total mechanical infrastructure, excising them leaves no functional overarching mental system capable of taking its place. Put another way, disputes about the legitimacy of "drive" theory misconstrue the true source of the problem which isn't the "drive" model per se, but the paradigm of motivation which underlies it. As such, a substantive critique requires deconstructing Freud's view of motivation in order to demonstrate that what's needed isn't the rebuttal of "drives," so much as a reformulation of motivation along *affective* lines.

To start, we may begin with Laplanche's observation that existing metapsychology utterly lacks a logical explanation for how unconscious life *originates*. That is, for Freud, it seems good enough to say that sexuality *becomes* a "drive" somewhat supernaturally, either because it is already a hardwired feature of every psychic system, or because it is the unavoidable outgrowth of physical-psychical development. In a sense, Freud asserts the ineluctable "fact" of unconscious sexuality – and then proceeds to trace all motivation to this sexual source – without ever explaining how or why this sexuality exists. One often wonders if Freud isn't so convinced of the inherent radicalness of his discovery that he feels no need to account for how he got there. Indeed, on more than one occasion Freud declares that anyone who doubts the "fact" of unconscious sexuality is guilty of resisting it, which has the effect of distracting readers from Freud's own systematic incoherence on the subject. As Laplanche's close reading shows, Freud repeatedly conflates "instinct" and "drive," leading to a deeply problematic misunderstanding of how *enlarged* sexuality works. Describing this theoretical problem, Laplanche explains that, "instinct is hereditary, fixed, and adaptive; it starts with somatic tension, has a 'specific action' and a satisfying object, and leads to a sustained relaxation of the tension. In contrast, drive in the pure sense would not be hereditary, nor necessarily adaptive. The model of source, aim, and adequate object cannot easily be applied to the drive. I have insisted more than once, notably in relation to the idea of 'source,' that is one can say with any rigor that the anus is the source of anal drive, then one must question with even greater rigor how one could ever maintain that the drive to see, voyeurism, aims at lowering something that one could call 'ocular tension'" (FS, 12). We know that instinctual life is predetermined by biology and we also know that adult sexuality is a fact of psychological experience, but we have no way of understanding how we get *from* basic, hardwired instinctuality *to* *enlarged*, unconscious sexuality. Existing metapsychology has never resolved Freud's conflation of instinct and drives and as such, faces an unexplained gap between instinctual life and unconscious sexuality.

Laplanche shows that in the absence of a logical explanation for *how* "drive"-sexuality originates, Freud resorted to Lamarckian ideas about the phylogenetic transmission of universal psychic fantasies. That is, unable to explain how certain powerful emotional experiences developed in the individual, Freud relied on the idea that ancestral social events could bridge the gap between "ancient interpersonal experiences and the universal underlying features of internal psychic structure," and that, when it came to "drive" sexuality, every individual acquired erotic interests out of some mysterious *endogenous* process. This move – from external events to internal reactions – was always Freud's particular talent; as noted earlier, he distinguished psychoanalysis from the therapeutic endeavors of Charcot precisely in this way, making subjective experience more psychologically meaningful than any particular traumatic event. However, while this move was extraordinarily successful in shining a light on a vast range of internal experience, it nearly immediately resulted in a well-worn philosophical problem, which was how then to account for the role of the *outside* world, and of the *other* person? As Mitchell and Greenberg have observed, classical drive/structure theories echo the "highly *individualistic, atomistic tradition* of Locke and Hobbes in British political philosophy" (Slavin and Kriegman, 1992, 30) wherein "man cannot live outside society, but society is in a fundamental sense inimical to his very nature and precludes the possibility for his deepest, fullest satisfactions" (30). While in the Anglo-American tradition, relational theory has ventured to remedy the psyche's atomism by dispensing with drive altogether and instead reorienting psychology toward the interpersonal context, Laplanche takes a different approach that retains sexuality as the primary object of psychoanalysis but fundamentally transforms our understanding of how it works.

Reconceptualizing metapsychology through affect theory introduces the concept of an "urge" to translate,[6] or what Laplanche sometimes calls a "drive to translate." While this idea has little meaning in metapsychology as it currently exists, re-situating the infant in the context of an *affective* event (the primal seduction) demonstrates the need for any coherent metapsychology to explain what sets unconscious sexuality in motion. To do this, Laplanche situates the emergence of sexuality in the communicative exchanges *between* the adult and child. Emphatically rejecting Freud's efforts to make "drive" the spontaneous outgrowth of instinctual life, Laplanche suggests instead that we view sexuality as the natural and inevitable result of the mind's developmental process which is fundamentally dependent on the other/adult person. The fact of this dependence is extremely important for Laplanche insofar as it establishes a *channel* for the exchange of material between adult and child. Why is it so important for a channel to exist? Because, as Laplanche will show, once you have a mechanism for transmitting information between an adult and a child, then you also have a way of explaining where "drive" sexuality originates – *which is in the unconscious of the adult.* According to Laplanche, *seduction* (chapter 3) names the fact that in order to survive, the human infant depends upon the adult as a caretaker but that this caretaker, who is an adult, also has an unconscious of his own. While in and of itself this statement hardly seems that controversial, what Laplanche goes on to describe is the impact – on the child – of encountering the adult's unconscious sexuality. Specifically, that when faced with the adult's sexuality, the infant sets about to "translate" what she is picking up on. Why does she do this? Because to the infant, experiencing the adult's unconscious sexuality is an *affective* event. Laplanche writes, "it is only because the adult's messages are compromised by his sexual unconscious that, secondarily, the child's attempts at symbolization are set in motion, where the child actively works on material that is *already* sexual" (FS, 47).

Laplanche does not explicate how "translation" or "symbolization" work at a technical or biopsychical level but our contemporary understanding of affect enables us to fill in the blanks. That is, understood in terms of affect, unconscious sexuality can be said to correspond to those areas of the adult's psychic life that have *not* been worked on by language or symbolization, meaning they are raw and largely unprocessed. While the adult may be undisturbed by what he doesn't consciously feel, the child has a different experience. For the child, repeatedly confronting large batches of unprocessed affect prompts regulatory action, propelling the child to diminish the intensity of incoming affect by setting to work on the material, "translating" it into images, fantasies, symbols, etc. It is precisely this process of "translation" that establishes 'drive' sexuality in the child. Understood functionally, affect is therefore able to explain what no theoretical program could explain without it – the development of unconscious sexuality. Laplanche calls this sequence of event the "Fundamental Anthropological Situation," by which he means that, it is "the truly universal relation *between a child* who has no genetically programmed unconscious ("genetically innocent") and *an adult* (not necessarily the mother) who, psychoanalysis tells us, is inhabited by an unconscious. It is a situation that is absolutely ineluctable, even if the infant has no parents, and even if he is ... a clone!" (FS, 48).

Now, before situating Laplanche's "translation" process in the context of contemporary biology, it is crucial to note that Laplanche himself never explicitly refers to "affect" or "affect theory" and seldom draws out the connection between his ideas of "translation" and contemporary attachment theory. That said, Laplanche is adamant that attachment must be "*accommodated* with the framework of a *rigorous metapsychology*" (FS, 36) and that the future of psychoanalysis depends on finding ways to formulate the unconscious in the context of attachment. Therefore, in my reading, Laplanche's account of the "translation" process only makes sense if we plug into his formula what science has recently taught us about the role of affect in the infant's regulatory mechanisms. Doing this enables us to see how Laplanche's concept of "translation" is not only compatible with current neurobiological understanding of the mind, but furthermore, offers a logically coherent paradigm of motivation that has attachment, and specifically affect regulation, at its center.

Among contemporary psychoanalysts, Peter Fonagy has worked intensively to show why recent scientific breakthrough require a psychoanalysis that is affect-oriented. Interested in moving past the "bad blood" that has characterized the relationship between attachment theory and psychoanalysis for decades, Fonagy has demonstrated that neither Bowlby's view of attachment nor the traditional Freudian rejection of it, offer a scientifically accurate depiction of mental development. As Fonagy readily acknowledges, Bowlby's bold intervention in psychoanalysis was urgently needed and tremendously evocative; whereas in the 1950s, psychoanalytic paradigms depicted the human infant as motivated by libidinal or aggressive "drives," Bowlby and his colleagues placed the need for attachment at the center of human behavior. Dissatisfied with the way psychoanalysts portrayed the need for a caregiver as merely secondary, a necessary vehicle for overriding oral drives, Bowlby was among the first to recognize that the human infant enters the world prepared and predisposed for social interaction. However, notwithstanding the immediate appeal of Bowlby's refreshing reconceptualization, it was nevertheless the case that it's underlying reasoning was tautological: as Fonagy puts it, "the response to separation is attributed to the disruption of a social bond, the existence of which is inferred from the presence of the separation response" (2001, 17). For many psychoanalysts, Fonagy included, there was something intuitively persuasive about Bowlby's prioritization of attachment over drives, but it wasn't until later research on affect – and on regulation specifically – that it became clear *how* exactly the adult affected the infant's developmental process.

In a watershed study of rodent pups in the 1990s, Myron Hofer revealed that the evolutionary survival value of staying close to the mother far exceeds simple protection from harm; the attachment "relationship provides an opportunity for the mother to shape both the developing physiology and the behavior of her offspring through her patterned interactions with her infant" (Fonagy 2001, 16). In other words, "attachment is not an end in itself – it is a system adapted by evolution to fulfill key ontogenetic physiological and psychological tasks. Hofer's reformulation of attachment in terms of regulatory processes, hidden but observable within the parent-infant interaction, provides a very different way of explaining the range of phenomena usually discussed under the heading of attachment" (16). This updated view of attachment puts affective regulation at the center, demonstrating that what makes attachment so important isn't safety per se, but the regulation of affect. Fonagy writes, "what is lost in 'loss' is not the bond but the opportunity to generate a higher order regulatory mechanism: the mechanism for appraisal and reorganization of mental contents. In this context attachment is conceptualized as a process that brings complex mental life into being from a multi-faceted and adaptable behavioral system" (17). This focus on how attachment works as a *regulator* of development echoes a range of findings in other disciplines which also confirm the importance of studying regulation. According to Damasio, "all emotions have some kind of regulatory role to play, leading in one way or another to the creation of circumstances advantageous to the organism exhibiting the phenomenon; emotions are *about* the life of an organism, its body to be precise, and their role is to assist the organism in maintaining life" (1999, 51).

To specify just how important it is, Allan Schore has shown the material "growth of the brain is dependent upon and influenced by the socioemotional environment" and that the "maturation of the orbitofrontal region, the cerebral cortical structure involved in the regulation of subcortically generated affect, is experience-dependent" (1994, 78). This "experience is specifically affective, or more properly socioaffective, since it is embedded in stimulation provided in the relationship between the primary caretaker and the child" (71). Drawing on multidisciplinary evidence, Schore has demonstrated that "during the earliest organismic-environmental transactions ... the mother serves as a hidden regulator of the infant's endocrine and nervous systems." Furthering Hofer's research, Schore presents evidence that "the infant's interactions with the mother directly elicit psychoendocrinological changes that influence the biochemical activation of gene-action systems which program the critical period growth and differentiation of a corticolimbic structure responsible for self-regulation" (18). Therefore, although the study of emotions has only recently become a legitimate scientific area, a vast body of research resoundingly confirms that emotions are responsible for every exchange of information between the body and the brain. As such, those who study the scientific underpinnings of brain development can claim the "infant is now conceptualized to be more of a sensoriaffective than a sensorimotor being" and that affect is *functionally* central to all aspects of mental development.

What does this mean for psychoanalytic theories of motivation? For one, it requires that psychoanalysis become thoroughly compatible with contemporary biology without losing its distinctive grasp on the realm of fantasy and unconscious sexuality. Speaking to the need for such compatibility, Laplanche writes: "For me, every human process is indissociably biological and psychical. Even the most abstract mathematical reasoning is inconceivable without a neurobiological corporal correlate" (FS, 105). At present this means that a "rigorous metapsychology" *must* accord with knowledge obtained in neighboring disciplines and more specifically, that our model of mental life *must* have affect at its center. This is why Laplanche's model of "translation" offers a necessary way out of the stale impasse between "drive" vs. "attachment" theories. Contrary to persistent debates about whether the infant is motivated by endogenous drives or the need for attachment, Laplanche demonstrates why the infant, as an affective being, is most clearly understood as someone motivated to achieve higher regulatory functions, which *of necessity* requires the adult-other. And yet, by virtue of this requirement, the infant is exposed to "more than he bargained for," insofar as there is *no such thing* as an adult who can regulate the baby but does not have an unconscious of her own. And if every regulating-adult is also a sexual-one then the infant will, by virtue of trying to grow, encounter "messages" he is capable of translating, and those which, unable to translate, become the core of his own unconscious.

According to Laplanche, we shouldn't be debating whether or not fantasies are endogenous to the infant, but instead concerning ourselves with how the infant's need to achieve a higher order regulatory mechanism results in an "urge to translate" the adult's enigmatic messages. The infant is motivated to develop and thrive, and since affect regulation is central to this biopsychical endeavor, the infant's motivation to "translate" is affective in nature. Since there is no adult without an unconscious, and no infant who does not need to grow, there is no way around the predicament of seduction and "translation."

Motivation and attachment: critique of the progressive view

While affect is conspicuously absent from traditional models of the mind, in recent progressive theory, there has been an increasing appreciation for the role of affect in mental life, and for the need to integrate scientific findings into existing metapsychology. In part owing to their comfort differentiating themselves from Freudian doxa, as well as to a longstanding tradition of drawing on developmental accounts cognitive and behavioral psychology, progressives seem, on the surface at least, to have already done some of the work Laplanche implores the field to do. Indeed, the frequency with which analysts of *any* orientation refer to the non-verbal dimension of unconscious processes suggests that nothing short of a sea change has occurred in psychoanalytic theory. Indeed, for many, not only has the field's founding Cartesianism been roundly overcome, but a new and flexible, dyadic, action-oriented psychoanalysis has successfully emerged to take its place. The popularity of terms like enactment, implicit memory and dissociation represents how thoroughly the tide has turned from having once been a theory and technique which privileged symbolization and interpretation to one that anticipates the necessity of action and unformulated experience (Stern, 1989). This rhetoric of our current progress – the insistence that our savvy new awareness of non-verbal communication signals our victory over the "bad old days" of an austere and intellectualizing theory – permeates the discourse, allowing each inch in the direction of affect to feel thousands of kilometers away from Freud. This sensation of our clinical enlightenment circulates so widely as to seem incontrovertible; and indeed, compared to the field's early days when countertransference was frowned upon and "acting out" was an aberration, our contemporary perspective is resolutely wider in scope and more flexible with respect to technique. But while affect is certainly more important than it has ever been, and our conceptualization of technique is less rigid than it used to be, a critical engagement with contemporary views suggests that even our most progressive models *do not go far enough* in conceptualizing the psychic role of unconscious affectivity.

The progress of psychoanalytic ideas is perhaps nowhere more clearly on display than in the wholesale denunciation of repression as an outdated and mechanistic concept, and the correspondent popularity of dissociation as an explanatory tool. In a statement that represents many working in the progressive tradition today, Jody Messler Davies declares that, "the unconscious structure of mind is fundamentally dissociative rather than repressive in nature" (1996, 564). According to this view, dissociation connotes a biologically based self-protective mechanism that gets triggered when an overwhelming event cannot be successfully processed by the psychological self. Dissociation represents a division in the personality; under extreme duress, like violence, trauma, or interpersonal abuse, the mind splinters so that one part stays technically present while another part, which is in touch with the pain, disconnects from everything else. As Elizabeth Howell explains, "when the continuity of being is traumatically interrupted, when whatever has happened is too frightening to be assimilated, people may "trance out," develop "psychic numbness" (Lifton and Marcuson, 1990), go into "neutral gear" (Terr, 1994), or all of these" (2005, 24). For this reason, dissociation is considered a failure of integration whereby the individual is "unable to assimilate the [traumatic] experience into already existing mental frameworks" (52).

For many who write on this topic, the popularity of dissociation signals a direct and powerful rebuke to the hegemony of repression in psychoanalysis. Moreover, the increasing acknowledgment of the important role dissociative phenomena play in a range of psychic defenses and pathologies is said to signal a new era of psychoanalysis in which the bad habits of Freud-the-Enlightenment-thinker have been *finally* and definitively renounced. In one powerful iteration of this narrative, Fonagy, Gergely, Jurist and Target contend that, "the relative neglect by psychologists and psychoanalysts of the developmental processes that underpin the agentive self may be seen as a residue of the traditionally powerful Cartesian doctrine of first-person authority that claims direct and infallible introspective access to intentional mind states, rather than seeing this access as a hard-won developmental acquisition... Both psychoanalysts and developmental science have often adhered to the Cartesian tradition in their assumption that the experience of mental agency is innately given" (2004, 3). Advocating for a radical break from Cartesian-Freudian ontology, these clinicians insist on a new understanding of mental life that adequately appreciates the role of affect in development. Motivated by major findings in infant research, ethology and neuroscience, a staggering number of recent books and articles have advocated for important revisions to the psychoanalytic model of the mind.

For example, in their groundbreaking study of parent–child interaction, the authors of the Boston Change Process Study Group skillfully draw out the connection between Freud's Cartesian bias toward affect and a range of enduring metapsychological problems. While acknowledging that "increasingly, psychoanalysis has been grappling with the interactive, intersubjective aspects of the psychoanalytic situation," the authors note that even popular interventions like those of the Relational school have yet to develop a "more encompassing theoretical foundation for grounding this clinical thinking" (2010, 143). In their effort to elaborate the groundwork for new theoretical foundations, the authors of the Boston Change Process Study Group correctly demonstrate that a major obstacle to a revised metapsychology resides in Freud's conviction that "before material could be repressed, it had to be in explicit domain, that is, in the preconscious or conscious domains" (2010, 158). Showing that "Freud was Cartesian in separating the mental from the physical," (156) they draw on extensive infant-child data to argue that "thought is not synonymous with verbal language and symbols. A primary source of confusion in previous theory stems from the equating of thinking and the generation of meaning with symbolic functioning. Analysts must now consider the possibility that the most important levels of psychodynamic meaning are carried, enacted, and expressed through nonsymbolizing processes" (149). The authors wonder if "perhaps the confusion surrounding this assertion stems from a belief that meaning can only be generated through symbolization, and that a being (the infant) incapable of reflecting on its actions cannot act meaningfully" (149). Drawing on decades of infant-adult experiments, these authors conclude that "reserving the more developmentally complex and relationally meaningful aspects of experience for verbally rendered forms of meaning is an example of the upside-down error of current theory. This version of theory is not now congruent with current understanding of the critical role of implicit meaning as foundational for verbal forms of meaning and thought (e.g., Hobson, 2002; D.N. Stern, 2004) (154)." As such, the attribution of all defensive activity to intrapsychic conflict is incompatible with recent breakthroughs in development and brain research. Moreover, "with this rich new view of all that happens in interactive and affective life, we would replace the idea of conflict between tripartite structures [id-ego-superego] with this more dyadic view of complex patterns of conflict between the intentional directions of the self and the intentional directions of important others, conflicts that are represented at the implicit level" (155).

Understanding the infant–adult relationship as a complex dyadic exchange has revolutionized the field; alongside infant researchers, a growing chorus of developmentalists have shown that, contrary to the long-held prioritization of verbalization, "we display affects automatically and often unconsciously and they affect those who observe them almost simultaneously, at split-second speeds" (Seligman, 2018, 87). These findings persuasively demonstrate that attachment relationships are primary, and that Freud's original drive model of human motivation was neither accurate, coherent nor sustainable. In illuminating the influential nonverbal rhythms and choreographies of infant-adult interactions, a growing body of work asserts the power of non-verbal affective patterns to shape intrapsychic and dyadic experience (Beebe and Lachmann, 2002; Beebe et al., 2005; Stern, 1985; Tronick, 2007). As Seligman explains, "since babies and their caregivers share an affective language from the beginning of life, and observe and imitate one another so naturally and frequently (many times per minute, if not per second), they are influencing each other's internal states immediately and very rapidly in the multiple pathways. All of this generates mutual regulation and understanding, when things go well enough, with these processes proceeding so quickly as to elude ordinary reflective awareness but becoming quite obvious when emerging video technologies slow down the action with slow, time-sequence analysis" (2018, 88). Sizing up this new view takes from Freud's original conceptualizations, Eagle notes that, "one can observe a radical shift from the classical unconscious of repressed wishes, dominated by irrational primary process thinking, to a contemporary unconscious of essentially *cognitive* representations, which, although cognitive, are associated with strong affects... Thus, the unconscious representations of contemporary psychoanalysis, although reflecting the immature cognition of the child, are not based on endogenous fantasies but are rather the result of implicit and explicit parental messages and communications" (129).

As this brief overview of contemporary theory makes clear, for progressives, it is no longer credible to claim that the human infant is motivated by endogenous fantasies. Instead, clinicians draw on a range of empirical and developmental research to argue that the infant is motivated by basic attachment needs and that when the infant encounters obstacles to attachment, as she invariably does, defenses such as dissociation invariably ensue. In this depiction of development, the infant is primarily motivated by the need for interpersonal interactions, rather than the drive discharge of the traditional model.

On the surface, the turn from instinct to attachment corroborates findings in other fields and moreover, echoes Laplanche's insistence on putting attachment at the center of a "rigorous metapsychology." But while emphasizing the primacy of attachment is an undeniable improvement, and reconfiguring the mind from one that was repression-based to one that is dissociative in nature obtains considerable theoretical progress, Laplanche's concept of "translation" reveals what's missing from this reformulation, namely, a true grasp of the infant's hermeneutic skills and concomitant vulnerabilities. As Slavin and Kriegman point out in their thoughtful deconstruction of prevailing progressive views, "in virtually no theory that we term 'relational' is a 'genuine clashing' (Goldberg, 1988) of individual aims and goals given a fundamental status as an inherent feature of the basic motives of normal individuals in the good-enough environment" (1992, 24). That is, while the emphasis on the infant's attachment needs is a welcome corrective to mechanistic formulations, the current understanding of attachment remains simplistic and utterly unable to explain the structural *origins* of *enlarged* sexuality. Whereas the traditionalists believe in a version of sexuality that is endogenous, and Laplanche (critiquing this traditional view), outlines a kind of sexuality that arises out the infant's encounter with the adult unconscious, progressives have no way of explaining why, or under what conditions, an *enlarged* sexuality – which is not instinctual or genital, is non-pathological – would develop at all. This is because, while progressive correctly recognize the importance of attachment, their view misconstrues what *underlies* this developmental need which isn't attachment itself, but higher order regulatory mechanisms. As the past two decades of research has shown, Bowlby's model of attachment was tautological insofar as it failed to provide an underlying motivation for attachment other than saying the loss of it is detrimental. What we have since learned via neurobiology and affect theory is that attachment isn't the primary need of the infant; affect regulation is the need and attachment is the necessary means.

When viewed in neurobiological terms, the infant's need for a caretaker can be understood as the need for an affective regulator. That this affective regulator is also an adult with their own unconscious sexuality means that the communication of affect is always inevitably compromised by sexual "messages" which the adult did not intend, and that the infant cannot escape. In other words, affect is a *necessary* and *contaminated* carrier. And while the contamination can vary in its nature and degree, it is the *fact* of this contamination, combined with the infant's supreme *dependence* on it, that accounts for unconscious sexuality. Although not discussed or labeled as such in his schema, we could hypothesize that Laplanche's process of "translation" and communication relies on affects which are *not* subjectively felt as such. Whereas the current model of repression and/or dissociation hinges on the mind's capacity to register, however non-consciously, threatening emotional experiences, Laplanche's model of "translation" describes affects that are happening all the time but not necessarily registered as such. Indeed, one way to understand Laplanche's intervention is as a rebuke of the longstanding phenomenological bias in psychoanalysis whereby accounts of mental processes are predominantly oriented toward subjective rather than structural events. Instead, what matters for "translation" is that the infant is understood as "working on" the adult's affective material as a necessary means for her own survival and growth.

For Laplanche, "the human being is an interpreter by nature: the only originary hermeneut; a hermeneut by virtue of his condition... From the very beginning, an interpreter of the enigmatic messages of the human adult other: this is what we propose with the general theory of seduction" (FS, 92). So far, this starting point is consistent with what we know from biology and infant research; namely, that from its earliest encounter with the outside world, the infant is motivated to "translate" what he encounters in the external environment into something he can use and understand. We also know that the regulation of affect subtends and enables every aspect of neurobiological development such that the mind's ability to achieve higher order mechanisms *depends* upon the success of its regulatory efforts. This means that developmental progress is contingent on the success of previous "translations." While psychoanalytic theory has recently acknowledged the unique role of the mother as the regulator of infant affectivity (Bion especially), the connection has yet to be made between the infant's dependence on the caretaker for regulation and the subsequent development of unconscious processes. That is, so far attention has focused on judging the quality of maternal attunement and exploring how this predicts a child's future pathology, without considering the broader, and distinctly psychoanalytic point, that every child's unconscious sexuality develops *in relation* to their parent's unconscious sexual life. In other words, it is not enough to merely say, as most psychoanalysts do, that the parent and child communicate non-verbally because what such a scenario ignores is the fact that these roles are neither equal nor symmetrical and that it is the *adult* – as a sexual being – who transforms the infant into someone with an "urge to translate" and this sequence happens by virtue of (1) the child's regulatory needs, (2) the fact that affect is the primary channel of communication, and (3) the caregiver is an adult who is sexual. Taken together, this new telos of mental development has little to do with hardwired aggression or endogenous fantasies, nor is it restricted to self-preservation and attachment needs. In its place, a portrait emerges in which the motivation to develop higher and more sophisticated regulatory functions is a fundamentally *affective* process.

Contrary to the recollections and patterns that are often reconstructed in treatment, the "work" the infant carries out is not necessarily either recorded nor symbolized; the child can make use of what *can* be successfully translated, and that which *resists* the child's attempts at translation become part of her developing unconscious. Laplanche writes: "the general theory of seduction provides a hypothesis that at the very least deserves to be examined: what from the beginning is 'to be bound,' 'to be translated,' does not come from the depths of an innate id but from the other human, the adult, in the essential asymmetry of our first months. The first attempts at 'treatment' are made in order to respond to the enigmatic messages (compromised by sexuality) coming from the adult other. The partial failure of these attempts at translation – by which the ego constitutes itself and begins to represent itself within a narrative – entails the exclusion of real elements, which then become the internal sources of sexual excitation against which the ego must continue to defend itself" (FS, 87). In Laplanche's schema, the unconscious is a structural inevitability because – in accordance with the dynamics of the "translation" process he describes – the child's necessary dependence on the adult produces an encounter with the adult's unconscious. It is because there is no alternative to this scenario – meaning, that the child is fundamentally motivated to further her own biopsychical developmental agenda – that the child will always require a caretaking adult whose regulatory skills are accompanied by affect the adult herself is unaware of, and has not, herself, worked on or understood. This encounter between the dependent and translating infant, and the regulating and unconscious adult, explains – in a way that no prevailing motivational paradigm does – the origins of *enlarged* sexuality.

The clinical implications of these ideas are tremendous, not least because, as Laplanche never tires of saying, every patient has been "translating" since infancy. What is more, "the individual will certainly not subsequently stop translating, as long as he lives" (IDH, 161). For psychoanalysis, this means that the goal of treatment is "not to restore a more intact past (*whatever would one do with that?*) but to allow in turn a deconstruction of the old, insufficient, partial and erroneous construction, and hence to open the way to the new translation which the patient, in his compulsion to synthesize (or, as the German Romantics might have put it, in his 'drive to translate'), will not fail to produce." (IDH, 164). Indeed, this reorientation toward "translation" as a process that draws on each infant's idiosyncratic disposition, skills, and temperament, confirms the findings of infant researchers that each child comes equipped with their own innate tendencies and harm is not reducible to the environment alone. For psychoanalysis, which has, from its inception, been divided between those who emphasize external trauma (such as Kohut) vs. those that focus on subjective fantasies (such as Klein), recontextualizing the infant in a rich and sophisticated affective encounter illuminates why there is no steady distinction between history and fantasy and why for psychoanalysis – as the study of unconscious sexuality – it is not what the infant came with or inherited but the intricate process of "translation" that matters. With that in mind, Laplanche nevertheless resists the all too familiar reliance on 'fantasy' as an alternative to 'factuality,' since for the most part this language is "liable to lead us on to the archetypal – i.e. to an atavistic experience" (IDH, 149). As such, Laplanche writes, "to the extent that the originator of the enigmatic message is unaware of most of what he means, and to the extent that the child possesses only inadequate and imperfect ways to configure or theorize about what is communicated to him, there can be no linear causality between the parental unconscious and discourse on the one hand and what the child does with these on the other" (IDH, 160).

What would it mean to view our patients as experts in "translation"? What impact would this have on our conceptualization of treatment and the labor of analysis? To start, we might begin by appreciating that the patient has an "urge to translate" which is a vital source of knowledge and development and that treatment is a powerful *affective* event which has immense potential to provoke both the patient and the analyst in unexpected ways. Furthermore, in viewing the patient as an expert translator, who has been translating her entire life, we shift our position so that treatment is less of a memorial reconstruction of events or a passive tracing of linguistic signifiers but instead a highly charged and potentially deeply threatening event in which the patient is offered an opportunity to encounter "his internal enigma but also the enigma of the other. In this sense, the analytic situation has in essence nothing to do with a simple transference of habits. It places the subject back within the originary situation, that of the genesis of infantile sexuality" (FS, 50). In Laplanche's view, current ways of understanding transference reflect a fieldwide neglect of *enlarged* sexuality and its origins in the exchange with the adult-other. Situating these ideas in the context of the therapeutic relationship, Laplanche writes: "With Freud, transference has a subject fully equipped with his conflicts; with Klein, someone burdened with instincts and objects, who brings them along to analysis. With Ferenczi, perhaps the notion of reciprocity is introduced, but only ever to relate two monads, about which *from that moment* that author is right to wonder why one should be termed the analyst, the other the analysand. Reciprocity, mutuality, the response of the shepherd/counter-transference to the shepherdess/transference, and the other way around – all of this stems from the fact that the arrow of analytic asymmetry has not been noticed. With Lacan, one sometimes seems to have emerged from monadology. But the Hegelian formulations on desire as desire of the other easily become circular (the desire of desire...); an endless circle which favors the assimilation of the unconscious to a language, and the claim that it is transindividual... Is it possible to conceive that the arrow, the originary vector, goes in a reverse direction? Reversing the arrow is not to fall back into the symmetry of transference and counter-transference, not to ask which desire of the analyst's would correspond to the analysand's desire. The 'desire of the analyst' – no doubt there is one, even several, and very diverse; but my question is a different one. Are we able to conceive that it is the offer of analysis, the offer of the analyst, which creates ... what? Not analysis, but its essential dimension, transference. Not, perhaps, the whole of the transference, but its basis, the driving force at its heart, in other words, the re-opening of a relation, the originary relation, in which the other is primary for the subject" (TPA, 226).

We can see here how Laplanche rejects *both* mutuality and neutrality because of how they each, in their own ways, neglect the role of the adult-other in the constitution of the subject. In a pointed rejection of neutrality, Laplanche writes that "the image of neutrality is inevitably that of the blank screen or, rather, the mirror. Offering projection as much room as possible, allowing solipsism its full space, finally to overthrow it in a confrontation: you clearly see that *it's you that... In short: you have projected, and I give you back your projection, I counter-project.* This is neutrality's artificial, almost experimental conception of the mirror: it should be possible to deduct the conditions of the experience or experiment, and for everyone to get back his marbles. One must arrive at a positive, creative conception of neutrality, productive of the enigmatic dimension. It is here that we should complete our short dialogue, with this response from the analyst:

Analyst: Yes, you can take me for an other, because I am not what I think I am; because I respect and maintain the other in me.

It is maintaining the dimension of interior alterity which allows alterity to be set up in the transference. Interior relation, relation to the enigma, 'the relation to the unknown'" (TPA, 229). Indeed, for Laplanche, the "inspired invention of the analytic situation cannot be properly understood unless it is coupled with a conception of the 'fundamental anthropological situation' (adult-*infans*) as originary asymmetry, another name for which is 'seduction.' It is only in relation to infantile asymmetry that the 'unbearable' analytic asymmetry can be explained and justified. 'Neutrality' is not primarily a refusal to give the other help, counsel, knowledge, etc. It is sustained only by what we must call the internal 'refusal' of the analyst: an understanding perhaps of his own unconscious mechanisms, a respect for unconscious alterity and also a sense of his limits, which implies a rejection of any aim to master, to fashion the other, of any *poiesis*" (FS, 280). Proposing a "benevolent neutrality" instead (TPA, 228), Laplanche rightly conceptualizes treatment as a "provocation" in which the patient is offered an opportunity to revisit a relation that is originary, constitutive and un-remembered. Demolishing a binary that has preoccupied the field since its inception, Laplance writes that, "*All psychoanalysis* is devoted primarily to psychotherapy: to the self-narration of the subject, with the more or less active assistance of the analyst. But the psychoanalytic act – sometimes quite rare – is something else. A work of unbinding, it tries to make new materials surface for a profoundly renewed narration" (FS, 282). This brings us back to the relevance of "unconscious affects" and their operation in the development of a sexuality which is "ours" and yet not our own, the extraordinary and inevitable consequence of translation, and its limits.

Notes

1 Quoted in Ruth Stein, who says it is from an unpublished address to British society (1976) as quoted by Limentani, 1977, p. 171.
2 Brierley called for affects to have a place in theory "more consonant with their importance in practice" and that what was necessary was a review of "cardinal problems of affect" (1937, 257).
3 Andre Green writes: "we are confronted with the following problem: either to treat affects that are not observable in the treatment of the classical neuroses by the Freudian model, feeling that this model is inadequate, or altering the theoretical framework of psychoanalysis in the light of knowledge deriving from these new clinical aspects by creating a new theoretical model that may be no longer suited to the classical neuroses and might run the risk of shifting the whole of psychoanalytic theory and practice in a different direction" (1999, 2).
4 Ruth Stein's chapter on Andre Green is very thorough and informative.
5 Johnston undertakes a close reading of Freud on this topic whereby he strives to show that Freud was actually more ambivalent and in various moments sought to conceptualize the possibility of unconscious affects; in large part, Johnston is

interested in distinguishing Lacan's interpretation of Freud – which is that Freud is categorically opposed to unconscious affects – from Freud himself.
6 I am grateful to Jonathan House for suggesting to me that "urge" might be a better word for what Laplanche describes (personal communication).

Bibliography

Beebe, Beatrice, and Lachmann, F.M. (2002). *Infant Research and Adult Treatment*. Hillsdale: Analytic Press.

Beebe, Beatrice, Steven Knoblauch, Judith Rustin, and Dorienne Sorter (2005). *Forms of Intersubjectivity in Infant Research and Adult Treatment*. New York: Other Press.

Bion, W.R. (1967). Notes on Memory and Desire. *The Psychoanalytic Forum* 2: 3.

Brierley, Marjorie (1937). Affects in Theory and Practice. *International Journal of Psycho-Analysis* 18: 256–268.

Boston Process Change Study Group (2010). *Change in Psychotherapy: A Unifying Paradigm*. New York: W.W. Norton

Damasio, Antonio (1999). *The Feeling of What Happens: Body and Emotions in the Making of Consciousness*. New York: Mariner.

Damasio, Antonio (2003). *Looking for Spinoza: Joy, Sorrow, and the Feeling Brain*. New York: Harvest.

Demos, E. Virginia (2019). *The Affect Theory of Silvan Tomkins for Psychoanalysis and Psychotherapy: Recasting the Essentials*. New York: Routledge.

Eagle, Morris N. (2011). *From Classical to Contemporary Psychoanalysis: A Critique and Integration*. New York: Routledge.

Fonagy, Peter (2001). *Attachment Theory and Psychoanalysis*. New York: Other Press.

Fonagy, Peter, Gyorgy Gergely, Elliot Jurist, and Mary Target (2004). *Affect Regulation, Mentalization and the Development of the Self*. New York: Other Press.

Freud, Sigmund (1895). "Project for a Scientific Psychology," J. Strachey (Ed. and Trans). *The Standard Edition of the Complete Psychological Works of Sigmund Freud* (Vol. 1, pp. 283–294). London: Hogarth Press.

Freud, Sigmund (1911). "Formulations regarding the two principles of mental functioning," J. Strachey (Ed. and Trans). *The Standard Edition of the Complete Psychological Works of Sigmund Freud* (Vol. 12, pp. 213–226). London: Hogarth Press.

Freud, Sigmund. (1923). "The Ego and the Id," J. Strachey (Ed. and Trans). *The Standard Edition of the Complete Psychological Works of Sigmund Freud* (Vol. 19, pp. 12–59). London: Hogarth Press.

Green, Andre (1999). *The Fabric Affect in the Psychoanalytic Discourse*, Trans. Alan Sheridan. London: Routledge.

Johnston, Adrian and Catherine Malabou (2013). *Self and Emotional Life: Philosophy, Psychoanalysis, and Neuroscience*. New York: Columbia UP.

Laplanche, Jean (1999). *Essays on Otherness: Jean Laplanche*, Ed. John Fletcher. London: Routledge.

Laplanche, Jean (2011). *Freud and the Sexual: Essays 2000-2006*, Trans. John Fletcher, Jonathan House, and Nicholas Ray. New York: Unconscious in Translation

Laplanche, Jean (2015). *The Temptation of Biology: Freud's Theories of Sexuality*, Trans. Donald Nicholson-Smith. New York: Unconscious in Translation.

Modell, Arnold (1973). Affects and Psychoanalytic Knowledge. *Annual of Psychoanalysis* 1: 117–124.

Modell, Arnold (1980). Affects and their Non-Communication. *International Journal of Psycho-Analysis* 61: 259–267.

Panskepp, Jaak and Lucy Biven (2012). *The Archeology of Mind: Neuroevolutionary Origins of Human Emotions*. New York: W.W. Norton

Rangell, Leo (1967). Psychoanalysis, Affects, and the 'Human Core' – On the Relationship of Psychoanalysis to the Behavioral Sciences. *Psychoanalytic Quarterly* 36: 172–202

Rapaport, David (1953). On the Psycho-Analytic Theory of Affects. *International Journal of Psycho-Analysis* 34: 177–198.

Sandler, Joseph (1985). Towards a Reconsideration of the Psychoanalytic Theory of Motivation. *Bulletin of the Anna Freud Center* 8 (4): 223–244.

Schore, Allan N. (1994). *Affect Regulation and the Origin of the Self: The Neurobiology of Emotional Development*. New York: Psychology Press.

Seligman, Stephen (2018). *Relationships in Development: Infancy, Intersubjectivity, and Attachment*. New York: Routledge.

Slavin, Malcolm O.and Daniel Kriegman. (1992). *The Adaptive Design of the Human Psyche: Psychoanalysis, Evolutionary Process and the Therapeutic Process*. New York: Guilford Press.

Spezzano, Charles (1993). *Affect in Psychoanalysis: A Clinical Synthesis*. New York: Routledge.

Stein, Ruth (1999). *Psychoanalytic Theories of Affect*. London: Karnac.

Stern, Daniel (1985). *The Interpersonal World of the Infant: A View from Psychoanalysis and Developmental Psychology*. New York: Basic Books.

Stern, Donnel (1989). The Analyst's unformulated experience of the patient. *Contemporary Psychoanalysis*, 25: 1–33.

Tronick, Ed. (2007). *The Neurobehaviorial and Social-Emotional Development of Infants and Children*. New York: W.W. Norton

Westen, Drew (2002). The Language of Psychoanalytic Discourse. *Psychoanalytic Dialogues* 12(6): 857–898.

Westen, Drew (1997). Towards a Clinically and Empirically Sound Theory of Motivation. *International Journal of Psycho-Analysis*, 78: 521–548

Index

action language 54
adult-*infans* relations 142
affect 35–6, 44; age of 152; and
  attachment 169; and contamination
  176; and human mind 41; and
  metapsychology 165, 167, 169–79; and
  motivation 152; as primary channel of
  communication 177; in psychoanalysis
  6, 42, 153–9; regulation of 167, 170,
  175, 176; versus unconscious 159–62;
  and unconscious sexuality 167;
  undischarged or strangulated 67, 163
affective responses 94
alien-ness 104, 112
analytic situation 3
anlehnung 123, 124
Aron, Lew 5, 29
atavism 77–81
atavistic unconscious 77–81
Atlas, Galit 86, 134
attachment 38, 115; and affect 169;
  versus drive 120–3; and motivation
  170–81; motivation for 41; patterns
  84; and psychic structure 120–3
autocentric system 91
autoeroticism 123, 127

Baranger, Madeleine 77
Beebe, Beatrice 84
befriedigungserlebnis 125
biases 94
Binet, Afred 161
Bion, Wilfred 154, 176
Birksted-Breen, Dana 33

Boston Change Process Study
  Group 172–3
Bowlby, John 40, 84, 167–8, 175
brain: cerebral cortex 169; emotional
  160; of infants 42, 59; maturation of
  42, 169; and mind 151; orbitofrontal
  region 169; power-engineering model
  of 56
breast 139
Breger, Louis 62, 64–5
Brenner, Charles 53
Breuer, Joseph 62, 64
Brierley, Marjorie 153
brute reality, brute 139

castration complex 73
celebrated parable of origins 125
cerebral cortex 169
Charcot, Jean-Martin 92, 161, 165
child abuse 79; representational
  structures of 97
"A Child in Being Beaten"
  (Freud) 105–7
children: disobedient 107; and female
  breast 139; instinctual tendencies of
  91; sexual theories of 71–4
classical narratives 116
classical relations 38
conscious fantasy 105
constancy principle 160
construction 118, 120
Cooper, Arnold 2, 4, 13, 15–17, 25, 27–8,
  29, 58, 61
Copernican discovery/reformulation/

revolution 8–14, 30–2, 43, 88, 91–2, 93, 138
Copernicus, Nicolaus 8–14
"Countercurrent" (Laplanche) 68
counter-transference 3, 179–80

Damasio, Antonio 39, 152, 160, 168–9
das andre 104, 138, 146
Davies, Jody Messler 79, 171
declarative knowledge 84
deficit 38
De-Idealizing Relational Theory 5
Demos, Virginia 6, 157–9
der andre 104, 138, 146
descriptive unconscious 162;
    see also unconscious
determinism 143–6
dissociated memories 118, 136;
    see also memories
dissociation 79, 171, 176; and
    repression 80
drive/drive theory 19, 38, 40, 59, 87, 112;
    versus instinct 89–90, 164; and model
    of the mind 159; object-seeking drive
    121–2; pleasure-seeking drive 121; and
    psychic structure 120–3
dual instinct theory 150, 157
dynamic unconscious 77–81, 105, 162;
    see also unconscious
dynamism 77–81

Eagle, Morris 37–8, 67–8, 82, 84, 95,
    103, 160, 162–3, 175
ego 111, 177; conceptualization of 54
ego psychology 21, 56
emotions and emotionality 39–40; and
    affect 157; bioregulatory role of 152,
    168–9; primordial 36, 152, 160–2;
    repressed 162
enactment 31, 171
enclosed unconscious 110
endogeny 130
enigma 145
enigmatic messages 108–9, 140
enlarged sexuality 9–10, 69, 100, 110,
    140–1, 164, 175
Erikson, Johann 51
Eros 91
erotogenic zones 127
exigency 1, 9; definition of 9
exigency of psychoanalysis 68–71
Exodus 23
external trauma 161

Fairbairn, W.R.D. 41, 84, 121, 136
faithful infidelity 9, 28, 36
false memories 95, 102
fantasy 82–8; conscious 105; primal 106;
    unconscious 105
female breast 139
Ferenczi, Sandor 143, 179
fidelity 9
Flanders, Sara 33
Fliess, Wilhelm 62, 64–5
Fonagy, Peter 120–3, 167–8, 172
forgotten man hypothesis 154–5
Freud, Sigmund 1, 2–5, 7–8; concept of
    enlarged sexuality 9; conception of the
    nervous system 56; and Cooper 15–17;
    and Copernicus 9–11; drive-defense-
    fantasy model of 79; fascination with
    Moses 27–8; and Laplanche 8–12; on
    metapsychology 51, 53; model of
    human mind 59; psychical reality
    105–6; question about Judaism 26–8;
    relationship to science 62–8; Sinai
    complex 26–8; treatment of heretics as
    idol-worshippers 24
fundamental anthropological
    situation 167
"The Fundamental Anthropological
    Situation" (Laplance) 141–3

Gedo, John 52, 55, 56
Gergely, Gyorgy 172
Gill, Merton 51–2
God 23
golden calf 24
Govrin, Aner 5
Grand, Sue 5
Grandma Moses 29
Green, Andre 156–7
Greenberg, Jay 37, 83, 121, 165
Grotstein, James 59
guilds 6

habitual relationship patterns 84
Hartmann, Heinz 52, 53–4
healing 1
heliocentrism 14
heretics 24
hermeneuticists 55, 57
hermeneutics 117–18, 143–6
hilflosigkeit 125
Hobbes, Thomas 165
Hofer, Myron 40, 168
Holt, John 55

Holt, Robert 56
homeostasis 39
Howell, Elizabeth 79, 171–2
hysteria 62–3

id 78, 142
implantation 110–11
implicit memories 93, 101, 102, 171;
    see also memories
implicit relational knowing 83, 94, 97
infant-adult relationship 134, 172–7
infanticide 79
infantile neurosis 25
infantile sexuality 69, 122–3, 123–4,
    141, 179
infants: brain development in 42, 59;
    object seeking 41–2; pleasure seeking
    41–2; as sensoriaffective being 59
inserted unconscious 110
instinct: death 150; versus deficit 38;
    versus drive 89–90, 164; dual 150, 157;
    self-preservative 122, 139–40;
    sexual 143
interactional structures 84, 94–5
internal working model 84
internalized objects 84
interpretation 171
intersubjectivity 38
Introduction Lectures (Freud) 68
intromission 110–11
Itzkowitz, Sheldon 79

Janet, Pierre 80, 82, 161
Jewish God 22
Johnston, Adrian 151, 159–60
Jones, Ernest 66
Judaism 26–8
Jung, Carl 118
Jurist, Elliot 172

Katz, Gil 80
Kernberg, Otto 83, 159
Klein, George 53
Klein, Melanie 85, 90, 179
Kovel, Joel 50
Kriegman, Daniel 37–8, 42, 80, 86–7,
    115–16, 136, 175
Kriegman, David 55
Kris, Ernst 52

Lacan, Jacques 9, 179
Lachman, F.M. 84

Lamarck, Jean-Baptiste 165
Laplanche, Jean 1, 7–8, 24, 87, 103–4;
    approach to critique 29–33; critique of
    traditional unconscious 88–93; on
    exigency of psychoanalysis 68–71;
    general theory of seduction 35;
    interventions in contemporary theory
    33–9; new foundations for
    psychoanalysis 38; on psychical reality
    105–6; theory of motivation 149–81;
    theory of psychic structure 115–46;
    theory of the unconscious 77–112; use
    of Ptolemaic/Copernican heuristics 88
leaning-on hypothesis 123–30
Leclaire, Serge 103–4
LeDoux, Joseph 160
Locke, John 165
Loewald, Hans 18
lumping 29

Mahler, Margaret 122, 131
maturity 62
memories: dissociated 118, 136; false 95,
    102; implicit 93, 101, 102, 171;
    procedural 83, 94, 100–1, 133, 144;
    repressed 84, 95, 118; in unconscious
    94, 101, 111, 133; unintegrated 82
memory wars 95
metaphor of the baby 85
metapsychology 9, 13, 15, 34, 35, 50–74,
    165; history 50–6; other-centered 44;
    scientific foundations 56–62; versus
    the sexual theories of children 71–4
metonymisation 128
milk, as object of self-preservation 128–9
mind-to-mind transactions 41
Mitchell, Stephen 17–22, 37, 41, 83, 84,
    95, 121, 165
Modell, Arnold 37, 55
Moses 22, 27–8
Moses and Monotheism 18, 65–6
mother-infant dyad 40
motivation theory 35, 149–81; and affect
    in psychoanalysis 153–9; affect versus
    unconscious in 159–62; and
    attachment 170–81; and drive 162–70;
    new foundations 149–53
Mount Zion Psychotherapy Research
    Group 84
murder 79
mutuality 179–80
mytho-symbolism 73

nature of the mind 115
neuropsychoanalysis 55
neurosis 118; as disease of memory 118;
    infantile 25; sexuality as cause of 63;
    transference 25
neutrality 180–1
Newton, Isaac 60
normal-neurotic unconscious 109–10

object relations 38, 115
*Object Relations and Psychoanalytic
    Theory* (Greenberg/Mitchell) 83
object-seeking drive 41–2, 121–2
ocular tension 164
Oedipus complex 3, 15, 24, 29, 67, 72, 79
orbitofrontal region 169
original phantasy 106
originary monad 121–2
other person 104, 138
otherness 12

Pappenheim, Bertha 63–4
parent–child interaction 172–7
pathogenesis 115–20
perceptual reality 107
pleasure-seeking drive 41–2, 121
Popper, Karl 73
preconscious 99, 109
primal fantasy 106
primal repression 78
primal scenes 98
primordial emotionality 161
Principia (Newton) 60
procedural knowledge 83–4, 94–5, 133
procedural memories 83, 94, 101, 133,
    144; *see also* memories
progressive unconscious 93–103;
    see also unconscious
A Project for a Scientific Psychology
    (Freud) 125
psyche-in-the- world 38
psychic numbness 171–2
psychic structure 35, 115–46; and
    attachment 120–3; and determinism
    143–6; and drive 120–3; and
    hermeneutics 143–6; leaning-on
    hypothesis 123–30; and pathogenesis
    115–46; progressive model of 132–8;
    and seduction 138–43; traditional
    model of 130–2
psychical reality 103–8
psychoanalysis 2–3; affect in 153–9;
    exigency of 68–71; new foundations

for 9; other-centered vision of 11;
    positivist era 5; postmodern era 5; and
    Sinai complex 17–29; two paths
    for 8–12
psycholinguistics 54
Ptolemaic 8, 12–15, 31, 32, 36, 88, 91
Ptolemaism 11
Ptolemy 9–10, 14

radical hermeneuticists 55, 57
Rangell, Leo 154
Rapaport, David 51–2, 153, 155
realism of the unconscious 103–8, 109
reality: versus fantasy 82–8; material 95;
    perceptual 107; psychical 103–8
reciprocity 179
reconstruction 118, 120
reizbarkeit 141
relational configurations 84
relational narratives 116
relational theory 19–20, 21, 115, 121, 165
religion-science dichotomy 26
reminiscence 92, 94
representation 83, 126; of brute reality
    139; conscious 161
representation of interactions
    generalized (RIGs) 83–4, 94
repressed memories 84, 95, 118;
    see also memories
repression 59, 72–3, 74, 78–81, 81, 95,
    101, 109–10, 160, 161–3, 171–2, 176;
    and dissociation 80; primal 78
Rorty, Richard 20
Rubinstein, Benjamin 55
Rudnytsky, Peter 17–19

Sandler, Joseph 158
Schachter, Stanley 84
Schafer. Roy 52, 54
Schore, Allan 40, 55, 60, 169
seduction 8, 14, 35, 39–44, 166; drive
    versus attachment 120–3; etiological
    82; fantasy 82, 92; general theory of
    35, 100, 138–43, 176, 177, 181;
    leaning-on hypothesis 123–30; other
    person 104; primal 165–6; psychic
    structure 115–20, 130–8;
    see also translation
self-begetting 9, 11
self-centering 9, 11, 102
self-critique 5, 6
self-preservation 122–3, 124–5, 126–30,
    128, 139

self-psychology 115
self-reflection 22
self-reflective turn 1–7
self-transformation 1
Seligman, Stephen 85, 174
separation-individuation 122
sexual intercourse 98
sexuality 8, 35, 39–44, 77–112; enlarged
    9–10, 69, 100, 110, 140–1, 164, 175;
    infantile 69, 122–3, 123–4, 141, 179;
    and self-preservation 122–3, 124–5,
    126–30, 139; unconscious 167
"Sexuality in the Aetiology of the
    Neurosis" (Freud) 63
shepherd/counter-transference 179
shepherdess/transference 179
Shore, Allan 59
Sinai complex 26–8, 60, 150
Slavin, Malcolm 37–8, 42, 55, 80, 86–7,
    115–16, 136, 175
Slochower, Joyce 5, 29
Solms, Mark 55
Spezzano, Charles 36, 60
splitting 29
Sroufe, Alan 40
Stein, Ruth 153
Stern, Daniel 83
stock of untranslated messages 111
Strachey James 123
strangeness 104
stranger 104
Studies on Hysteria 62
Sullivan, H.S 136
Swanson, Don 57, 61
symbolization 166, 171

Target, Mary 172
tendencies 94; Copernican 8; defensive 1,
    7; instinctual 91
The Interpretation of Dreams
    (Freud) 125–6
theory of the unconscious: fantasy
    versus reality 82–8; progressive
    unconscious 93–100; realism of the
    unconscious 103–8; traditional

unconscious 88–93; unconscious
    content 108–12
traces 94, 125
traditional Freudians 31
traditional unconscious 88–93;
    see also unconscious
transactional patterns 95
transference 3, 179–80; neurosis 25
translated messages 111
translation 8, 14, 35, 39–44, 71–2, 96,
    150, 166, 167, 175, 176, 177–9;
    see also seduction
translation-resistant messages 111
trauma 79–81, 81, 98, 134, 171; external
    82, 161, 178; intergenerational
    transmission of 110
trauma external 82, 161, 178
triebkraft 146

unconscious 24, 34, 59, 77–112; versus
    affect 159–62; atavistic 77–81;
    communication 31; content 108–12;
    critique of 88–103; descriptive 162;
    dynamic 77–81, 162; fantasy 105;
    fantasy versus reality 82–8; features of
    109; inserted/enclosed 110; memories
    in 94, 101, 111, 133; normal-neurotic
    109–10; pathogenic beliefs 84;
    progressive 93–103; realism of 103–8;
    sexuality 167; as storehouse of
    repressed mental content 81, 83;
    traditional 88–93

verfuhrbarkeit 141

Waters, Everet 40
Westen, Drew 60, 61, 150, 159
Whitebrook, Joel 62
Wolf Man 118, 122
worldviews 115

Yerushalmi, Yosef Haim 27, 28, 65

Zweckmassigkeit 90